GENERALS-AT-SEA

Naval Operations during the English Civil War
and the
three Anglo-Dutch Wars
by
Colonel H.C.B. Rogers, OBE

GALAGO

All Rights Reserved
ISBN 0 946995 84 2

Published by Galago Publishing Ltd
42 Palace Grove, Bromley, Kent, BR1 3HB

Photosetting in 10½/12pt Melior
WHM Photosetting
David Mews, 11a Greenwich South Street, London, SE10 8NW

Printed in England by Antony Rowe Limited

In memory of Eileen who loved the sea

Contents

Chapter   Page

 1 Introductory   1
 2 The Ships   6
 3 The Civil War   12
 4 The Start of the First Dutch War   31
 5 The Battles of 16 August and the Kentish Knock   42
 6 The Battle of Dungeness   48
 7 The Battle of Portland   64
 8 After Portland   73
 9 The Battle of the Gabbard   80
10 The First Battle of the Texel   90
11 The End of the First Dutch War   96
12 The Restoration   101
13 The Second Dutch War   104
14 The Battle of Lowestoft and After   110
15 The Four Days Battle   116
16 The St. James's Day Fight   125
17 The Medway Raid and the End of the Second Dutch War   130
18 The Opening of the Third Dutch War   133
19 The Battle of Sole Bay   139
20 The Two Battles of Schooneveld   145
21 The Second Battle of the Texel   149

Index   156

Illustrations

All these are by courtesy of the National Maritime Museum

1 A Battle in the First Dutch War by Pieter Coopse.

2 A Dutch Ship before the Wind, c.1650 by W. Hollar.

3 An English 4th Rate in the Second or Third Dutch Wars by Van de Velde the Elder.

4 The Battle of the Kentish Knock, 28 September 1652 Artist unknown.

5 The Battle of the Kentish Knock by J. Pass.

6 The Battle of Dungeness (the date shown is New Style) by C. Jannson.

7 The First Battle of the Texel, 31 July 1653 Artist unknown.

8 An English 5th Rate about 1654 by W. Hollar.

9 The 2nd Rate *Royal Katherine* in 1664 by I. Sailmaker.

10 The Four Days Battle, 1 to 4 June 1666 by Soest.

11 The Four Days Battle by A. Storck.

12 The Surrender of the 1st Rate *Royal Prince*, aground on the Galloper, in the Four Days Battle by Wetterwinkel, after Van de Velde.

13 The Four Days Battle by A. Storck.

14 Dutch Flagships *Eendracht* and *Zeven Provincien* (the latter being de Ruyter's) with other Dutch Men-of-War, c.1666 by C. Van Mooy.

15 The English Fleet riding before Vlie Island at the burning of 150 Dutch merchant ships by Sir Robert Holmes on 9 August 1666 by W. Hollar.

16 The 3rd Rate *Resolution* (built 1667) in a gale during that year by Van de Velde the Younger.

17 An action in the Second Dutch War by Renier Zeernam.

18 The Dutch Fleet off Sheerness during the attack on the Medway, June 1667 by Van de Velde the Elder.

19 The Dutch attack on the Medway by Jan Peeters.

20 An action in the Second Dutch War by A. Willaerts.

21 The 1st Rate *St. Andrew*, built 1670 by Van de Velde the Younger.

22 The Battle of Sole Bay, 28 May 1672 by P. Monamey.

23 The Battle of Sole Bay by Van de Velde the Younger.

24 The Burning of the Earl of Sandwich's flagship, the 1st Rate *Royal James*, at the Battle of Sole Bay by Van de Velde the Elder.

25 The Second Battle of the Texel, 11 August 1673 by Van de Velde the Younger.

26 The Second Battle of the Texel — the defence of the new 1st Rate *Royal Prince* (centre) (built 1670) by Van de Velde the Younger.

27 Cornelis Tromp's flagship, *Gouden Leeuw*, at the Second Battle of the Texel by Van de Velde the Younger.

28 The *Royal Prince* in 1679 by Jan K.D. Beech.

Charts

The English and Dutch coast lines from the latitude of the Texel to the Straits of Dover.

A large chart of the Downs.

From 'Great Britain's Coasting Pilot' by Captain Greenville Collins, Hydrographer to King Charles II.

Facsimile of the 1753 edition.

Published by the Sudbrook Press.

Bibliography

1 Frank Fox, Great Ships: *The Battlefleet of King Charles II* (Greenwich, Conway Maritime Press, 1980).

2 E.H.H. Archibald, *The Wooden Fighting Ships in the Royal Navy* (London, Blandford Press, 1968).

3 J.R. Powell & E.K. Timings, ed. 'Documents Relating to the Civil War 1642-1648', *The Navy Records Society*, Vol. 105, 1963.

4 W.G. Perrin, *British Flags* (Cambridge, At the University Press, 1922).

5 Colonel H.C.B. Rogers, *Battles and Generals of the Civil Wars 1642-1651* (London, Seeley Service & Co., 1968).

6 S.R. Gardiner, ed. 'The First Dutch War', Vol. I, *The Navy Records Society*, Vol. 13, 1898.

7 S.R. Gardiner, ed. 'The First Dutch War', Vol. II, *The Navy Records Society*, Vol. 17, 1905.

8 S.R. Gardiner & C.T. Atkinson, ed. 'The First Dutch War', Vol. III, *The Navy Records Society*, Vol. 30, 1906.

9 C.T. Atkinson, ed. 'The First Dutch War', Vol. IV, *The Navy Records Society*, Vol. 37, 1910.

10 C.T. Atkinson, ed. 'The First Dutch War', Vol. V, *The Navy Records Society*, Vol. 41, 1912.

11 C.T. Atkinson, ed. 'The First Dutch War', Vol. VI, *The Navy Records Society*, Vol. 66, 1930.

12 A.C. Dewar, 'Corrigenda to Letters and Papers Relating to the First Dutch War', *The Navy Records Society*, 1931.

13 Oliver Warner, *Hero of the Restoration* (London, Jarrolds, 1936).

14 Robert Latham & William Matthews, ed. *The Diary of Samuel Pepys*, Vols. I-XI (London, Bell & Hyman, 1970-1983).

15 J.R. Powell & E.K. Timings, ed. 'The Rupert and Monck Letter Book', *The Navy Records Society*, Vol. 112, 1969.

16 R.C. Anderson, ed. 'The Journals of Sir Thomas Allin', Vol. I, *The Navy Records Society*, Vol. 79, 1939.

17 R.C. Anderson, ed. 'The Journals of Sir Thomas Allin', Vol. II, *The Navy Records Society*, Vol. 80, 1940.

18 Captain A.T. Mahan, *The Influence of Sea Power upon History 1660-1783*, (London, Sampson Low, 1890).

19 E.H. Jenkins, *A History of the French Navy* (London, Macdonald & Janee's, 1973).

20 J.R. Tanner, ed. 'Samuel Pepys's Naval Minutes', *The Navy Records Society*, Vol. 60, 1926.

21 R.C. Anderson, ed. 'The Third Dutch War', *The Navy Records Society*, Vol. 86, 1946.

22 Edwin Chappell, ed. 'The Tangier Papers of Samuel Pepys', *The Navy Records Society*, Vol. 73, 1935.

23 N.A.M. Rodger, *The Wooden World* (Glasgow, William Collins, 1986).

Acknowledgements

For the sources of the operations narrated in this book I am indebted above all to the contemporary documents contained in the many publications of the Navy Records Society which deal with the period — a Society to which I have had the honour to belong for over a quarter of a century.

The Navy Records Society has kindly given me permission to cite those volumes of which I have made use, and I would mention particularly the kindly help I have received from the Society's Honorary Secretary, Mr. N.A.M. Rodger MA, D.Phil, FSA, FRHist.S.

I am also indebted to the National Maritime Museum for all the illustrations of ships and naval actions which appear in the book, and to my friend Commander P.T. Lawman RN, who visited the Museum on my behalf and, with the assistance of the Museum staff, chose this selection of the works by eminent contemporary artists.

Documents in Crown Copyright appear by permission of the Comptroller of H.M. Stationery Office.

1

Introductory

The wars covered in this book are probably the most fascinating in our naval history; for it was during them that, from a comparatively minor and ill-organised force, the English Navy grew in strength and efficiency to become the greatest maritime power in the world — a position it was to retain for three hundred years.

The growth of England's Navy began during that paradoxical Civil War between King and Parliament on one side and the King on the other. In this war the bulk of the Navy took up arms with the side which favoured Parliament and a constitutional monarchy; partly because the King had not been able to obtain the money to pay the seamen, and they thought that they would have more sympathetic treatment from Parliament.

This book starts, therefore, with the English Civil War. The close of that war was soon followed by the First Dutch War, waged by the Commonwealth (established after the execution of King Charles I), and then by the Protectorate of Oliver Cromwell which followed his dismissal of Parliament and assumption of supreme power. The Second and Third Dutch Wars came after the Restoration of the Monarchy.

After the Restoration, the Navy, without any change in its organisation, returned smoothly to its Royal allegiance, and officers who had recently been fighting each other were soon appointed to commands at sea and administrative posts ashore without reference to which side they had supported in the Civil War.

The term 'Generals-at-Sea' for the Commanders-in-Chief of the fleet, which had been used during the Interregnum (following tentative earlier use) and which was retained, was more appropriate than intended, for the officers who were appointed to these posts were soldiers and it was they who moulded the Navy of England and trained it in the tactics which they had derived from their experience of fighting on land and which proved so successful at sea that they were copied by the Dutch, learned by the French, and subsequently adopted by all European maritime powers.

Of these great soldier-admirals, the first to make his name was Robert Blake. Before the outbreak of the Civil War he had been in business as a merchant. He fought in the Parliamentary Army during that war, becoming Lieutenant-Colonel in the Regiment of Colonel Edward Popham (who also commanded later at sea as an Admiral), and distinguishing himself in the defence of Lyme against the Royalists in 1643-44. In the latter year he captured Taunton and held it successfully against Royalist attacks. In 1649 he was appointed General-at-Sea and pursued Prince Rupert to the Mediterranean, sinking many of his ships. With Richard Deane as his fellow General-at-Sea he defeated the great Dutch Admiral Tromp at the Battle of Portland in 1652. In 1653, when the Protectorate was established, he nearly lost his command because, as a Parliament man, he was opposed to Cromwell's seizure of power. Perhaps his greatest exploit was the destruction of the Spanish West Indian fleet at Santa Cruz in 1657. He died of fever on his way back to England.

Richard Deane was a gunnery expert in the Parliamentary Army and commanded the artillery under Sir Thomas Fairfax at the decisive battle of Naseby in 1645. At the battle of Preston in 1648 he commanded the right wing of Cromwell's army. In the following year he was appointed a General-at-Sea, with responsibility for the defence of the coast from Portsmouth to Milford Haven. His appointment may well have been due to his reputation as a gunnery officer. He returned to the Army and fought as a Major General at the battle of Worcester in 1651. Afterwards he was Commander-in-Chief of the Cromwellian Army in Scotland, but on the outbreak of the First Dutch War he returned to the Navy as a General-at-Sea and was killed at Monck's side on their flagship at the battle of the Gabbard in June 1653.

Edward Mountagu, First Earl of Sandwich, raised a regiment of foot in Cambridgeshire for Parliament and commanded it at the battle of Naseby and at the storming of Bristol in 1645. He was a member of Cromwell's Council of State in 1653 and in 1656 was appointed a General-at-Sea, commanding the fleet in the Downs the following year. In 1660 he commanded the fleet which sailed to Holland to convey Charles II to England on the Restoration of the Monarchy. In the same year he was nominated a Knight of the Garter, created Earl of Sandwich, and appointed Admiral of the Narrow Seas and Lieutenant-Admiral to the Duke of York. He distinguished himself in the Second Dutch War at the battle of Lowestoft in 1664. On the outbreak of the Third Dutch War in 1672 he was appointed Second-in-Command of the fleet under the Duke of York and was killed at the battle of Sole Bay in the same year.

George Monck had been a professional soldier well before the Civil War and when it started he was commanding a regiment of foot fighting with distinction against the Irish rebels. In September 1643 a peace was made with the rebels, and some of the troops thus made available were despatched to reinforce the King's forces fighting in England. These troops from Ireland were defeated and captured by Sir Thomas Fairfax, the great Parliamentary General, and Monck was amongst the prisoners of war. Most of the soldiers, who were professionals with no pronounced leaning to either side, re-enlisted in the Army of Parliament. Monck was committed to the Tower of London as a prisoner in 1644. In 1646, the King being then a prisoner of Parliament, Monck was freed. He had agreed to raise a force for employment against Irish insurgents, with the proviso that he would not be employed against the King's forces in England. In 1647 he was a Major-General commanding the Parliamentary troops in Ulster.

For the invasion of Scotland in 1650, Cromwell chose Monck and John Lambert as his principal officers. As all general officers at this time had to be commanders of a regiment (though the operational command of such a regiment would normally be exercised by its Lieutenant-Colonel) Cromwell formed a regiment for Monck by taking companies from other regiments. (Monck's Regiment exists today as the Coldstream Guards.) After the successful conclusion of the campaign Monck was left in command in Scotland.

After the outbreak of the First Dutch War in 1652, Monck was appointed a General-at-Sea, along with Blake and Deane, and proved as able a commander at sea as he had been on land. In fact it has been said that he revolutionised naval tactics by introducing fighting in line. His orderly military mind had rejected the customary deployment into groups of ships 'charging' an enemy fleet, and substituted the army system of deploying in line so that the broadside of every ship could be brought to bear on the enemy. With Mountagu he was instrumental in the Restoration of the Monarchy and was rewarded by being created Duke of Albemarle. In the Second Dutch War he and Prince Rupert were joint Generals-at-Sea.

Prince Rupert had also been a soldier and a gallant, if too impetuous, cavalry leader. Indeed, it was his wild and uncontrolled charges which twice deprived the King of victory in the Civil War, firstly at Edgehill and secondly at Naseby. At sea he had gained maritime experience by fighting against the Parliamentary Navy with his comparatively few Royalist warships. But he was to display the same incapacity for high command at sea as he had on land.

Sir George Ayscue was another Parliamentarian who, knighted before the Civil War by Charles I, became a Captain in the Parliamentary Army. By 1646 he was in the Navy, and a Captain, and in 1649 was Admiral of the Irish Seas. After fighting successfully against the Dutch in the Downs in 1642 he (also no lover of Cromwell) retired under plea of ill health. By 1658 he was commanding the Swedish fleet, and after the Restoration he was made a Commissioner of the Navy.

The flamboyant Irishman, Sir Robert Holmes, served under Prince Rupert during the Civil War. He was mainly responsible for the start of the Second Dutch War by seizing Dutch possessions on the Guinea Coast of West Africa and also in North America. He was knighted in 1666.

Sir Jeremy Smith had been a close adherent of Cromwell, but after the Restoration he became a Vice-Admiral and commanded the Blue Squadron of the fleet in the 'St. James's Day Fight'. After that battle Holmes, who had been temporarily serving under him, accused him of cowardice (an accusation strongly rejected by Monck in a letter to the King). The result was a duel which

3

both survived. The enmity between them may well have been due to some confrontation at sea during the Civil War.

Sir William Batten was a seaman who had been appointed Surveyor of the Navy in 1638 under Charles I. He took the side of Parliament in the Civil War and became Second-in-Command to the Earl of Warwick, the Commander-in-Chief of Parliament's Navy. Batten achieved notoriety by shelling King Charles I's Queen when she arrived in England from Holland with ammunition for the Royalist forces. In 1647 he resigned his command and went to Holland and, joining the Prince of Wales (later King Charles II), was knighted. He came back to England later and after the Restoration was reinstated as Surveyor of the Navy.

Sir William Penn was another seaman who served under Blake in the First Dutch War with distinction. In December 1653 he was appointed one of the Commissioners of the Admiralty, and in the following year he was selected as General and Commander-in-Chief of the expedition against the West Indies in conjunction with General Robert Venables. Though he failed in an attack on St. Domingo, he captured Jamaica in 1655. He was imprisoned in the Tower for returning to England without leave, but was released after a few weeks. Disgruntled, he retired to his Irish estates in Munster and corresponded secretly with the Royalists. He was knighted at the Restoration and made a Commissioner of the Navy.

Batten and Penn were colleagues of Samuel Pepys on the Navy Board, and both the 'Sir Williams' are the subject of frequent uncomplimentary remarks in his famous diary.

Sir John Lawson was another distinguished Admiral in both Parliamentary and post-Restoration naval service. He was dismissed from public service on political grounds in 1656, during the Protectorate. The following year he was implicated in the conspiracy of the Fifth Monarchy men and was arrested. However, he was back as Commander-in-Chief of the Fleet in 1659, and cooperated with Monck in the Restoration of 1660. He was knighted in that year by King Charles II.

Sir Thomas Allin was a noted Royalist who left a valuable and detailed journal of his sea service to posterity.[1] He was a merchant and shipowner in Lowestoft when the Civil War began, and fought at sea on behalf of the King. He was captured and imprisoned by Parliament. After the Restoration he had a distinguished naval career and was Vice-Admiral of the Fleet in the Second Dutch War.

One other officer must be mentioned, Major Nehemiah Bourne, an officer in the Parliamentary Army. And another soldier who served with distinction in the Navy both at sea and ashore. In the First Dutch War he commanded a squadron as Rear Admiral under Blake. Subsequently he was transferred to a shore appointment as Commissioner of equipment of Fleets in 1652. On relinquishing 'occasional' (i.e. acting rank) of Rear Admiral, he reverted to his Army rank of Major (at that time senior to a captain in the Navy, which

---

[1.] *The Navy Records Society*, Vols. LXXIX and LXXX, 'The Journals of Sir Thomas Allin', Vols. I and II, ed. R.C. Anderson.

equated to the Army rank with the same title). Bourne, an immensely capable and conscientious officer, could not reconcile himself to the Restoration and emigrated to America.

Omitted from the above list, because he did not hold any naval appointment after the end of the Civil War, is Robert Rich, Earl of Warwick. He started his active military service as a soldier in the Low Countries, and later commanded at sea in naval operations against Spain. It was this great man who created the efficient nucleus around which the Navy grew to its subsequent stature.

The Duke of York, who was Lord High Admiral at the Restoration, learned his military trade as a soldier on the Continent, and then became the competent commander of a fleet in battle. During the tension that preceded the Second Dutch War, Samuel Pepys recounts the reception of the Dutch Ambassador by the Duke of York[2]. The Dutch believed that the Puritan fanatics in England would, in the event of war, rise in their favour. To a politely worded suggestion to this effect, the Duke replied: 'The English have ever united all their private differences to attend Forraigne', adding that in Cromwell's time the Cavaliers did never 'interrupt him in his foreign business.'

But to two men was due the efficiency in ships and maritime administration of the Restoration Navy, in the face of political opposition in this post-Cromwellian nation: King Charles II, the one man who had the genius to run England on a light rein, whilst disarming opposition to its essential needs, and Samuel Pepys, the great administrator, who eventually advised the King on the Navy's needs.

King Charles, indeed, was one of the greatest monarchs this country has ever had; for despite the moral laxity, which was his refuge from the strains of government, he was able to unite a country, so recently torn by the schism of civil war, by turning its attention towards a foreign threat to England's trade. The King saw clearly, too, where the priorities in defence lay, when he wrote in the preamble to the Articles of War in 1662, 'It is upon the navy under the Providence of God that the safety, honour and wellfare of this realm do chiefly attend.'

Pepys, who as a schoolboy, had watched and welcomed the execution of King Charles I, wrote[3]: 'If it had not pleased God to give us a King and Duke that understood the sea, this nation had 'ere this been quite beaten out of it, such was the deplorable condition of our Navy when they came in, in comparison with the Dutch'.

'Understood the sea'; is that perhaps the secret of maritime strategical success throughout the ages?

---

[2] The Diary of Samuel Pepys, ed. Robert Latham & William Matthews, Vol. V 1664, p. 264 (London, Bell & Hyman 1971).
[3] Navy Records Society, 'Samuel Pepys's Naval Minutes', ed. J.R. Tanner, 1926, p. 84.

2

The Ships

It is not intended to give a detailed description of the ships of this period, for this has already been done in publications devoted to the subject. But in order to understand the naval operations one needs to have some general appreciation of the different classes of warship and of their functions, methods of employment and armament. Through much of the seventeenth century (and all of the eighteenth) the size and power of a man-of-war was assessed by its 'Rate': a 1st Rate being the most powerful, a 2nd Rate the next, followed by a 3rd Rate, and so on. It seems that the term 'Rate' originated in the rate of pay authorised to the captain of a ship, which depended on the size of the ship's company; for just as a company of foot was the basic unit of infantry in the Army, commanded by a captain, so the term was used for a captain's command at sea — the company of his ship. But whereas the company of infantry was of the strength fixed by the establishment of the day, the size of a ship's company depended on the size of the ship and the strength of her armament. Hence the rate of pay of her captain was assessed according to the number of officers and ratings he had to command. This is clarified by a letter written on 20 January 1653 by the Navy Commissioners to the Admiralty as follows: 'We have considered how to distinguish the State's ships into ranks and are of the opinion that the respective numbers of men set under each rate (i.e. rate of pay of the captain and others), and so upwards to the ranks next before should be settled, and so all officers to receive their pay accordingly, viz:

'1st Rank	2nd	3rd	4th	5th	6th
Men	Men	Men	Men	Men	Men
400 and	300	200	140	80	40

upwards'

(Below these figures there followed the rates of pay for all ranks and appointments from Captain downwards.)

The table concluded with the following statement:

'And for all small vessels under forty men to be without rates and to be paid as the service shall deserve.'[1]

So it would appear that ships were initially classified officially by ranks, and that since these ranks were determined by the number of men, which in turn determined the rates of pay, the term 'rate' had been by popular usage substituted for 'rank'.

By the Second Dutch War, with ships of generally increased size, the number of men required for the various rates was somewhat greater. The table below shows the pay laid down for captains of ships according to their rates. The numbers of men and guns are average figures for ships of different rates in the fleet of 1665. It will be noted that some of the ships were armed with more guns than those carried by the next rate above; but the guns varied in size and a ship with fewer guns than one in a lower rate probably fired a heavier broadside.

Class of ship	Captain's pay per month	Ship's company	Number of guns
1st Rate	£21	over 500	82-93
2nd Rate	£16 18s	320-500	60-80
3rd Rate	£11	250-320	56-70
4th Rate	£10 10s	150-250	34-54
5th Rate	£ 8 8s	70-150	20-34
6th Rate	£ 7	up to 70	4-14

Of the guns carried, some were still known by their ancient names, while others were now called by the weight of shot. The principal ones are given below, though there are a few other varieties.

Title of piece	Weight of shot in lbs
Cannon of 7	42
Demi-Cannon	32
Culverin	18
Demi-Culverin	9
Saker	6
12-Pounder	12
24-Pounder	24

The scale per ship of these pieces varied considerably, and probably reflected

---

[1] *Navy Records Society*, Vol. XXX 1906 'The First Dutch War' Vol. III ed. S.R. Gardiner and C.T. Atkinson.

the contemporary policy of arming the various Rates at the time they were
built, modified by the number of guns in each category that the Board of
Ordnance was able to supply. Typical ships in the first four Rates in the fleet
of 1665 were armed as follows:[2]

Name	Rate	Cannon of 7	Demi-Cannon	Culverin	Demi-Culverin	Saker	12-pdr
Royal Charles	1	26	6	26	30		
Swiftsure	2		22	28	16		
Victory	2	22	4	26	24		
Lion	3	22		2	32	2	
Mary	3	20		4	8		26
Princess	4	10		12	4	6	20
Kent	4			22	20	4	

The two most powerful types of the men-of-war, the 1st and 2nd Rates,
were known as 'Great Ships'. They were the capital ships of the period and
were all 'three-deckers' — that is, having three gun decks, each with a tier of
guns, of which the heaviest were on the lowest gun deck for stability. The 3rd
and 4th Rates were two-deckers with two tiers of guns, and both of these
rates were included in the battle line. The 5th Rates were small two-deckers,
not powerful enough to be included in the battle squadrons for a fleet action,
but invaluable for scouting, escort, and naval 'policing'. In the Civil War they
were called 'whelps' and bore numbers rather than names — e.g. the 10th
Whelp. The 6th Rates had only a single gun deck and were lightly armed.
They were used on somewhat similar duties as the 5th Rates.

In 1644 there occurred something of a revolution in naval ship design with
the first appearance of the English frigate. King Charles II told Samuel Pepys
something of the background to the construction of this remarkable ship,
and Pepys recorded it in his *Naval Minutes*.[3] A renegade from St. Malo came,
in about 1630, to Sir George Cartaret, then a Captain in the Navy, and offered
to build a vessel of about 20 guns that would outsail any ship that the King
of England (Charles I) had, and would not ask for any money but would rely
on the King's generosity if he succeeded. Cartaret brought this man to the
King, who recommended him to the officers of the Navy (i.e. the Navy
Board). They, however, were indignant that any Frenchman should pretend
to build better ships than they could and discounted his proposal. The man,
not being able to live in England without employment, was advised by
Cartaret to go to Dunkirk, which was then at war, and where Cartaret thought
his proposal would be welcomed. He accordingly did so, and there 'first
invented and built there the ships called frigates.' Charles II gave it as his

[2] *Navy Records Society*, Vol. 112, 1966, 'The Rupert & Monck Letter Book', ed. Rev. J.R. Pownall &
E.K. Timings.
[3] *Navy Records Society*, Vol. 60, 1926, 'Samuel Pepys's Naval Minutes' ed. J.R. Tanner.

opinion that this man got the idea for his invention from the shape of the St. Malo shallops (small gaff rigged two-masted vessels), which were the best in the world. The Dunkirkers had subsequently derived *their* shallops from this man's frigates. Later, one of these frigates came into the Thames and 'the shape of her body was taken very strictly by Sir Peter Pett's father'. He was the master-shipwright at Deptford and also had a private yard at Ratcliffe, where he soon afterwards built the first frigate England had, the *Constant Warwick*. She was constructed for the Earl of Warwick as a privateer, and she did so well that he sold her to the State 'and was the best sailor that ever England had'. (The name 'shallop' came from the French 'chaloupe', which in turn came from the Dutch 'sloep' or, in English 'sloop'.)

Sir Phineas Pett, master shipwright at Chatham, told Pepys some more about this ship. His father, Peter Pett, built it for Robert Rich, 2nd Earl of Warwick, appointed Lord High Admiral of England by Parliament in 1643. Warwick told Pett that he 'aimed at nothing but sailing'. He did not want many men; only a few light guns, limited accommodation, and scant accommodation for provisions. Nor did he want a ship to last, so that 'she was but very weak of timber, trembling in the sea . . . and was always kept in trim by filling with salt water the victualling casks as fast as they were emptied of provisions. By which means she is said to have cut through the water so that the waves have gone over her head in such a manner that her commander has told Sir P. Pett that he has sometimes been afraid that she would never have appeared above water again.' She was, indeed, an ideal privateer — fast enough to overhaul any merchant ship and with sufficient armament to overpower her.

Sir Phineas Pett told Pepys 'that he does not know that we are at this day one bit improved in the shape or building of our sailing frigates, though we are in our greater ships of the first- and second-rates, which are built for burthen, force and battery.'

The famous shipwright, Sir Anthony Deane, also had some comments to Pepys on the *Constant Warwick,* saying that the shape of this frigate was taken from the Dunkirk frigates and that upon this foundation 'our frigates from the 3rd rate downwards were built'.

It would appear that the shape of the *Constant Warwick's* hull was copied for all subsequent frigates, and that from some date during the regime of Parliament all 3rd, 4th, and 5th Rates were built as frigates. The 3rd and 4th Rates were apparently classed as 'large frigates', and the 5th Rates, together with those 6th Rates of frigate design, as 'small frigates'. In scouting, large frigates were expected, if necessary, to fight for information, whilst the small frigates obtained it solely by reconnaissance.

It is to be noted that in the First Dutch War, English commanders in their reports gave the strength of their commands in 'ships and frigates'. It is a fair assumption that 'ships' referred to the 1st and 2nd Rates, or 'Great Ships', and that 'frigates' included the 'great frigates' (3rd and 4th Rates) that could lie in the line of battle, and the 'small frigates' (5th and 6th Rates) used for scouting and escort.

A very important element of the battle fleet was the fireship, the function of which one could perhaps liken to the submarine of later days. It was filled with combustible material and the task of its commander was to steer it towards an important enemy ship. As soon as contact seemed ensured, he would ignite his fireship and he and his crew tumbled rapidly into a boat that was towed astern, and cast off. The moral effect of a blazing vessel bearing down on a ship was tremendous — so great that sometimes a crew would abandon ship rather than face it. A favourite method of defence was to try and destroy the boat towed by the fireship, before it was set alight, and so remove the crew's chance of escape.

A humble, but very useful, addition to the fleet was the ketch (a small two-masted sailing vessel fore-and-aft rigged). Armed with only a few light guns, ketches were always in great demand, and there never seemed enough of them. They were used for communications, bringing provisions and ammunition, and even, on occasions, for supplementing the small frigates in scouting. The fleet flagship generally asked for two in permanent attendance on her, and one for every other flagship in the fleet was often requested, though seldom with success.

Sir Anthony Deane told Pepys some of the lessons that would be learned from foreign warships. He said that in 1663-64 the Dutch and French built ships which two gun decks, carrying 60 to 70 guns and 'so constructed that they carried their lower guns 4 foot from the water' and could stow four months supply of provisions; whereas the English frigates carried their guns little more than three feet from the water and could only provide space for ten weeks provisions. The height above water of the lowest (and heaviest) tier of guns was important, because, when fighting to windward in a heavy sea, they could be unusable if too low, thereby giving an enemy to leeward a considerable advantage in gunpower. Deane says that in 1665 the Duke of York 'beat the Dutch fleet (in the battle of Lowestoft) and destroyed upwards of 20 of their men-of-war, upon which the Dutch built 34 ships with two decks and a half, carrying from 70 to 84 guns. These ships could carry six months provision and their guns to lie 4½ foot from the water. They are the best ships at this day belonging to Holland'.[4].

With its heavy armament, the keeping of a big warship's centre of gravity low was very important, and the decks were therefore placed as low as possible, with only about 5½ feet between each deck and the overhead beams — a source of considerable discomfort to other than short men. The most common design error lay in building a ship with poor stability, a defect which was commonly corrected by 'girdling', that is, adding an extra thickness of planking along the outside of a ship's hull to lower the centre of gravity — with the possible loss of some speed.

At this period, whilst the captain of a ship was responsible for fighting her, navigation was the responsibility of the master, as was also the operation of rigging and sails. This was a relic from the days when seamen navigated and

---

[4] Op. cit. pp 241-2.

manoeuvred the ship for soldiers to board and capture an enemy. The master, though of warrant rank, was graded socially with the lieutenants and excelled them in practical authority. The firing of the ship's guns and their maintenance was carried out by the gunner, assisted by quarter-gunners. The carpenter and his assistants looked after the woodwork, and the boastwain maintained sails and rigging, ground tackle, deck fittings, etc. The ship's boats were the responsibility of the coxswain. The most important post for the quartermaster and quartermaster-mates was at the helm, but they were also responsible for stowage in the hold. Pay and supply came under the purser.

A large proportion of both English and Dutch warships were merchantmen, requisitioned and armed. They were a particularly important element in the Dutch Navy because their East India merchantmen were amongst the biggest ships in the Dutch fleet, and were necessarily heavily armed in peace for protection against the formidable vessels possessed by Arab and other pirates. The Dutch Navy was a powerful force, for that small country depended for its livelihood on its overseas trade. As compared with English men-of-war, those of the Dutch had a much shallower draught for navigation amongst the shoals and sandbanks of their harbours and shoreline.

3

The Civil War

The England over which the King's war standard was raised on 22 August 1642 was largely disarmed. Apart from the small garrisons of coastal fortresses, there were no standing forces on land, and the security of the Realm was entrusted to the small regular Navy.

The operations on land during the approaching civil war have been dealt with elsewhere by the present author.[1] In this narrative, therefore, there appear only those movements and actions on land which bore on or affected the operations at sea.

Dates during this period are confusing, because in England the 'Old Style' of dating was in use, whilst Holland and other Continental countries had adopted the 'New Style', or 'Gregorian', calendar which did not come into use in England until 1752. Furthermore, for legal purposes in England the New Year did not start till Lady Day, 25 March; so that between 1 January and 25 March two years were quoted, e.g. 1660/1661. Throughout this book the Old Style dates (ten days earlier than the New Style) are used, and the year has been taken as starting on 1 January.

Though small, the English Navy had fine ships with competent officers and well-trained crews. Its allegiance, therefore, to either side could be of decisive influence in the approaching conflict between King and Parliament. Unfortunately for the King, during the years when he had tried to rule England without a Parliament he was unable to raise sufficient money to pay the officers and seamen of the fleet. There was, therefore, considerable stress and bitterness among these men over the way in which they were being treated. When the King was forced to recall Parliament, and the Lord High Admiral, the Earl of Northumberland, was at last able to start the issue of pay and clothing, the bitterness remained, and it is small wonder that most of the officers and practically all the seamen sided with Parliament. It is difficult to overestimate the advantage that Parliament gained by its aquisition of the fleet. Not only was it possible to curtail the supplies which could reach the

---

[1] *Battles and Generals of the Civil Wars 1642-1651* by Colonel H.C.B. Rogers (London, Seeley Service, 1968).

Royalists from overseas, whilst safeguarding Parliament's own connections with the Continent, but the ports held for Parliament could be succoured by sea, and heavy guns could be moved in ships over the longer distances instead of being hauled by long teams of labouring horses over the desperately bad roads of the time. In addition, Parliament's command of the sea served to deter the foreign help for which the King had so confidently hoped.

The person in whom the command of the fleet was vested was obviously of considerable importance. As stated above, the Lord High Admiral was the Earl of Northumberland, but he viewed the coming war with considerable distaste. He pleaded that he was too unwell to exercise command at sea and announced his intention of exercising his constitutional right to appoint a deputy. The King wanted him to select Sir John Pennington, who had experience in a naval command, but Parliament persuaded Northumberland to appoint Robert Rich, Earl of Warwick, as his Vice-Admiral. In addition they got Sir George Cartaret chosen as Rear-Admiral. The enthusiastic Parliamentarians who were dealing with naval affairs presumably did not know that Cartaret was a Royalist. Luckily for Parliament, the King was so angry at Warwick's appointment that he refused to let Cartaret serve under him. (Cartaret was, indeed, to render distinguished service to the King, including the capture of Jersey from Parliament, and he was Treasurer of the Navy after the Restoration.)

The Earl of Warwick was an able operational commander at sea and a very competent naval administrator. He had seen active service as a soldier in the Netherlands and had commanded a squadron in semi-piratical sea warfare against the Spaniards.

Whilst the Navy kept the ring for Parliament (or 'King and Parliament', as that side preferred — maintaining that they were not against the Monarchy), both rival parties set about raising armies, initially from the Trained Bands. These were militia units of horse and foot, intended for defence against invasion. The eight infantry regiments of the City of London (which opted for Parliament) were comparatively well trained, but most of the county troops and regiments lacked any but the most elementary drill.

The populace of London being for Parliament, the King had ridden out of the capital towards the north and reached York on 19 March 1642. His immediate objective was Hull, for its arsenal had been stocked with weapons and ammunition in preparation for a war against Scotland. He arrived before Hull on 29 April, but Sir John Hotham, the Governor of the town, was for Parliament, and he had been told not to admit the King's troops, and Charles, with only a small body of soldiers and no artillery, was unable to enforce entry. Parliament had ordered Warwick on 26 April to send two warships to Hull, and the bulk of the contents of the arsenal were loaded into ships and sent to London under naval escort.

The Queen at this time was in Holland buying munitions, and the King had sent the 4th Rate *Providence* there to await her orders. Newcastle had been secured for the King and to that port, early in June the *Providence*, loaded with arms and ammunition, was directed. Warwick had ships on the watch for her and chased her into the Humber, but she slipped into a narrow creek and unloaded her cargo, including four big guns, under the guard of the local trained bands, before she was captured. Hostilities had not yet been opened, and a furious King despatched Sir John Pennington to take command of the fleet. The attempt was unsuccessful, for it was obviously far too late. However, the King secured two more ships of his Navy, the 3rd Rates *Swallow* and *Bonaventure*, and on 18 August he ordered them to sail to Holland, as soon as conditions allowed, and, having contacted the Queen, to follow her instructions. Looking ahead, they were both captured by Captain William Batten with his squadron of six ships.

About 10 July fighting broke out at Hull, where the Earl of Lindsey had started to invest it and built three forts commanding the Humber. Command of the sea again saved the situation for Parliament. Transports carrying troops under the command of Sir John Meldrum arrived in the Humber under naval escort, and the warships opened fire, destroying all three forts. Meldrum's troops then disembarked and drove off Lindsey's investing force.

On 22 August, as stated above, open hostilities began. Parliament's fleet, now that the King's three ships had been captured, consisted of three 1st Rates, thirteen 2nd Rates, ten 3rd Rates, three 4th Rates, two 5th Rates, and four 6th Rates. It was little enough; some were in poor condition and four others were graded as 'not fit for service'. There was an urgent need for the fleet to be reinforced by armed merchantmen and Warwick secured the requisitioning of a large number of these vessels, of which 24 were soon armed and at sea to supplement the warships detailed for the 'Summer Guard' of 1642.

Main interest now centres on the land, where both sides were assembling their armies. The Parliamentary Army concentrated in the Northampton and Coventry areas, and on 10 September the Earl of Essex, an experienced soldier, arrived to take command. He had a strength of about 20,000 men, but they were largely untrained. The King was in a far worse position, for the force over which he raised his standard consisted of only about 800 horse, most of them armed with swords only, and some 1,000 foot. Portsmouth, which was held for the King by Lord Goring, was soon captured for Parliament by Waller. Goring was allowed to depart overseas, but the Royalists had lost a most important port.

However, during September the King's Army began to increase rapidly. He arrived at Shrewsbury on 20 September and immediately despatched a force to seize Chester in order to make sure of his communications with Ireland where he hoped to get substantial reinforcements.

On 23 October the two armies clashed at the battle of Edgehill. It was at this battle that Sir Jacob Astley, commanding the Royalist foot, uttered the prayer that has become famous: 'Lord I shall be verie busie this day. I may forget Thee but doe not Thou forget me. March on boys!' And drums beating, the King's infantry advanced to the attack.

Though the Royalists had the better of the battle, it was indecisive. It could have been a complete victory for the King and ended the war at a stroke, if Prince Rupert, commanding the cavalry of the right wing, had not thrown away the chance by a mad charge and lost control of his horsemen, who, after breaking the opposing horse, galloped on in search of plunder, instead of wheeling left to shatter the Parliamentary infantry. (Rupert was to do the same thing three years later at Naseby costing the King both the war and his head; and similar impetuosity in the Third Dutch War at the naval battle of the Texel deprived Charles II of a decisive victory over the Dutch fleet. He was a very gallant soldier, the limit of whose command ability was a single cavalry regiment on land and a squadron of ships at sea.)

After the battle Essex retired towards London and the King followed him, but now the Trained Bands of the City of London came into action for the first time. Faced on 19 November by these sturdy regiments, the King had to fall back.

Fighting for the year ended with a naval action on 5 December. Goring had collected seven ships, filled them with 1,500 French and German mercenaries, and sailed with these to the King's assistance. He encountered Warwick with the 2nd Rates *James* and *St. George* and the little 6th Rate *Greyhound*. Grossly overpowered, and after four hours action, two or three of Goring's ships had been sunk and the remainder made off. Later in the month Goring succeeded in landing at Newcastle.

In the West Country, Plymouth was held for Parliament, but Cornwall was strongly Royalist and Sir Ralph Hopton, Royalist commander, there, took Launceston and Saltash from Parliament, and in November 1642 was threatening Plymouth. He was not strong enough to force the defences and, short of supplies, he had to retire into Cornwall. But on 17 January 1643 he had a windfall. Some 40 Parliament merchantmen were driven by bad weather into Falmouth harbour, under the guns of Pendennis Castle (held by the Royalists) and captured. They were bound for London, and laden with arms and such a large amount of money that Hopton was able to pay his soldiers their arrears and to give them a fortnight's pay in advance.

On 19 January Hopton attacked a Parliamentary force at Liskeard and, after routing it, attacked and captured Saltash and armed merchantmen, and again threatened Plymouth. But Plymouth had now been reinforced by sea with men, supplies, and ammunition, and Hopton was once more forced to withdraw to Cornwall. Warwick was determined that Plymouth should be held at all costs.

Warwick's greatest concern at the start of 1643 was the convoy of arms and ammunition which the Queen was preparing in Holland for the supply of the Royalist Army in England. He had already sent the 4th Rate *Providence* and 6th Rate *Greyhound* to watch her activities, and he followed these by despatching his Vice-Admiral William Batten in the 2nd Rate *Rainbow* to take charge in intercepting the Queen's ships.

The States General of the United Provinces were supporting the Queen's efforts and the 'High and Mighty Lords' had provided five merchant ships to carry the arms and ammunition that she had purchased, together with an escort of nine men-of-war. Loading having been completed, Queen Henrietta Maria embarked at Scheveningen, near The Hague, on 16 January 1643. There was little wind, but the following day the convoy was able to get clear of the land. However, the favourable wind soon increased far more than was pleasant and by midnight it 'blew a fearful and furious storm' which continued for the next six days. Eventually the Queen, who was apparently in charge of the whole operation, decided to return to Holland; although attempts were made to dissuade her on the grounds that it was far safer to stay at sea in sound ships than to return to that dangerous coast in a storm. Nevertheless she insisted, and Admiral Maarten Tromp, commanding the convoy (who was later to be such a formidable opponent of the English fleet), agreed reluctantly to make the attempt. To everybody's relief the ship, in which Henrietta Maria had embarked, returned safely, as did two other ships; but the remaining eleven were as yet unaccounted for. Two of them, it was learned later, had not seen the signal to return and reached Newcastle. Another seven arrived at various Dutch ports; one, carrying men and horses, ran aground, but all men and horses were saved. The remaining ship, carrying all the coachmen, was feared lost.

If an Admiral of Tromp's eminence considered it was safer to proceed than to return, he was undoubtedly right. Why the Queen, who was a very courageous woman, should have insisted on returning, is one of the minor mysteries of naval history.

A convoy was reassembled for her with seven, though larger, warships, together with a ship of her own which was loaded with ammunition. This ammunition ship was lying in the estuary of the River Maas, watched by two of Batten's ships, the *Providence* and the *Greyhound*, from which a message had been sent ashore that if the ship sailed they would seize it or sink it. Tromp, armed with a warrant from the States General and the Prince of Orange, went with two warships to take possession of the ship. In spite of this, the local administration, the States of Holland, refused to release her. Tromp so informed the States General and the Prince of Orange, whilst Henrietta Maria wrote a furious letter to the States General. The States of Holland gave way and the ship sailed. The *Providence* fired some ineffectual shots, presumably more in protest than anything else, because Tromp was in considerably superior strength.

This time the weather was good and the wind favourable and the convoy was soon in sight of Flamborough Head, and the next day was near Scarborough on its way to Newcastle. The wind then turned adverse and the ships turned back and anchored in Bridlington Bay. This was an area that favoured the Royalists and local people arrived with provisions. The Queen sent a message to the Marquess of Newcastle, who was some 20 miles away, informing him of the convoy's arrival. Two hours later some of his cavalry trotted into Bridlington and the Queen landed. Tromp, with the naval escort, was lying well off shore, for it was not the policy of the Dutch Government to get actively involved in the hostilities.

During the night Batten arrived with the 3rd Rate *Antelope* and four armed merchantmen. The Queen, in a letter to the King, said that the alarm was given about 4 o'clock in the morning, with the advice that the ammunition ships, which had not yet been unloaded should be secured. An hour later

Batten's ships opened fire. The Queen and her companions rose hastily and left the village whilst the soldiers took up defensive positions around the ammunition ships. In her letter the Queen added, 'In case of a descent I must act the captain, though a little low in stature myself. One of these ships has done me the favour to flank my house, which fronted the pier, and before I could get out of bed the walls were whistling upon me in such style that you may easily believe I loved not such music.'[2]

This bombardment continued for two hours, until Tromp sent a message to Batten that if he did not stop he would open fire. Batten was in no position to withstand a superior force lying between him and the open sea. He accordingly ceased fire, and, as the tide was ebbing and there would soon be insufficient depth of water, he was forced to withdraw. So, with Dutch naval support, this important convoy was safely unloaded. Parliament was furious, but was in no position to take on Holland as well as the King.

On 7 March Prince Rupert made an unsuccessful attempt to take Bristol by surprise. This great port, with its wealth, its ships, and its trade, was a prize dearly coveted by the Royalists. Rupert had arranged that some Royalist adherents amongst the City merchants should open a gate for him; but the Roundheads discovered the plan and the merchants were arrested.

In April 1643 Parliamentary forces made another attempt on Cornwall. The object was twofold: to remove the threat to Plymouth and capture Falmouth, which was invaluable to the Royalists for the import of munitions and other supplies, whilst Warwick had all too few ships to blockade it. After some initial success, the Parliamentary forces were defeated by Hopton on 16 May at the battle of Stratton, and driven out of the County.

The fortunes of Parliament declined during the summer of 1643. In June and July, respectively, their forces were defeated at the battle of Lansdown, near Bath, and Roundway Down, outside Devizes. And then on 25 July the King's troops stormed and captured Bristol, in the harbours of which lay the potential nucleus of a Royalist fleet. Eight large armed merchant ships greeted Prince Rupert, commanding the Royalist troops with a salute of 60 guns (the even number displaying some ignorance of naval protocol) and merchants of the City offered him ships and crews. Eight ships were made available immediately and others also declared for the King's service, including a 5th Rate of the Navy, the 10th Whelp. Command of this start of a Royal fleet was vested in Sir John Pennington. By 4 August Pennington had 18 ships armed, manned, and ready for sea. The citizens of Bristol undertook to raise this number to 50.

Parliament's reaction to this disaster was to order Warwick to send a squadron of his best ships 'to lie in the mouth of the Severn, to stop all ships coming in or going forth of Bristol'.[3] Before these ships arrived, Pennington had despatched the armed merchant ships Fellowship and Hart to try and secure Milford Haven harbour and achorage; for this was a port where the

---

[2] Navy Records Society, 'Documents Relating to the Civil War 1642-1648', ed. J.R. Powell & E.K. Timings. Vol. 105, 1963, p. 61.
[3] Op. cit. p. 55.

King hoped to land troops he was intending to withdraw from Ireland. The two ships found Milford Haven empty, for Parliament's Vice-Admiral William Smith, who had been based there, had been sent to relieve the besieged town of Galway. He had arrived there too late to save the hard-pressed garrison from surrender to the King's troops.

At the same time as Bristol was being attacked Warwick had suffered a reverse before Exeter which, held by Parliament, was besieged by Royalist forces under Sir John Berkeley. Warwick's ships, trying to sail up the river, came under heavy fire from the Royalist gun emplacements which had been hastily prepared by Berkeley. Three ships were set on fire, three were captured, and two lighters carrying ammunition were sunk.

Parliament had a slight compensation at sea to offset these dismal reverses. At the beginning of August a 300-ton ship, bound from Denmark to Newcastle with a large consignment of arms and ammunition, was captured; and about the same time another ship, on her way from Newcastle to Holland, was seized in which, hidden amongst a cargo of coal, was found about £4,000 in cash to purchase arms for the Royalists.

The Royalist triumph at Milford Haven was brief. Smith sailed from Kinsale on 2 August 1643 in his ship the 3rd Rate *Swallow*. Arriving before Milford harbour on 7 August, a fisherman came on board and told him that there were two King's ships, men-of-war, in the harbour, the 400-ton *Fellowship* of Bristol with 24 guns and four captains, and the *Hart*. He added that the captains had summoned the local gentry to tell them of the King's capture of Bristol and other successes. Smith sailed into the harbour where he saw the *Fellowship*, commanded by Captain Burley, at anchor. The two Royalist ships were no match for a 3rd Rate, and one of the four captains on board her, John Brooks, came out in a boat carrying a white flag and asked for a parley, to which Smith consented. 'Then', said Smith, 'he came aboard; and leaping down into the waist, he cried, "God bless King Charles"; to which we all said, "Amen".'[4] The parley effected nothing. The *Swallow* came to anchor alongside the *Fellowship*, which suddenly cut her cable and was under sail, intending to run ashore. Smith ordered one gun to fire; both ships ran aground, and after Smith had fired a further two guns, Captain Burley surrendered. The *Hart* had fled eight miles up river and run ashore, where most of her company ran away. She was captured and brought off. And so failed Pennington's attempt to secure Milford Haven.

Warwick's main problem was lack of ships. He was writing to Parliament at the time of his failure against the Royalist defences around Exeter, asking for more ships. Obviously men-of-war could not be built quickly, but he had his eye on suitable merchant ships which could soon be provided with guns. In November 1643 he wrote again, repeating this request. He knew that Parliament was reluctant to take ships up from trade, but he pointed out that if the Royalists succeeded in capturing Plymouth, the merchants in the West would be unable to trade anyway for lack of a port. Finally he wrote again

---

[4] Op. cit. p. 89.

later that month, saying that if Parliament 'wanted their business done' they must give him the ships to do it.[5]

Meanwhile a Royalist campaign in Devon had been having considerable success. Barnstaple and Bideford surrendered to the King's troops, and on 4 September the garrison of Exeter, which Warwick had been trying to relieve, surrendered.

But this was the high tide of Royalist victories. The Earl of Essex, perhaps the greatest of Parliament's generals, by a brilliant march from London, relieved the Parliamentary garrison of Gloucester, entering the city on 8 September. After leaving supplies, heavy guns and ammunition, he started on his return journey. Following able manoeuvres to mislead the King and his commanders, he encountered the Royalist Army, commanded by the King in person, at Newbury on 19 September 1643. The battle the next day was indecisive, but the advantage lay with Essex, and when he prepared to renew it the following morning, the Royalists had gone.

The Earl of Ormonde, the King's commander in Ireland, had defeated the rebels at Ross in March 1643. In April the King ordered him to conclude a truce, in order to free soldiers to be transported to England. Ormonde arranged this in September. On 19 October Ormonde wrote to Sir Orlando Bridgman, the Lord Keeper, saying that by His Majesty's command he was preparing to transport about 3,000 foot and 300 horse. His main difficulty was in finding the ships to transport them safely to Chester, to which they had been directed. On 23 October some troops were landed at Minehead and a little later at Bristol. But the despatch of troops to Chester had become too dangerous because there was a Parliamentary squadron of six ships in the Dee estuary.

On 26 November Ormonde wrote to the Archbishop of York, who had taken refuge in his own town of Conway, seeking his assistance in the reception of the troops. He was worried, too, about the steadiness of the soldiers' allegiance to the King, because efforts had already been made in Ireland 'to corrupt the officers and debauch the soldiers', and, as they were short of clothing and money, it would be essential to have these things ready for them when they disembarked, for otherwise they could easily be seduced by promises from Parliamentary agents of the supply of these wants.

As a result of this letter, transports and escorting warships were sent to Ireland from Bristol, and, through the arrangements made by the Archbishop of York, some 2,000 to 3,000 soldiers were landed at Mostyn, near Prestatyn, in November. The Parliamentary squadron was too weak to interfere, and an indignant Warwick complained that this movement could have been prevented if the Winter Guard had taken up its positions at the time he had ordered. He had been warned by the master of a merchant ship of the approaching embarkation of six regiments of foot and six troops of horse.

Up till this time Warwick had been in intermittent communication with the Earl of Northumberland, who, whilst 'sitting on the fence', was still Lord

---

[5] Op. cit.

High Admiral. To him, on 22 November, Warwick wrote complaining of his shortage of ships for the tasks required of him. He said that the Royalists had fitted some 16 sail at Bristol and Barnstaple and were fitting more as fast as they could manage it.

Some of the troops from Ireland were soon in action and justified Ormonde's fears. Lord Byron was besieging Nantwich in Cheshire, when on 25 January 1644 Sir Thomas Fairfax arrived to relieve the town and attacked the Cavalier army which was divided by the swollen River Weaver. Two unreliable regiments from Ireland broke and fled, and a sally by the beleagured garrison completed the defeat of the Royalists. Byron got away with his cavalry, but most of the rest of his troops were taken prisoner, a total of 72 officers and 1,500 men. Of these, some 800 officers and men joined the Parliamentary Army. One of the officers taken prisoner was Colonel George Monck, who was sent as a prisoner to the Tower of London.

On 5 December 1643 the Commissioners of the Navy had sent to Warwick the 'Certificate and Estimate of the Charge of the Fleet' for 1644. They had considered the number of men required to man the fleet and conceived that this could not be less than 5,000 if the seas were to be kept in safety. They calculated that these 5,000 would suffice to man 46 sail, made up of two of the second rank, nine of the third rank, twenty of the fourth rank, and five of the sixth rank. (The term 'rates' had not yet been adopted into official usage, though it had been employed by William Batten in his 'Fleet Survey' of 1642.[6]) Of these 46 ships, 26 were to be of His Majesty's 'that may be fitted to service', the remaining 20 were to be taken up from the merchants of those lying in the River Thames. The Commissioners thought they might be distributed as follows: 8 to the West, 16 for Ireland and the Severn, 8 for the Downs, 8 for the Scottish Coast, and 6 for the North Coast of Ireland.[7] It is apparent that, from the number of ships in the Navy, Parliament had sanctioned further building.

On 7 December 1643 Warwick was created by Parliament Lord High Admiral of England in succession to the Earl of Northumberland.

On 13 January Ormonde wrote to Lord Digby saying that he was sending two more regiments to England and four troops of horse. It may well have been the necessity to cut communications between England and Ireland that prompted Warwick to write to Parliament on 10 February 1644 notifying them of his dissatisfaction at the Commissioners' proposals for the fleet. Amongst the points that Warwick made were:

1. Of vessels from 50 to 300 tons the Royalists now had at least 260.

2. That at least 50 warships were necessary for the safeguarding of 'His Majesty's Dominions' and the security of trade, for which 6,000 men would be needed.

3. That these 50 ships would have to be distributed in so many small squadrons that at least 10 would be needed to prevent a foreign invasion or a threat by a large foreign fleet.

---

[6] Op. cit. p. 7.
[7] Op. cit. p. 108.

4. That naval stores were nearly exhausted and it would take a lot of money and considerable time to replenish them.

5. If the above deficiencies were not remedied quickly the country would lie open to invasion, it would be impossible to prevent importation of arms from abroad, and the merchandise of the Kingdom would be transferred to others.

At the start of 1644, however, affairs for the Royalists had taken a turn for the worse, for Scotland had entered the war on the side of Parliament. On 19 January the Scottish army of 18,000 foot and more than 3,000 horse, under the command of Lord Leven, crossed the Tweed. The King's troops in Northumberland retreated into Newcastle before the Scottish advance.

Leven halted for some weeks before the City of Newcastle and then, by-passing the town, he forded the Tyne with most of his army and pushed on southwards. By 2 March he was across the River Wear and on 4 March he entered Sunderland. The Marquess of Newcastle, with his very much smaller force, did nothing more than fight a delaying action and then fell back on Durham. Leven followed him up, but the country had been stripped bare of provisions and supply problems forced him to stop in the northern part of the county and he laid siege to the Royalist forts protecting the mouth of the Tyne.

On Newcastle's southern flank Lord Fairfax had sent Sir William Constable northwards against the Royalist coastal garrisons. He captured Whitby but was not strong enough to take Scarborough.

As a result of these operations, the Royalists lost the use of the ports of the North-East and Warwick was relieved of one of his problems.

In April 1644 Ormonde, in Ireland, wrote to Lord Digby, the King's Secretary of State, about the hazard that would be run by any ships approaching the English or Welsh coasts, owing to the blockade by ships of Parliament. For this reason, and also on account of the shortage of money to hire ships from the merchants, he was unable to send the arms and ammunition that Digby had requested.

On 27 May Ormonde wrote to the Archbishop of York, informing him that he had a detachment of 300 soldiers with 20 barrels of powder ready to embark for the defence of Anglesey, but their despatch had been prevented by the arrival of Parliamentary warships. He added that the brutality by which 70 soldiers and two women from Ireland had been bound and thrown overboard as Irish rebels made men fearful of embarking. In fact, the number so outrageously treated was even greater; for in South Wales the brutal Parliamentary Captain Swanley, commanding at sea in that area, had tied back to back 150 soldiers brought from Ireland by Colonel Willoughby and thrown them into the sea 'to wash them from the blood of the Protestants that was upon them.'

In the West Country, a Royalist force under Prince Maurice had given up the siege of Plymouth and arrived before Lyme Regis, which was held for Parliament and which Prince Maurice was determined to take. It was important because it was the end of a string of fortresses which ran across the neck of land between the Bristol Channel and Lyme Bay. All except Lyme were in Royalist hands, and if this were captured Maurice reckoned that he would be able to complete the reduction of Plymouth without Parliamentary interference.

Maurice arrived before the Lyme Regis defences on 20 April 1644. The official commander of the fortress was Colonel John Weare, but the actual command was exercised by Lieutenant-Colonel Robert Blake, the future General-at-Sea and Commander-in-Chief of Parliament's fleet. The garrison was small — little over 1,000 soldiers with some assistance from seamen and civilians. Blake realised that the perimeter was too long for his small garrison. He shortened it and used the steep fall of the ground towards the sea to neutralise the Royalist artillery fire.

Against Blake's defences, Maurice was unable to make any impression, in spite of a succession of fierce assaults. But the garrison was in sore need when Warwick, the Lord High Admiral, arrived off the town on about 23 May. He had despatched ships from Plymouth with troops, supplies, and munitions. On 30 May he sent a report on the situation to the Speaker of the Lords. He had arrived at Lyme Regis, he said, to find the garrison very short of food and ammunition; even though three armed merchantmen he had sent to assist them had landed powder and provisions from their own ships' stores. After his arrival Warwick landed 300 seamen to reinforce the garrison. In addition, he despatched ships' boats filled with men to threaten a landing at various places east of Lyme; and these succeeded in drawing off some of the besieging troops.

On 12 June Warwick rendered a report to the Committee of Both Kingdoms (i.e. that appointed jointly by England and Scotland). The Royalists, he wrote, were daily bringing their approaches nearer to the Parliamentary lines, and the defenders were very short of ammunition. He could spare no more from his ships without diminishing their fighting ability. Warwick added that he was going to stay before Lyme, but was retaining only his own ship and that of his Vice-Admiral, Batten; the rest he had despatched to their various duties — the Irish Seas, the North, Weymouth Road, Dartmouth, Guernsey, the Downs, and the Thames (the last two for convoys and services).

But help was at hand. Essex's army, disposed about Stow-in-the-Wold or Chipping Norton, had about 130 miles to march to Lyme. Marching 110 miles in seven days — a phenomenal effort, hauling guns and wagons over the roads of that time — the approach of his cavalry advanced guard caused Maurice to raise the siege of Lyme, and on 15 June Warwick's secretary wrote to the Speaker of the House of Commons to say that the Royalists had departed at 2 a.m. that morning.

Apart from Warwick's assistance, the successful conduct of this epic defence had been due to the leadership and tactical ability of Blake.

Whilst the siege of Lyme Regis had been in progress most of the Parliamentary naval activity had been in connection with operations in South Wales. The Royalists had taken advantage of the absence of the Parliamentary squadron to send supplies to a fort which was under construction at Pill, opposite Pembroke, with the object of denying access into Milford Haven by Parliamentary ships. On 23 January 1644 a squadron under the command of the beastly but able Swanley, consisting of two 3rd Rates, one 6th Rate and three armed merchantmen, appeared off Milford Haven. Pennington, the Royalist naval commander, had sent ships carrying guns and supplies for the Pill fort under the escort of two armed merchantmen. When it arrived, the Parliamentary squadron found these two warships lying at anchor. Faced by such a vastly superior force, the two ships 'cut and ran'. Parliament's conquest of Pembroke followed and was completed on 10 March.

On 12 July Colonel Sir Charles Gerard landed at Black Rock in Monmouthshire with Irish troops and captured Cardiff and Carmarthen Castle, as well as several other places. Parliament's chances of retaining their South Wales conquests looked poor, but on 1 August Warwick received a report that Gerard and his troops had left the area. They had indeed been recalled by the King following the defeat of the Royalists under Prince Rupert and the Marquess of Newcastle at the battle of Marston Moor on 2 July 1644.

Attention now switches to the West Country, for the Queen had given birth to a daughter in Exeter and on 10 July she sailed from Falmouth for France. A Parliamentary squadron under the command of William Batten lay off Falmouth, and when some of the ships in the harbour were seen to set sail, Batten got ready. The first to come out was a Dutch warship and as soon as she was within range, Batten opened fire. The ship did not reply and got away. Ten more followed and, having the advantage of the wind, were able to avoid interception. Parliament's ships followed, but the only one fast enough to overhaul the ships of the Queen's squadron was the new frigate *Constant Warwick* (described in Batten's report as 'a nimble frigate of ours'), which was able to get within range and open fire on the fleeing ships which 'replied for their own safety'. However, all the Queen's ships got safely to Brest.

The Queen, with her newly born infant, had been apprehensive (one hesitates to use the word 'afraid' with regard to this indomitable lady) that her squadron might not be able to evade Batten's ships, and had acquired a 16-oar galley, 'which the best vessel in the world could never have coped with', to which she might transfer if necessary.[8] Batten does not seem to have distinguished himself, and this was the second time that the Queen had foiled him.

Warwick, reporting the episode to the Committee of Both Kingdoms, said that at the time he had only eight ships available, of which the *Reformation* (2nd Rate) (Batten), *Paramour* (armed merchant ship), and *Warwick* (5th Rate — Frigate) were three of the fastest sailers and had been sent to Falmouth. The *Dreadnought* (3rd Rate) and *Mary Rose* (4th Rate), being but heavy (i.e. slow) ships were kept to look after Dartmouth. The *Providence* (4th Rate) was sent to Salcombe, where there were some Royalist ships. The *Hind* (5th Rate) and *Nicodemus* (6th Rate) were off Topsham, and his own ship the *James*

---

[8] Op. cit. p. 163.

(2nd Rate) was alone at Torbay, 'ready to assist the several services and the Army as occasion should require.'[9]

On 22 June the Speaker of the House of Lords read a letter from Essex saying that Warwick had assured him that if he advanced further west the men of the Western Counties would flock to join him. Essex was sure that the Parliamentary Army under Sir William Waller's command would safeguard his own rear from Royalist attack. There would be good strategic reasons for Essex to move west and conquer Cornwall. It would relieve Plymouth and also result in the seizure of the important Royalist port of Falmouth. Warwick, concurring with the importance of these objectives, had promised to keep him company by sea. On 23 July Essex reached Tavistock; but he had now learned that the King had defeated Waller at Copredy Bridge, and that the safety of his rear no longer existed, for the King was following him and was reported to be already in Somerset.

At Tavistock Essex was well positioned, and he had already relieved Plymouth, for the Royalist commander, Sir Richard Grenville, with his communications threatened, had raised the siege and retired across the Tamar. Nevertheless, although his strength had been depleted through the need to leave garrisons behind him, Essex decided to push ahead with his invasion of Cornwall because he had arranged with Warwick that it would be a joint operation; he would advance overland whilst Warwick kept pace by sea. To strengthen his depleted forces, he took one regiment of horse and one of foot from the Plymouth garrison — a step that worried Warwick because if Essex were defeated the Plymouth garrison might not be strong enough to resist Royalist assault.

On 2 August Essex was informed that the King had entered Launceston, and he withdrew southward towards Lostwithiel to make contact with the fleet. But a detachment sent ahead to seize the port of Fowey saw no sign of Warwick's ships — and nor were those ships ever to turn up! Warwick gave the reason in a letter to the COBK on 18 August 1644. The wind, he said, had been in the west for such a long time and had blown so hard that he had been unable to send any relief to Essex's army, and he added that the army was provided solely from Plymouth and that its supplies would be exhausted if they were not replenished soon.

In fact, the Lord General and his army were trapped. Their defeat followed at the battle of Lostwithiel and the bulk of them were forced to lay down their arms. Essex himself rightly embarked on a fishing boat for Plymouth in order to present his report to Parliament. Adverse winds and the King's defeat of Waller had turned a very promising joint navy and army operation into a disaster.

The year 1645 opened with important Parliamentary operations in the South Wales area. Major-General Langharne captured the family Langharne Castle from the Royalists and then advanced north to attack Cardigan Castle, which he also successfully captured, with the assistance of a naval detach-

---

[9] Op. cit. p. 164.

ment and a demi-cannon piece from the 3rd Rate *Leopard* which battered a breach in the walls. Subsequently, these operations served to retain Sir Charles Gerard (who had returned to South Wales) in the country and thus contributed to the decisive Parliamentary victory at the battle of Naseby.

On 5 February 1645 Vice-Admiral W. Smith (commanding in this area during Swanley's absence) wrote to Warwick from his ship, the 3rd Rate *Swallow* in Milford Haven, reporting an attempt by Gerard to recapture Cardigan Castle. The garrison was, indeed, on the verge of surrender when a party of 120 seamen in boats succeeded, in the face of the fire from some 300 musketeers on shore, in getting a supply of provisions into the castle. In a subsequent attack, Langharne drove off the Royalists.

On 16 February Batten, who had heard of a successful Royalist assault on Weymouth, went there with his own and another ship. He reinforced the garrison (which had retreated into neighbouring Melcombe) with 150 seamen and a supply of ammunition. Thus reinforced, the garrison counter-attacked the Royalists and, after bitter fighting, recaptured the town.

On 9 April 1645, the Earl of Warwick, in compliance with the 'Self-Denying Ordinance', which had just been passed by the House of Lords and under which none of their House could command in the field (including presumably a wet one!), resigned as Lord High Admiral, and on 19 April an Admiralty Commission of six Lords and twelve Members of the Commons was appointed to fill the post. (The Lords had opposed this measure, but the Commons, who had passed a similar Ordinance in their own House, insisted.) Warwick was appointed head of The Commission of Admiralty and Batten was selected to command the fleet for six months as Vice-Admiral.

On 14 May Warwick, at the request of the Lords, submitted a report on the state of the fleet as then at sea. His main points were:
1. The number of ships available for the summer's requirements was 49, plus 6 as escorts for fishing vessels and colliers. These 49 were to be employed as follows:
(a) The Guard for the Irish seas 9 (of which 2 were packet boats
(b) The Scottish Guard 7
(c) Blockading Bristol 7
(d) Guernsey 3
(e) The Downs (for convoy) 5
(f) In port (revictual, repair, etc.) 5
(g) Other services (including watching enemy ports) 13
2. It should be considered whether the public service would suffer unless more ships were provided.

On 14 June 1645 all hopes of a Royalist victory vanished after the disastrous defeat at Naseby. Nevertheless the King struggled desperately on. Gerard was again recalled from South Wales and Swanley was thus relieved from further worry. His Vice-Admiral, W. Smith, had been killed and William Penn was promoted Vice-Admiral in his place. On 11 July the COBK warned Batten that the King was intending to transport what remained of his army by sea from South Wales to join the Royalist troops in Somerset, commanded by Lord Goring. They ordered Batten to send an appropriate number of ships to prevent this, and he despatched four men-of-war into the Severn on 31 July. They discovered that in Bristol there were 38 flat-bottomed boats waiting to transport the troops, and captured all of them.

The King had been joined by Gerard with 2,000 Welsh foot, so that, with reinforcements from garrisons and detachments, he now had about 4,000 horse and 3,000 foot; but his infantry were nowhere near of the same quality and the morale of the horse had suffered. But the move to Somerset had been called off before his landing craft had been captured because on 9 July Fairfax had defeated and routed Goring's army at the battle of Langport.

On 19 August Batten reported to the Speaker of the Commons that he had assisted Major-General Langharne in South Wales with the frigate *Constant Warwick* and 200 seamen. This reinforcement led to the defeat of the Royalist troops still remaining in that area, with the loss of four guns and about 1,000 small arms.

On 10 September Fairfax launched the crowning stroke on Bristol, which was defended by Prince Rupert. After a fierce defence, Rupert surrendered on terms, and left for Oxford. There, a furious King (a far abler general than Rupert) dismissed him from all his appointments and directed him to depart overseas.

The First Civil War was now drawing to a close. In January 1646 Fairfax opened the last campaign in the West. With Batten's support from the sea, he stormed Dartmouth Castle on 18 January. On 16 February he defeated the Royalist force under Lord Hopton at Chumleigh, and on 25 February he entered Launceston. Fairfax's troops marched into Bodmin on 2 March and the next day the Prince of Wales (later Charles II) sailed for the Scilly Isles. Truro fell to Fairfax on 10 March. Terms were agreed, and on 20 March the Royalist field army in Cornwall laid down its arms and was disbanded.

A squadron under Batten had been waiting outside Falmouth to intercept the Prince of Wales, but once more he was eluded. After capturing Portland at the beginning of April, Batten, too, sailed for Scilly, arriving at St. Mary's Island on 12 April with nine ships. He then surrounded the island; but once more Batten was unlucky for a storm arose that scattered his screen of ships, and the Prince seized the opportunity to escape and reached Jersey.

On Christmas Day 1646 Batten was ordered to sail north and station himself about Tynemouth to stop any attempt by the King to escape overseas. As his ship, the *Leopard* (3rd Rate), had a 'great draught of water making it unsafe for her to go within the bar', he was asked to consider going aboard the *Fellowship* (armed merchantman) or *Constant Warwick* (frigate). In fact Batten took the *Leopard* and the *Constant Warwick* and 'two or three ships more'.[10] Here Batten, in January 1647, established relations with the Scots, and also with the King, who was then in their captivity.

In about March 1647 troubles began to arise in the Parliamentary Army which was owed a large amount in arrears of pay. The predominantly

---

[10] Op. cit. p. 209. [10] Ibid, p. 209.

Presbyterian Parliament was too broke to find the money readily and would have liked to have cut the strength of the Army, which was under the control of the Independents. By August 1647 the Army had triumphed, the Independents became the majority in the House of Commons and some of the Presbyterian generals of the Army were fleeing overseas. Batten, Vice-Admiral of the Fleet, and a Presbyterian, not only disliked the Independents, but he was disgruntled because he had expected to be given command of the Fleet, whereas he had been appointed an Admiral only on a temporary basis.

As a result of the Army's triumph, charges were brought against eleven Members of Parliament. Six of them got passes from the Speaker and embarked for France. However, they entrusted their passage to a scoundrel who, in August 1647, brought them before Batten, the Vice-Admiral. Batten, who had already offered to join the Earl of Lauderdale (who was with the Royalists in Holland) with 22 ships, provided he could get them victualled in France, allowed the six Members to continue their journey. The Independents arranged that Batten should be summoned to appear before a Committee of Both Houses, and he was directed to lay down his commission. Colonel Rainsborough, a particularly unpleasant commander of a regiment of foot, was appointed to succeed Batten as Vice-Admiral. He was the leader of a party called the Levellers, and Parliament considered this a way to get him out of politics!

These political wrangles and manoeuvres were suddenly interrupted by the outbreak of the Second Civil War. On 22 February 1648 Colonel Poyer, Governor of Pembroke Castle for Parliament, refused to deliver up the castle to Colonel Fleming whom Fairfax had sent to replace him. Poyer said that he was only holding out till his troops had received their arrears of pay. Reinforcements were sent to Fleming from Bristol and guns were landed from the 4th Rate *Expedition*, riding in Milford Haven. Poyer promptly broke out into open revolt and on 23 March attacked and defeated Fleming, who had to take refuge on board the *Expedition*. Poyer now overran most of Pembrokeshire, seized Tenby Castle and declared for the King. Fairfax sent Colonel Horton to South Wales with a small force; but on 29 April Fleming was surprised and killed near Carmarthen, and all over South Wales revolt flared up. On 28 April Sir Marmaduke Langdale, with a Royalist force from Scotland, surprised and took Berwick, though Captain Ball, in the new 4th Rate *Adventure*, did his best to support the garrison with gun fire.

Fairfax, Parliament's Commander-in-Chief of the Army, was faced with a rising in South Wales, an impending invasion by a Scottish army, outbreaks threatened in Essex and Kent, and disaffection in Devon and Cornwall. In addition, the loyalty of the fleet could not be relied upon. The officers of the Navy were strongly Presbyterian; they disliked and distrusted the Independents, and they loathed Rainsborough. The seamen were angry because their victuals were bad and their pay was in arrears, and Batten, whom they trusted, had been replaced by Rainsborough.

Fairfax despatched Cromwell, with his own regiment of horse and three regiments of foot, to South Wales to reinforce Horton. Captain Crowther was ordered to abandon the blockade of Irish harbours, in which he had been engaged, and sail to Penarth.

By the time Cromwell arrived in South Wales, Horton, with Crowther's assistance, had largely restored the situation.

While Fairfax had been issuing orders to deal with the troubles on land, Parliament had hurriedly re-appointed the Earl of Warwick as Lord High Admiral. Warwick reached the fleet in the Downs on 1 June, but was unable to gain control because the seamen refused to accept him. On 3 June he went to Portsmouth, the fleet there being still dubiously loyal to Parliament. Batten had been ordered to accompany him, but he claimed that business prevented him and said that he would arrive a day or two later. Batten, in fact, had been round spreading disaffection himself. This was found out and he was ordered to appear before a Parliamentary Committee. However, Batten boarded the *Constant Warwick* (of which he was part owner with the Earl of Warwick), persuaded the crew to join the Prince of Wales, and escaped to Holland. At Portsmouth, everything appeared to Warwick to be in order and he returned to London.

On 4 June an insurrection broke out in Essex. In the Downs the Royalists had ten ships placed between the Parliamentary fleets in the Thames and at Portsmouth, but they were out of provisions and could get no supplies from the Kentish ports and on 10 June they sailed for Helvoetsluys in Holland. The next day Fairfax crossed the Thames at Tilbury Fort, with such troops as he could make available, and marched to Billericay on his way to crush the Essex revolt.

In Holland the Royalist-manned ships from the Downs were joined by the Prince of Wales, who had embarked at Calais in Batten's old flagship the 2nd Rate *Constant Reformation*.

On 8 July the Scottish army crossed the Border, faced by a much smaller Parliamentary army under Lambert. Fairfax had ordered Cromwell to go to Lambert's assistance as soon as he could leave South Wales, and on 11 June he set off, meeting the retreating Lambert on 13 August. Cromwell took command of their united forces and on 17 August defeated and routed the Scottish army at the battle of Preston.

On the day of the battle of Preston the Prince of Wales sailed with his fleet into the Downs. His Vice-Admiral was Lord Willoughby, who had transferred his allegiance from Parliament, and his Rear-Admiral was Batten, who had been knighted. Contrary winds drove Prince Charles into Yarmouth, where he purchased supplies, and left again for the Downs on 25 August. He had 12 ships with a total of 199 guns. Warwick had the same number of ships in the Thames but with 312 guns; the crews of some of his ships, however, were disaffected. There was also the Portsmouth fleet, in uneasy allegiance to Parliament, of 9 ships and 185 guns.

To the Prince the situation looked bleak. He had heard of the Royalist defeat at Preston and Colchester had just capitulated to Fairfax. He decided to return to Holland, but the crews of his leading ships forced their captains to sail up the Thames, and the Prince with the remaining ships followed.

On the morning of 29 August, as Warwick's ships came down the river on the ebb tide, they saw the Royalist ships coming up the river. Warwick, after anchoring, weighed and manoeuvred towards the Oaze shoal, keeping to windward of the Royalists. Both fleets anchored for the night.

The Prince of Wales sent a summons to Warwick to surrender his ships in exchange for a general pardon. Warwick rejected it and held a Council of War, which decided to await the arrival of the Portsmouth fleet before attacking.

Owing to his shortage of provisions and water it was essential for Prince Charles to force Warwick to action and to beat him decisively. The land war had been lost, but a naval victory might still swing popular opinion towards the Royalists.

The following day both fleets weighed with the tide and worked to windward. At 4 p.m., when action seemed imminent, the wind changed and increased in strength, forcing both fleets to anchor. The Royalist ships could stay no longer and the next day they retreated reluctantly. Under cover of darkness the Prince put to sea. Some of his ships passed others lying at anchor; they were the ships of the Portsmouth fleet waiting for the tide to carry them in. The next day Warwick followed the Royalist fleet across to Holland.

Cooped up in a foreign land, the seamen of Charles's little fleet soon grew discontented, and they levelled accusations against Batten. The fleet thus gradually disintegrated and Batten resigned his commission and retired to The Hague, from whence, availing himself of Warwick's indemnity, he returned to England. Prince Rupert was then placed by Charles in command of what remained of the Royal fleet.

On 21 November Warwick sailed for England, arriving in the Downs on 23 November. On 20 February 1649 he was dismissed, owing to the impending trial of his brother, and replaced by Popham, Blake, and Deane as Generals-at-Sea.

On 31 January 1649 King Charles I was executed and the designation 'King and Parliament' was replaced by Commonwealth'. New flags were now designed for the Navy's ships. Nevertheless, there was now a new King for the Prince of Wales was proclaimed King in Edinburgh as Charles II.

The Navy had one more major task before these wars finally drew to a close. On 12 June 1650 Fairfax was appointed General of the field army, with Cromwell as his Lieutenant-General, for Parliament had decided on a preventive invasion of Scotland, thereby initiating the Third Civil War. To this Fairfax objected. He was overruled and resigned; Cromwell being appointed in his place.

On 22 July the army crossed the Border and marched north without opposition, and on 29 July the cavalry drove back the Scottish outposts to within a mile of Edinburgh. The troops attacked in heavy rain, and the next morning Cromwell withdrew his wet and weary troops to Musselburgh. Sir David Leslie, commanding the Scottish army, followed up with a mounted attack which was repulsed after a hard struggle. On the following day the Scots attacked the English position at Musselburgh but were beaten off.

Cromwell was short of supplies and on 6 August he was forced to withdraw to Dunbar where there was an adequate harbour. His intention now was to march round Leslie's right flank to Queensferry, where the fleet was to join him so that he could seize both banks of the Forth and cut Leslie's communications.

After various manoeuvrings by Cromwell and Leslie, the latter had only to stay where he was to force Cromwell to evacuate such of his army as he could by sea (a 300 years anticipation of Dunkirk). Fortunately for the English army, Leslie, under pressure by the ministers of the Kirk, who persuaded him that the English were at his mercy, moved down from his strong hill top position, and was defeated at the battle of Dunbar the following morning. So the fleet was saved from a perilous evacuation and Cromwell from the pages of history due to his incompetent generalship.

Though defeated, the Scottish army was still very much in being. On 1 January Charles II was crowned King of Scotland at Scone. He believed that all the northern parts of England favoured the Royalist cause and he decided to march south through Lancashire with the Scottish army, and notified the leading Royalists there of his intention.

During the march south the King noticed that Sir David Leslie looked melancholy and asked him why, when he was at the head of such a good army. Leslie whispered to him that 'he well knew that army, how well soever it look'd, would not fight.' The King never repeated this to anyone, as he told Clarendon many years later;[11] but Leslie was right, as was soon shown at the disastrous battle of Worcester. On that 28 August the Scots were routed, and after leading one last mounted charge (from which all the soldiers melted away except his own servants!), King Charles II was a fugitive.

---

[11] Edward Earl of Clarendon, *The History of the Rebellion and Civil Wars in England*, Vol. III (Oxford, The Theater, 1704), p. 312.

4

The Start of the First Dutch War

The civil wars in England had hardly ended before Parliament found itself embroiled with Holland — indeed, these wars had not really ended, for Prince Rupert still commanded at sea the remains of the squadron which had taken refuge in Dutch ports. Friction between the new English Commonwealth and the Dutch Republic could of course be anticipated, for the States General had given as much maritime help to the Royalists as the Americans gave to the British during the period preceding their entry into the Second World War.

But their previous support for the King's party was not the reason for the conflict. Holland and England were the great trading nations of the world, and their trading interests clashed from the American and African shores of the Atlantic to the Indian Ocean. There were feelings on both sides of the North Sea that there was insufficient trade for both countries. During the years of war in England the Dutch were free from competition in their chosen trading areas and resented the fact that English merchants were now able to divert their ships from war to commerce. For trade was not only a major interest to the Dutch, it was nearly their sole livelihood.

As in many wars, the immediate cause for the start of hostilities was only the match applied to the bonfire. Two ordinances of 1650 and 1651 by the English Parliament, the 'Navigation Acts', banned foreign trading in English colonies, restricting such trade to English or Colonial ships, manned by predominantly English crews, and forbade the importation into England of goods not the produce of the country to which the importing vessel belonged. These Acts were clearly aimed at the Dutch, whose ships would not only be prevented from carrying goods to and from English colonies, but would no longer be allowed to carry merchandise into English ports which was the produce of a country other than Holland.

On 5 March 1651 it was announced that the Dutch, with 76 ships afloat, were adding another 150. (Unless otherwise stated, all dates are in the 'old style' [OS], used in England. The Dutch used the 'new style' [NS], which was ten days later in the calendar.)

31

The organisation of the English Navy under Parliament had been established on 23 February 1649. Its supreme control was vested in a Council of State (COS) consisting of members appointed by Parliament. But the ordinary, or day-to-day, direction of naval affairs was in the hands of the Admiralty Committee (AC), the members of which also belonged to the COS. Under this body were the Commissioners of the Navy (also known as Navy Commissioners [NC]), who were responsible for most of the administrative work. Admirals and captains at sea corresponded with the AC on important operational matters, and with the NC on matters relating to officers, seamen, and ships.

As noted in the last chapter, command of the fleet had been entrusted in 1649 to three Generals-at-Sea, Popham, Blake, and Deane; but in 1651 Popham was dead and Deane was still on military duties in Scotland, leaving Blake in sole command. An Order of the Council of State, dated 4 March 1652, states: 'Colonel Blake shall have a commission to command the fleet for nine months. . . . Consideration of another person to be general-at-sea be respited till further occasion.'[1]

After the establishment of the Commonwealth the flags worn by the ships of the Navy were changed. The Union between England and Scotland was dissolved by the execution of Charles I. The Council of State decreed 'That the Ships at Sea in service of the State shall onely beare the red Crosse in a white flag'. Nevertheless, the COS apparently wished to continue the concept of a 'Union' so that they could have a Union Flag and decided that a union existed between England and Ireland. The new Union Flag for naval use would be 'the Armes of England and Ireland in two severall Escutcheons in a red flag within a Compartment or'. The arms were (for England) 'argent a cross gules' and (for Ireland) 'azure, a harp or'; which flag was to be 'borne by the Admirall'.[2] What this meant (for those unversed in heraldry) was that in the centre of a red flag there was a yellow rectangle on which were two shields (actually, of an extraordinary shape with a convex curved top and straight sides) sided by side, with the dexter (i.e. right; but left as you look at it) a red cross on a white field, and the sinister (i.e. left) a yellow harp in a blue field. As regards this flag, Blake and Deane wrote to the Navy Commissioners pointing out that they would need sufficient for issue to each admiral, vice-admiral, and rear-admiral. They also needed for each ship jacks, ensigns, and pendants.

In the Standard (intended to replace the Royal Standard), which was to be flown by the Generals-at-Sea, the yellow compartment was abandoned and the shields bearing the arms of England and Ireland were surrounded by green laurel and bay branches.

The jack, the flag worn on the jackstaff at the bow or bowsprit, consisted of the impaled arms of England and Ireland, that is the red cross on white and the yellow harp on blue side by side, with the former next to the staff.

---

[1] *Navy Records Society*, 'The First Dutch War', ed. Dr. S.R. Gardiner, Vol. 13, 1898.
[2] W.G. Perrin, *British Flags* (Cambridge University Press, 1922).

The command organisation of the fleet followed that first used in an expedition against Cadiz in 1625. On this occasion the fleet was divided into three squadrons. One squadron, the 'Admiral's', commanded directly by the Commander-in-Chief of the Fleet, wore a red flag and red pendant on the main topmasthead of the flagship. The second squadron, in order of seniority, was commanded by the Vice-Admiral of the Fleet, and his flagship wore a blue flag and a blue pendant on the main topmasthead. The flagship of the third squadron had a white flag and white pendant, similarly displayed on the main topmasthead, and this squadron was commanded by the Rear-Admiral of the Fleet.

Each squadron was divided into three divisions commanded by squadron flag officers. The 'Admiral' of the three squadrons was, respectively (as stated above) the Commander-in-Chief of the Fleet, the Vice-Admiral of the Fleet, and the Rear-Admiral of the Fleet. These also commanded directly the senior division of their squadron. The vice-admirals and rear-admirals of the squadrons flew the colours as above, appropriate to their squadrons, a vice-admiral at the fore topmasthead and a rear-admiral at the mizzen topmasthead. The vice- and rear-admirals of squadrons were normally senior captains, who were only 'occasional' flag officers, or, in modern terminology, acting. Thus the status and identity of a flagship could be seen at a glance.

The private ships of each squadron wore pendants of the squadron colour, those of the red squadron at the main topmasthead, of the blue squadron at the fore topmasthead, and of the white squadron at the mizzen topmasthead. The term 'Admiral', 'Vice-Admiral', etc., denoted the ship as well as the officer in command. The red, blue, and white flags of command were of plain colour throughout, and the pendant was flown below the flag on each flagship. In addition to these plain flags, squadron flag officers also probably flew the Union flag. If the fleet was small and had only three flag officers, the senior had the Union flag at the main topmasthead and the vice- and rear-admirals flew the Union at fore and mizzen topmastheads respectively.[3]

This was the system adopted by Parliament for the fleet fitted out at the start of the First Dutch War, but with of course the Commonwealth flags. At some stage, however, there was a change in the order of the colours. Red still remained the senior, but white now came next, with blue as the junior. The reason is not known.

The private ships in each squadron (i.e. those which were not flagships) wore a pendant of the squadron colour at the topmasthead — main, fore, or mizzen according to the seniority of their division in the squadron. All ships wore an ensign of the squadron colour at the stern, and all pendants and ensigns had the red cross on white of St. George — in chief (i.e. next to the hoist) on pendants and in the canton (i.e. in the top corner of the flag next to the hoist) on ensigns.[4]

---

[3] Perrin, op. cit.
[4] Ibid.

Whilst the fleet organisation of the Dutch Navy was very similar, its higher direction differed because of the loose organisation of the Dutch Republic, which was a confederation of seven Provincial States. Inside each State, municipalities sent deputies to the States General, and sovereignty rested ultimately in the municipalities. This constitution had only been adopted in 1650 when, on the death of William II, the Stadholdership of the House of Orange had been abolished. Nevertheless, it appears that throughout the First Dutch War the Dutch warships wore the flag of the House of Orange (known as the 'Prince's Flag') of equal horizontal stripes, orange, white, and blue (the same as the present flag of South Africa — without, of course, the emblems on the centre stripe). During the Second and Third Dutch Wars the flag of the States General was used — the present national flag of Holland, with the stripe at the top being red instead of orange.

In Tromp's instructions to the captains of ships under his command in 1652, he said that the signal for fighting would be a red flag under the Prince's, flying on the Admiral's main mast. The States General took umbrage at the expression 'Prince's' flag in this instruction and did their best to substitute the red stripe of Holland for the orange one, but apparently without success. The old flag doubtless had a sentimental value, for it had been adopted as a national flag soon after the revolt against Spain.[5]

The great disadvantage of the political constitution was that no important resolution could be taken until it had been discussed and approved, not only by the Provincial States, but also by the municipalities! The arrangements for the several Boards of Admiralty made for even more delay and confusion. There were five of these Boards, one for each of five Provinces as follows:

1. Middleburg for Zeeland
2. Rotterdam for South Holland
3. Amsterdam for North Holland
4. Hoorn or Enkheizen for West Friesland (usually known as the North Quarter)
5. Haslingen for Friesland.

Each Board consisted of seven members — four appointed by the States General on the nomination of the Provincial State to which the Board belonged and three from Provinces to which it did not belong.

The post of Admiral-General had been abolished with the Stadholdership. Tromp was the Lieutenant-Admiral of Holland, i.e., Lieutenant of a non-existent Admiral-General.

Dutch ranks are here referred to, in general, by their English equivalents; but for one temporary rank there was no equivalent; this was *Commandeur*, which was given to a captain placed in command of a squadron on detachment.[6]

The first shots that heralded the outbreak of hostilities were fired on 12 May 1652 by the hired ship *Recovery* commanded by Captain Anthony Young.

---

[5] *Navy Records Society*, Vol. 13 'Papers Relating to the First Dutch War 1652-54' Vol. I, ed. S.R. Gardiner 1898.

[6] *Navy Records Society*, 'Corrigenda to Letters and Papers referring to the First Dutch War' by Captain A.C. Dewar 1931.

A letter of 15 May from one of the ship's company relates what happened. They discovered three Dutch warships escorting seven merchantmen with an 'Admiral' leading, followed in turn by a 'Vice-Admiral' and a 'Rear-Admiral' (these terms being applied, as customary, to the ships of the officers leading each of the three small squadrons). As the Dutch Admiral approached, the *Recovery* sent a boat to him with instructions to lower his flag (i.e. recognising to an English warship, English sovereignty in the Narrow Seas). He complied and fired a salute of three guns, which the *Recovery* returned. The Vice-Admiral then approached but refused to lower his flag and fired 13 shots at the *Recovery*. Captain Young sent a boat to persuade the Dutch ship to comply but received a curt refusal. The *Recovery* then prepared to fight; but before she did so, a small 24-gun English frigate appeared and fired three guns at the Dutch Rear-Admiral to make him strike. He did not return the fire but said he could not lower his flag as long as the Vice-Admiral kept his up. The frigate captain asked him if he supported the Vice-Admiral, to which he replied that he did not, but that 'as they had brewed up so they should bake'. Thereupon the *Recovery* fired a broadside at the Vice-Admiral with 19 guns, causing considerable damage. The Dutch ship returned the broadside, but after a considerable fight her captain was forced to take down his flag and submit. The rest of the Dutch ships kept half a league off and took no part in the contest. The letter concludes that 'having banged them handsomely, they began to fawn like spaniels and so in the conclusion we parted friends.'[7]

An account of this action was included in a report sent by Tromp to the States General on 20 May. On 19 May his fleet encountered two Dutch captains coming out of the Straits who had been escorting some rich merchantmen. They gave an inaccurate account of the action and said that they had left the merchantmen behind and were afraid that the English frigates had taken them. Tromp then set off to try and secure them.

On that same 19 May the Council of State had appointed Captain William Penn Vice-Admiral of the Fleet and Major Nehemiah Bourne Rear-Admiral. This signalled the division of the fleet into squadrons, but the appointment did not carry with it a permanent rank. Letters to Penn, for instance, were addressed 'Captain William Penn, Vice-Admiral of the Fleet and Captain of the *James*'. Blake, on the other hand, whilst referred to as 'Admiral', was addressed as 'General', his permanent rank.

To return to Tromp and his report to the States General; on 14 May he said that he and his fleet were sea off Ostend, when they were forced to anchor owing to bad weather. On 16 May the weather got worse while they were under sail and it was decided to shelter under the South Foreland. At 1.0 p.m. they were off the Downs and Tromp sent two captains to inform Admiral Bourne, who lay there with some Parliament ships, that they had been forced in by bad weather. Bourne greeted them with courtesy and thanked them for giving him notice.

---

[7] 'The First Dutch War' op. cit., pp. 179-180.

A letter from Dover reported Tromp's arrival before the town with a fleet of 41 ships, 'with his flag at the main top. The Castle fired a shot to order him to strike but he would not'.[8] He departed at noon the next day.

Tromp continued his report to the effect that after sailing from Dover he met with 15 'ships and frigates' of Parliament, among which was an Admiral's. He intended to speak with him and took in all his sails except the topsails, which were lowered to the middle of the mast. As soon as they were within cannon shot the English admiral shot a ball over his ship. He did not answer. The English shot another and Tromp answered with one. He then says that the English admiral being within musket shot fired a broadside through his ship and sails. A general fight followed. Bourne came out from Dover with 12 ships and frigates. (As Bourne had told Tromp's delegates, the ships were armed with 60 or 70 guns and the frigates with 38 to 50 guns.) Bourne's squadron assailed the Dutch fleet from astern and the fighting lasted from 4.30 p.m. till 9.0 p.m.

Blake's account of the action differed from that given by Tromp. He had been on the way from his anchorage off Fairlight to see what the Dutch fleet was doing off the English coast. On 20 May he wrote to the Speaker to tell him what had happened. He said that Major Bourne had informed him that Tromp with 40 sail was off Sand-Head, whereupon he made all possible speed towards Tromp and saw him on the morning of 19 May at anchor in and near Dover Road. When he was within three leagues of the Dutch they weighed and stood eastwards. About two hours later they altered course and bore directly towards the English fleet. When they were within musket shot Blake gave orders to fire at Tromp's flag, which was done thrice. After the third shot Tromp fired a broadside. Major Bourne with his ships from the Downs was then approaching. The fighting continued till night. By this time Blake's ship, the *James*, had all her rigging and sails destroyed and her mizzen mast shot off, so that she was unable to sail. They anchored and worked all night in repair. The next morning they saw the Dutch fleet about four leagues away towards the French coast. They had taken one Dutch ship and thought another had sunk, and they had the captains of both. The *James* had about 70 great shot in her hull and a number of casualties — six men killed, nine or ten dangerously wounded, including the master, one of his mates, and other officers.[9]

In this action Tromp had 42 ships and Blake 22, though the English ships had the heavier armament. The particular interest in these accounts is that the opposing commanders, in the action to their governments, both accused the other of firing a broadside first. In the heat of action, these things happen in war, and no doubt both believed they were right.

Although this battle signalled the effective start of hostilities, it was not till 30 June that negotiations were finally broken off.

After the battle, perhaps in an attempt to avert war, Tromp wrote to Blake, on 23 May, saying that his intention had been to greet him, and asked him for

[8] 'The First Dutch War', op. cit.
[9] Ibid.

friendship's sake to restore to him the only one of his ships that was missing. But an indignant Blake, convinced that Tromp had fired first and probably thinking of his dead and wounded officers and seamen, would not accept this conciliatry approach.

On 21 May Blake wrote to Penn: 'Foreasmuch as the Council of State have thought fit that you should command as Vice Admiral of the fleet, these are therefore to authorise you forthwith to wear a flag on the foretop of the ship *Triumph* under your charge. Dated this 21 May 1652. Rob. Blake.'[10] (i.e. the Union flag.)

With the advent of a primarily naval war, the manning of ships became a major problem for Parliament. The Council of State accordingly wrote to the 'Vice-Admirals' of the south-eastern counties of Norfolk, Suffolk, Essex, Kent, Sussex, and Hampshire on 24 May, authorising them to summon all 'seamen and mariners' from 15 to 50 years of age in their counties and acquaint them of the State's need of seamen to man the fleet in preparation in the Thames and press for service as many able seamen as they could get, giving each man 12d prest money and 1d a mile conduct money.[11]

A 'prest', or imprest, was an advance of pay on account, and equated with the 'Queen's shilling' later given to voluntarily enlisted soldiers. A 'prest-man' was therefore a volunteer. There was nothing in the above letter to say that a man should be taken by force; but forcible impressment did increase and became a form of conscription as the war went on.

Ships too were needed. In those days, when warships and merchant ships were of somewhat similar design and build, the arming of them converted vessels used for trade into far more effective warships than can be done at the present day. A list of merchant ships suitable for requisitioning (as for horses before the First World War and motor vehicles before the Second) was needed. Dr. Stephens (a doctor of law) was therefore directed on 29 May to produce a list of ships he considered fit to be converted into men-of-war, and to give their tonnage and the number of guns they already carried. The Council of State also directed that the letters from Captain Moulton at Portsmouth, of 26 May, be sent to the Commissioners of the Navy to show what he was doing there about taking up ships for the public service.

Dutch commerce was an obvious target for the English Navy, and this raises an issue which has been much argued over the ages. Conventional naval wisdom, following the arguments of the brilliant American naval writer, Captain Mahan, is that the primary naval objective is the destruction of the enemy's battle fleet. But this, as has been shown in both World Wars, is not always true for both antagonists. In the First Dutch War the aim of the English fleet was not the destruction of Tromp's warships, but the collapse of Dutch commerce, on which the very existence of the nation depended; whereas the aim of the Dutch fleet *was* the destruction of the English fleet, which could cause such a collapse.

---

[10] Ibid.
[11] Ibid.

To prosecute the attack on Dutch commerce, Blake sailed northwards because the Dutch East India fleet of merchantmen was on its way home and it was expected that, instead of facing the dangers of the Straits of Dover, it would take the long route to the west of Ireland and round the north of Scotland. In addition, the Dutch herring fleet of fishing vessels would by this time be in the North Sea.

Tromp, writing to the States General on 2 July,[12] had heard from a small fishing vessel he had captured that Blake with the main fleet had gone north and that in the Downs there was only a squadron under the command of Sir George Ayscue. This was correct, for Ayscue's squadron was awaiting the hired merchant ships which were being fitted out in the Thames. However, Tromp, who had been ordered to follow Blake when the wind allowed, left the tempting target of Ayscue and followed Blake with his whole force of 83 men-of-war, 'great and small', and nine fireships.

Fireships, those seventeenth century equivalent of submarines, were receiving the attention of the Council of State, and on 11 June they had written to the Navy Commissioners instructing them to order the despatch of these vessels 'and to place in them commanders, boatswains, pursers, gunners, carpenters, and cooks.'[13] It was a hazardous service and all officers and seamen in these ships were volunteers.

Tromp, on 20 June, issued orders for the distribution of his fleet in action. Every captain was to keep close to his flag officer; the Vice-Admiral of the Fleet, with his squadron, was to sail immediately ahead of the squadron, and immediately under the command of the Admiral; whilst the Rear-Admiral was to remain with his squadron close astern of the Admiral.

Sir George Ayscue, in Tromp's absence, was engaged in worthwhile activity, which he reported to the Council of State on 3 July 1652. He had been informed of the approach of 30 or 40 Dutch merchantmen, homeward bound, with an escort of four men-of-war — some of the merchant ships being heavily armed. On receipt of this information he stood over to the French coast at first light and came on this Dutch fleet. There appears to have been something of a panic; for he said that most of them 'made little or no dispute', but 26 ran directly on shore upon Calais sands. He captured three, secured another two of those that had run ashore, and burnt three. He believed that the ships ashore would never get off, 'being very deep ships'. The French, he says, did their best to defend those on shore, but he saw some of them cutting holes in these ships and loading the cargo on to carts. The Dutch crews had run away, so there was no opposition to this operation. Three ships of Ayscue's squadron pursued the eight Dutch ships which had managed to escape, but were only able to overtake one, which 'defended herself stoutly'. However, she, 'a very rich ship' was at last forced on shore and burnt.[14]

---

[12] Ibid.
[13] Ibid.
[14] Ibid.

Tromp, during his journey northwards, was joined by de With with eight ships, which Tromp reported as being 'very foul and scantily manned'. He now had 94 warships and 10 fireships 'which we fear will sink or have their sails blown away'. Tromp frequently complained about the wretched vessels that he was given as fireships.[15] It seems that the Dutch government was so mean that they could not bear the thought of a sound vessel being deliberately set on fire.

On 11 July the Council of State sent a message to Blake that Ayscue had informed them of Tromp's appearance in the Downs with 102 men-of-war and 10 fireships, the whole divided into three squadrons. Ayscue, who had only 14 or 15 ships, had put himself under the protection of Dover Castle.

Tromp had also rendered a report on his way north, on 12 July, telling the States General (in reference to Ayscue) that he had tried all means of getting into the Downs, but was hindered first by calms and then by strong adverse winds which compelled him to anchor. He rubbed home the state of his deplorable fireships. He had had 16 but of these only seven had survived, and of these seven, three might sink in bad weather. He added, again in reference to Ayscue, that at daybreak on 11 July he had been near the North Foreland and, with a favourable wind and weather, had held on to the Downs to attack Ayscue; but it suddenly became calm and they drifted backwards and had to anchor. Soon afterwards the wind did get up, but it shifted and rose into a stiff gale, against which it was impossible for his ships to get through the Narrows. But it was favourable for them to shape their course for the North, and so he set off to look for the main English fleet.

Tromp was bothered, he says to the States General, about the victualling of his fleet, for they had forbidden him to enter Dutch harbours for provisioning and cleaning, and their plans to provision his ships at sea were impracticable; firstly because in bad weather a boat could hardly go once a fortnight from one ship to another, and secondly because, as he was unable to appoint a rendezvous, it was difficult to see how the victualling ships could meet him. He had 11,000 men, and they consumer 50 or 60 barrels of beer and the same amount of water every day, and ate over 60,000 lbs of bread every week.[16] There is no recorded reply to this broadside, but the ignorance of the States General as regards the provisioning and maintenance of ships obviously infuriated Tromp.

On the same day that Tromp was writing this report, Blake had sent some frigates to scout in front of the fleet. They soon spotted 12 Dutch men-of-war, which, as they discovered, were guarding the Dutch herring fleet. One of the men-of-war had a flag on the main topmasthead (the 'Admiral') and another one on the fore topmasthead (the 'Vice-Admiral'). The Vice-Admiral opened fire. An English frigate replied with a broadside. Five more English frigates arrived and the subsequent fight lasted for three hours. Captain Taylor, commanding the English frigates, claimed to have 'subdued three' and made

---

[15] Ibid.
[16] Ibid.

a fourth strike. All the Dutch warships were taken, but some were too damaged for service in the English Navy and were sunk.

When the main body of the English fleet arrived some of the Dutch fishing vessels fell amongst them. Blake made the skipper of a Dutch 'buss' come on board his flagship. He asked him where he was born and the Dutchman said, 'Schiedam'. Blake replied, 'I lived at Schiedam in my youth for five or six years. Come into my cabin and let us drink a glass of wine together to the welfare of the town.' Blake asked the Dutchman to let him have two or three tons of herrings of the best quality, which was done at once. Blake said he was going to pay for them, but the Dutch skipper refused to take any money; whereupon Blake threw some English money on board the herring buss, and by his orders most of the herrings were thrown back too. He also directed that the buss was to be taken in tow for the night.[17] This incident reflects a very kindly aspect of Blake's character.

On 30 July 1652 Tromp and his principal flag officers (Evertsen, de With, and Florizoon) submitted a report to the States General. Since the latter's resolution of 29 June (on the victualling of the fleet) no provisions had reached them. On 24 July they had reached the latitude of the Orkneys. The next day two ships were sent to Fair Isle to get news of the English fleet, as well as the Dutch merchant fleet returning from the East Indies and of the fishing fleet. They returned with news only that they had learned that the English fleet was near or in the roadstead of Shetland.

This information was received at 4.0 p.m. on 25 July. At 5.0 p.m. on that day Fair Isle lay to the south-west, two (Dutch) miles off (i.e. eight English miles), with a strengthening wind, heavy rain, and thick weather. About 7.0 p.m., the rain slackening a little, they were so near to Shetland that several of their ships to leeward had been driven close to the shore and could not weather it without great danger. The whole fleet accordingly made their way SW by S so as to sail free of the land. At night the wind shifted to the southward 'with an extraordinary tempest' and by degrees got round to the west, so that it was impossible to clear the land. It blew so hard that they could not tack and the sails were either ripped up or actually blown into shreds. On the morning of 26 July the whole Dutch fleet was scattered. By the evening they had collected 34 men-of-war. During the night the expected East Indiamen arrived and joined them. The next morning all the flag officers and captains from the ships that had managed to assemble came on board Tromp's flagship. Out of the 92 ships of the fleet there were 40 present, so that there were 52 men-of-war missing, as well as six fireships, the supply ships, and two galliots. They cruised for two days without finding any more and did not know how many had been sunk or wrecked. Several captains, however, reported that they had seen a number of ships under sail to the windward.[18]

This was the end of the report to the States General, but on his return to The Hague on 10 August Tromp discovered that many of his missing ships had taken

---

[17] Ibid.
[18] Ibid.

shelter in different parts of Shetland, whilst others had gone to Norway. In fact the majority had survived the storm and had got home at about the beginning of September.

Blake's fleet, being north of Shetland, suffered less damage. Both the rival commanders had achieved part of their objectives. Blake's ships had destroyed or captured all the escorts to the herring fleet, whilst Tromp had managed to contact the East India fleet and escort it home.

5

The Battles of 16 August and the Kentish Knock

When Tromp sailed after Blake, he had left Ayscue in a position to dominate the Channel and the States General had consequently to form a squadron to provide protection for Dutch merchant ships. They accordingly granted a commission to Captain de Ruyter to command, as *Commandeur*, a fleet then assembling in the Wielengen (a channel and anchorage off the Scheldt). On his arrival there de Ruyter found 20 men-of-war and 4 fireships. On 2 August he was off Calais with the slightly increased strength of 22 warships and 6 fireships.

On 16 August the Council of State, alive to possible dangers in the Channel, had ordered Ayscue to stand to the west to ensure the security of English shipping, and on 20 July, as a further precaution, they directed two armed ketches to ply about the Land's End and inform incoming English merchant ships of the outbreak of war with Holland. They were also to inform Ayscue of any ship movements and they were to seize any Dutch or French ships (within their power to do so), except such French ships as were authorised to trade or fish.

On 15 August 1652 Ayscue left Plymouth in search of the enemy. The next day, having received information about a Dutch fleet, he stood over to the French coast on the most probably course to meet it. He sighted the Dutch between 1.0 and 2.0 p.m. and came up with them about 4.0 p.m.

Ayscue had 38 men-of-war, 4 fireships, and 4 small vessels (probably ketches) as scouts. De Ruyter's fleet had now increased to 30 men-of-war and he was escorting 60 Dutch merchant ships. In addition to having more ships and a greater armament than de Ruyter, Ayscue had the advantage of the wind.

The battle started when Ayscue was 9 or 10 leagues from the French coast. He says that he started the fight with his own and six other ships, and 'charged them quite through, and, not being able to go windward of all, received forty broadsides and afterwards got away'. He had sustained many shots in the hulls of his ships, but more in their masts, sails, and rigging, the reason for this was 'the enemy's main design being to spoil them in hope thereby to make the better use of their fireships upon us'. Then he 'charged

42

them again and made another furious assault'. Ayscue said that, 'Our shot took most place in their hulls, as theirs had in our masts and rigging'.[1]

Neither the English nor the Dutch fleets fought in line at this period, nor did any other navy. The 'charge' of a group of ships was apparently normal in battle tactics, but depended on the attacking fleet being to windward of their opponents. But if the charging ships broke through the enemy's fleet, they would in turn be to leeward and faced with the problem of tacking back to windward to renew the assault; which it appears Ayscue managed to do. His account of the battle is sketchy, but presumably other 'charges' were carried out, headed by his vice- and rear-admirals.

The Dutch practice of trying to make a ship immobile by destroying masts and rigging, so that fireships could be used, was of frequent occurrence in these wars, whereas English ships generally preferred, with their usually heavier guns, to fire at the hull. There was an additional reason for this preference. English ships were far more solid in construction than the Dutch. They had thicker scantlings, and their wood, tough English oak, was unequalled by any other timber. Dutch hulls were therefore far more vulnerable to a broadside.[2]

The battle went on till dark, and then Ayscue put back into Plymouth. De Ruyter sent the merchant ships off towards their destinations, whilst he pursued Ayscue into Plymouth. However, owing to bad weather and adverse winds, he was forced to give up this plan.[3]

A note from the Admiralty Commissioners of 11 September refers to a petition from the captain of the fireship *Charity* of Ayscue's fleet, asking for recompense to the ship's company for clothes lost when the ship was fired, which shows that fireships were used by Ayscue during the engagement.

There is an interesting letter from the Council of State to the Navy Commissioners on 23 August relating to the 1st Rate *Sovereign*. This was the great *Sovereign of the Seas*, the 100-gun ship conceived by Charles I in 1634, built by Phineas Pett at Woolwich dockyard, and launched in October 1637. Under Parliament she was re-named *Sovereign*, and after the Restoration *Royal Sovereign*.[4] Parliament's plea to the Navy Commissioners said: 'We left it to you to provide such vessels to attend the *Sovereign*, to prevent the danger of firing her, as were fit for that service either with or without oars. We hear that there are two ketches in the river, which we desire may be sent, and also the two shallops in Dover pier may be ordered to meet her in the Downs';[5] all of which shows what a prestigious vessel she was.

A short time after the battle Ayscue departed for London, saying that he was not feeling well. A Venetian, resident in London, wrote on 22 January 1653 that Ayscue had found a way to excuse himself from the Service. Hugh Peters

---

[1] *Navy Records Society*, Vol. 17, 1899 'First Dutch War' Vol. 2, ed. Dr. S.R. Gardiner.

[2] F.L. Robertson, *The Evolution of Naval Armament* (London, H.T. Storey, 1968).

[3] *First Dutch War* op. cit.

[4] Frank Fox, *Great Ships* (Greenwich, Conway Maritime Press, 1980), pp. 33-37.
Robertson, op. cit., p. 24.

[5] *First Dutch War*, op. cit.

(the militant Independent divine, who was a great friend of Cromwell and Chaplain to the Council of State) had, it was said, urged Ayscue to take no further part in a war against a Protestant enemy. Peters, who was heartily disliked by the Presbyterians, wished the war to be stopped. Ayscue forwarded Peters' letter to Parliament, but he did resign. It is possible that he wished the war to end, but for entirely different reasons to those urged by Peters; for, though he took no further part in this war, he was commanding the Swedish fleet in 1658, and after the Restoration he served as an Admiral in the Navy of Charles II. The French Ambassador, in 1657, said that Ayscue disliked serving under Cromwell.

On Tromp's return from the northward voyage, there was a row between him and the States General. The cause appears to be unknown, but it may have been the business of provisioning his ships at sea. A letter from Rotterdam on 21 August reported that Tromp had desired to be excused from going to sea any more.[6] The States General ordered Vice-Admiral de With to take over command of the fleet. It was not a happy choice, for de With, though a very brave man, had a violent temper which he used to ventilate in abusive language, and he was noted for finding fault in everything. He was disliked intensely by the seamen.

On 14 August de With went on board to take over command. His flagship was an East Indiaman of 45 guns. According to a letter from Rotterdam of 27 August, the remainder of his ships had 32, 20, or 16 guns, but they were so short of men that de With could not sail. Rather strangely, so the letter said, many of his gunners, junior officers, and several other men were English, Scots, and other non-Dutch nationalities.[6]

The manning of the fleet seems to have been hampered by political differences. The two States of Holland were at odds with Zeeland. Holland would not agree to the young Prince of Orange being General, while Zeeland insisted on it. When recruiting drums beat in Zeeland in the name of the States General, the seamen, according to the above letter, cut the heads off the drums because they did not bear the name of the Prince of Orange.

It was 4 September before de With was at last ready, and he put out into the Schoonevelt with 31 ships and galliots. Four days later he was conveying merchant ships down Channel. On 19 September he was reinforced by seven men-of-war, and on 22 September by de Ruyter, with the sizeable addition of 28 ships, but 9 of these were fireships and 4 of them were in so bad a condition that they had to be sent back.

De With now set off to seek Blake and the English fleet, announcing, 'I shall bring the fleet merrily to the enemy, the devil may bring it off'.[7] Blake spotted the Dutch fleet outside the Goodwins on 25 September.

De With had originally intended to hoist his flag on board Tromp's old flagship, the *Brederode*, but the crew would not let him board the ship. The only other ship suitable and available was the *Prins Willem*, which a disgusted de With said was the worst sailer in the fleet.

---

[6] Ibid.
[7] Ibid.

According to de Ruyter, Blake had 68 ships against de With's 62. The latter had decided to attack the English fleet as it lay in the Downs. De Ruyter was to lead with his squadron, followed by de With with the centre squadron and de Wilde with the rear squadron. Cornelis Evertsen was given the task of going to the help of any ship which was hard pressed.

The plan was never put into effect because in the evening of 25 September a SSW gale made it impossible, and the weather did not improve until the evening of 27 September. By the following morning the English fleet was no longer in the Downs, for Blake had taken advantage of a SW wind to slip out and was bearing down on the Dutch fleet which was in disorder, owing to the gale. It had caused some ships to drag their anchors and scattered others. Two of the East Indiamen and three men-of-war had been blown off, or had made off, and de With's fleet had been reduced to 57.

In his report to the Council of State, on 2 October, Blake said that they had caught sight of the Dutch fleet at noon on 28 September. Between 3.0 and 4.0 p.m. they got their fleet of 60 sail (a smaller number than de Ruyter had estimated) and, 'hauling their foresails' upon their masts, made ready to fight.

Captain John Mildmay, in his 'Relation of the Sea-Fight with the Dutch', says that in the morning of 28 September, the wind westerly, the whole fleet weighed from the Downs and about noon sighted the Dutch fleet, then about six leagues east of the North Foreland. Mildmay says that his ship, the Nonsuch frigate, was sailing very well. He stood ahead of the fleet until he came within gun shot of the Dutch, and then waited for it to come up.

According to Blake, most of his fleet were well astern 'by reason of their late weighing from the Downs'. He had, indeed, only three ships with him (in addition to his flagship), so he waited until a 'considerable part was come up' and then attacked. He had ordered no guns to be fired until they came very close to them.

Mildmay continues that the Admiral (Blake), Vice-Admiral (Penn), and others arrived. Then Blake 'hauled on the backstays', because the greater part of the fleet lay far astern, some being about two leagues from the Dutch. The fight began, he said, about 5.0 p.m. and lasted till about 7.0 p.m.

The battle was fought near the sand bank known as the Kentish Knock, about 20 miles north east of the North Foreland.

The following account of the battle was given in a letter from Blake's fleet: 'First Major Bourne with the Andrew led on and charged the Hollanders stoutly, and got off again without much harm. Captain Badily with his ship also, he charged exceedingly gallantly; but was in very great danger to have lost his ship, for the Hollanders were so close on both sides of him charging against him that one might have flung biscuits out of his frigate into the Dutch ships. . . . The Sovereign — that great ship . . . — did her part; she sailed through and through the Holland fleet, and played hard upon them, and at one time there were about 20 Holland frigates upon her; but blessed be the Lord she has sustained no very great loss, but in some of her tacklings, and some shot in her, which her great bigness is not much prejudiced with.'[8]

Mildmay noticed three Dutch ships in distress, one of them, which had lost all her masts, was the Dutch Rear-Admiral (i.e. de Wilde). Another, of 30 guns, which had lost her mainmast, was being towed by the third of about 500 tons and 30 guns. Mildmay 'stood to them', and coming within half a musket shot, the third of the trio cast off her tow which was a 'gallant frigate of 30 guns'. Mildmay 'fired a few guns' into the latter, and 'ran directly on board him, entering about 30 men, so that he presently yielded'. Mildmay then pursued the ship which had been towing his prize. He continues: 'In about half an hour I got up by his side, and laid him on board upon the weather. Entering my men, he called for quarter, so I entered about thirty men more aboard him, at which time several Holland ships were close by, yet none came to help them.' The *Ruby* frigate had followed the *Nonsuch*, but seeing that Mildmay 'had done his work', she tacked away to the English fleet, by which time it was dark. Mildmay, having taken the ship which had been towing his first prize, gave orders for it to ply to windward towards the English fleet. He then put off himself as soon as he could, for the *Nonsuch*, he says, had received some hard blows in the contest. He stood back to the first ship he had captured and sent off his boat, which returned with the captain of the Rear-Admiral's flagship and also the captain of his first prize. (The Rear-Admiral himself is not mentioned as having been captured, though he had apparently transferred to this ship when his own was dismasted. He may have moved again to a third ship.) Mildmay lay by the Dutch frigate all night, losing sight of the English fleet. He was then driven to leeward of the whole Dutch fleet which was less than a mile away from him. Then, as the frigate (the ship he had first captured) was in a sinking condition, he took on board the two captains and all of the remaining 80 men of the crew who would come, and made all sail to the windward, to get clear of the Dutch fleet and rejoin his own.

Blake said that many broadsides were exchanged and that the engagement was fierce until night fell. Penn's ship, the *James*, and the great *Sovereign* both grounded on the Kentish Knock, 'the *James* touched once or twice and the great ship had 3 or 4 rubs', but both got off it. This, in fact, turned to their advantage because after the main English fleet had fallen on the enemy, they were able to pour their fire into the Dutch as they stood to the southward and on the starboard tack. According to Blake, the Dutch had the worst of it because so many of their ships 'held back', and some of them, trying to fire over their own ships which were nearer to the English, fired into the Hulls of the former! In his report, Blake didn't know what loss the Dutch had sustained, other than that occasioned by Mildmay's exploit.

Next morning there was only a light variable wind at first, but it later blew more strongly from the north and the Dutch made off towards their own coast — Blake's leading ships firing at them at long range.

---

[8] Ibid.

46

In the afternoon the wind shifted so that the Dutch were to windward and de With wanted to renew the action; but in addition to the ships captured many others had left the fleet, and de Ruyter persuaded him to make for home.

A furious de With made many accusations and excuses after the battle. He claimed that before the engagement he had warned the captains, by message conveyed by a galliot, to do their duty. He and de Ruyter had done theirs but had been badly seconded; many captains having slunk away. This same Dutch 'Account of the Proceedings of the Flet' added to the above by saying that de With went to The Hague and made his report, 'tending in everything to cast the blame on the other captains as cowards.' It is easy to understand why de With was an unpopular commander! A 'Letter from The Hague' said that de With tried to excuse his loss in the late engagement on the grounds that the English had exceeded him in number and had fresh supplies, and that some of his own fleet stole away without fighting.[9]

De With wrote to the States General on 13 October reporting on gun cartridges.[10] He said that in an engagement he fired his guns as quickly as anyone else, and that this was possible because he used parchment cartridges, which was unusual, but if this was always done no gun ought to miss its mark. In addition, guns loaded with such cartridges carried more than half as far, and of this the ships under his command had proof. He asked that a greater quantity of parchment might be sent to him in suitable boxes or chests so that each ship should have enough cartridges for 500 charges, and amongst 25 ships this came to 2,500 cartridges for 25-pdr, 18-pdr, 8-pdr, and 6-pdr guns.

But the States General had had enough of de With, and Tromp was recalled.

A printed pamphlet giving an account of the battle, emanating from 'Aboard the *Garland*, October 2, 1652, Northward of the Downs', contained the statement that, 'The Hollanders' Rear-Admiral sank carrying 50 guns. Their great new ship, carrying 68 guns, sunk, being the biggest that was ever yet sent forth by their States, and the first time she ever went upon service. Six of our men that boarded her perished in her.'[11] The *Garland* was a 3rd Rate.

It is a little difficult to follow this battle, which seems to have been a rather untidy affair of charges by groups of ships and actions by individual ships. The exploit by Captain Mildmay in his 4th Rate frigate *Nonsuch* seems to have been the most distinguished stroke in the battle and was singled out for special mention by Blake.

---

[9] Ibid.
[10] Ibid.
[11] Ibid.

6

The Battle of Dungeness

The Dutch, who believed themselves with some justification, to be the leading maritime nation, were shaken by the defeat at the Kentish Knock. They assumed that it must have been due either to the unfitness of de With to command or to the incompetence of his captains.

A large and valuable convoy of merchantmen had to be escorted to the Isle of Ré, off Rochelle, which was the standard dispersal and assembly point for Dutch merchant shipping trading with the European continent. Tromp, back in command, was to conduct the operation.

On 9 October 1652 the States General issued their operational instructions. Tromp was given a dual objective; 'to do damage and offence to the English fleet and also to give convoy to the West.'[1] A convoy of merchantmen were due to return from France and those parts on 20 November. They were to assemble at a rendezvous off the Isle of Ré (called by the Dutch the Island of St. Martin) and be conveyed by such men-of-war as the commander of the fleet might despatch. This convoy was to return under cover of the main fleet, which was to remain in the Channel to await them and to look out for the English. The convoy would then continue its homeward journey, escorted by men-of-war that were unable to remain longer at sea.

The main fleet was to remain in or about the Channel to protect ships homeward bound from Brazil, the Caribbean Islands, the Barbary Coast, the Straits of Gibraltar, Spain, and Portugal.

An abstract of letters from Holland of 22 October 1652[2] announced that the fleet of 100 to 120 vessels, of which 20 were fireships, was ready to sail. This formidable armada was to convey some 200 merchantmen bound for Spain, France, and Portugal. The start had been somewhat delayed due to shortage of men to man the ships and the unreadiness of some of the merchantmen.

A 'Resolution of the States General of the United Netherlands' of 23 October 1642 announced that Lieutenant-Admiral Tromp and Vice-Admiral John

---

[1] Navy Records Society, Vol. 30, 1906, 'The First Dutch War' Vol. 3, ed. S.R. Gardiner and C.T. Atkinson.

[2] Ibid.

Evertsen, together with Vice-Admiral Witte Cornelis de With, Vice-Commandeur de Ruyter, and Rear-Admiral Peter Florizoon, were appointed commanding officers of the fleet at present lying in the Goeree Gat (estuary of the River Maas). Two days later de With resigned his post because he was placed under Evertsen who was junior to him.

Tromp had some criticisms of his instructions. It will be noted that, contrary to the accepted principles of war, he had been given two separate and possibly conflicting tasks: firstly to find and defeat the English fleet, and secondly to convey an outward bound fleet of merchantmen, and then another such fleet homeward bound. He commented that:

(a) To carry out both tasks he would need all the men-of-war in the country.
(b) If the English fleet was in such strength that he would need all his ships to confront them, was he to stay by the merchantmen, or leave them unescorted and a possible prey to fast frigates?
(c) To send warships to escort merchantmen to the Isle of Ré whilst the main fleet remained in the Channel would be unsafe at this season of the year, as it would be difficult for the two bodies to meet again.
(d) If some ships homeward bound from the West were unwilling to remain with the convoy, were they to be forcibly detained or allowed to proceed independently at their own risk?
(e) When the fleet arrived at the Isle of Ré, could not the escort remain six or eight days longer than the scheduled date of return 'to careen and clean their foul ships for there is an opportunity to careen twenty-five or thirty at once, as the greater part will be so foul that, in case of a storm, they will run great risk of being driven on a lee shore'.[3]

From subsequent actions it is apparent that the States General satisfied Tromp on these points. They illustrate the danger of civilians issuing instructions on operational matters without the benefit of Service advice.

On 28 October Tromp wrote to the States General[4] saying that he was shortly going to Rotterdam to arrange for the crews of his ships. He had found that the majority of his men-of-war were so foul that from the rudder of his own ship alone there was taken over half a barrel of mussels. Ships, he said, in that state would not be able to stop the fast-sailing English frigates from getting amongst the merchantmen. 'I see', he wrote, 'that your H.M. and all the good citizens have very great hopes that this fleet with its great number of ships will accomplish wonderful things, as indeed it could and ought to do if all the ships were built as men-of-war and were properly cleaned; but as this is not the case . . . there may easily fall on me great ingratitude from the ill-affectioned.' Towards the end of a very long letter he hoped that, 'When I return home I may be free from the annoyances of investigations of accounts, examinations &c, it being unheard of that a commander-in-chief of a whole force should have to answer all kinds of

---

[3] Op. cit. pp. 23-5.
[4] Op. cit. pp. 19-22.

subtle questions, why did he not rather do this, and he rather did that.'[5] (Tromp knew his country's bureaucrats!)

De With, having taken umbrage at being put junior to Evertsen in the 'Resolution' of 23 October, had written on 25 October to the States General protesting at his supersession and hoping to receive an order to go to Rotterdam and restore his health.

A 'Letter from Rotterdam' of 29 October stated the trouble the Dutch were having in manning their fleet. Numerous seamen were deserting, leaving even without the pay due to them rather than serve any more. Serving in privateers was so much more attractive that the States had to put up notices threatening the death penalty to any seaman found deserting State service to join a privateer.

On 3 November the English Council of State took a step which was to be repeated many times more in naval history. They directed the Committee for the Admiralty 'to consider how the ships which shall be hereafter built for the civil trade between London and Newcastle may be so built as they may be serviceable upon occasion as men-of-war for the Commonwealth.'[6]

Tromp issued some sailing orders on 4 November. Captain Haecxwant, with the ship under his command and those of four other captains, which were to be subject to his orders, was to remain with or ahead of the flag as far as the longitude of approximately Calais. He was then to separate from the flag as escort to the merchant ships 'that may range themselves with them in accordance with the orders of the HM', and thereafter at as follows. Those merchant ships bound for Calais, the Somme, Dieppe, Havre, and St. Malo were to sail with the main fleet and then in the van under the above escort as far as St. Malo. The above mentioned men-of-war were then to rejoin the main fleet cruising in the Channel, or, if it had left there, sail to the general rendezvous at Ré.

Captain Jeroeuz, with his ship, was to go to Havre and remain there until the merchantmen bound for the Seine (i.e. Le Havre) had sailed into it, and then rejoin the flag in the same way as the above escort.

Two days later Tromp wrote to the States General telling them that he was ready to put to sea with the first favourable wind. He had 60 ships of war and about 80 merchantmen at Helvoetsluys and he had sent an express message to Vice-Admiral Jan Evertsen asking him to hold himself in readiness to sail with the fleet lying in Zeeland to join Tromp.

On 21 November Tromp reported to the States General that they had got out of the shallows with the largest ships that day at 3.0 p.m., with the rest following slowly. If the 8 men-of-war and 70 merchantmen from the Texel joined him that day 'pray that this fair wind holds'.

On 24 November Blake wrote to the Council of State that he was awaiting provisions from Dover and hoped to be ready to meet the Dutch fleet 'which is not yet come together, as I am informed by a scout of the enemies, a small Dutch hoy which was brought in yesterday by the *Sapphire*.' The master of

---

[5] Op. cit. pp. 19-22.
[6] Op. cit. p. 35.

the vessel had said that van Tromp with his party was at Goeree Gat, and the others in the Wielings and the Texel. Blake thought that this hoy had been sent to discover the location, movements and strengths of the Englishfleet. If so it was strange that he should have believed him; for Blake had been deceived by the master of the hoy and was completely taken by surprise. Later the same day he wrote again saying that soon after the despatch of his previous report 'there was descried from our top-mast head to be off the North Foreland about 80 sail of ships plying to windward conceived to be Dutch'.[7] Still later intelligence arrived that from the church steeple at Margate over 400 ships had been sighted. Blake called a council of war at which it was resolved that, the wind being SW by S and likely to blow and rain, the fleet should lie moored during the night and that commanders should meet at daybreak to decide further action.

However, the impending battle was not to take place immediately. On 26 November, in accordance with instructions from the States General, Tromp ordered de Ruyter to take command of the squadron which had previously been under de With. On the same day he furnished the following situation report to the States General.

On 22 November he had been joined by de Ruyter with 10 men-of-war, fireships and merchantmen, with more to follow, so that he eventually had 450 ships with which to put to sea. That evening they were off West Kapelle. The next day it was calm and the fleet was well scattered, but in the evening there was a slight NE breeze and they set course towards Dover. It then fell calm. On 24 November, the wind WSW by W, 'we beat over in bad weather'. This was the day when they had been sighted by Blake's flagship off the North Foreland. The following morning the wind was SW and it was very dark with drizzling rain and very few of their own ships could be seen. Soon afterwards a great storm arose, many ships were wrecked and great damage caused, bowsprits and beak heads being carried away. The merchantmen were back in the Goeree Deep and the Maas, and the men-of-war lay between Dover, the Downs and the Maas. He suggested that 'your HM' might think it fit that the men-of-war should be ordered to enter Goeree and remain there until an East wind should blow.

Tromp referred to the galliot (the craft called by Blake a hoy) which had been sent by the Deputies to get information of the English fleet and inform him, but which had not yet appeared. (It had, of course, been captured.) He had been ordered to attack in the light of its information, if that were possible, but at the same time arranging for the security of the merchantmen. He pointed out the difficulties on account of the large number of merchant ships. He added, 'I could wish to be fortunate as to have only one of the two duties, to seek out the enemy or to give convoy; for to do both is attended by great difficulties'. (The cry of commanders throughout the ages who have been given two conflicting objectives!) He concluded by asking for the punishment of those who had gone home 'without orders or pressing necessity'.[8]

---

[7] Op. cit. p. 75.
[8] Op. cit. pp. 78-88.

On 30 November 1652 the Dutch and English fleets engaged; Tromp, having about twice the number of men-of-war as were at Blake's disposal, got the better of it.

Blake sent an account of the action to the Admiralty Commissioners on 1 December. Other accounts are contained in a letter to the Council of State of 30 November and a 'Letter from the Fleet' of 1 December.[9] From these it is possible to compile a rough narrative of the battle of Dungeness.

On Monday 29 November the Dutch fleet was discovered 'on the back of the Goodwin Sands'. Blake called a Council of Officers at which it was resolved to engage them. At about 9.0 a.m. the scouts from each fleet made contact, one Dutch scout being captured. The wind was then SW, but before the fleet got clear of the land there arose a fresh gale, at first variable, but later turning NW, so that it was not possible to engage that day, but the English fleet tacked to 'keep the weather gage' of the Dutch. At night the wind increased and the English fleet anchored in the Dover Road; the Dutch anchoring about two leagues to leeward.

The Dutch had 95 men-of-war and 11 fireships, organised in three squadrons. The English fleet consisted of only 42 men-of-war in one body, but less than 20 engaged in the battle. The remainder abstained on the pretext that they were undermanned and had not enough men to 'ply their tackle'. Amongst these were some frigates as well as armed merchant ships. According to a 'Letter from the Fleet', of those ships that did engage 'not more than eight did so whole heartedly'.

The next morning (30 November) the weather was fairer than it had been during the night and in Blake's ships trumpets sounded and drums beat. The Dutch weighed first, followed by the English, 'keeping,' says Blake, 'the wind to the Ness (i.e. Dungeness) to get clear of the Rip-vaps (a bank about half-way between Dungeness and Calais) before engagement'. Both fleets plied to the westward. Between 11.0 and 12.0 'about half the pitch of the Ness' the leading English ships met and engaged the Dutch. The 'Letter from the Fleet' says that 'One half of the small fleet we had — I will not say would not, but I am sure — did not engage; and it is a moderate expression if we say that some did not well, in regard they lay out of danger of gunshot, to the extreme hazard of the whole fleet.' Blake agrees that the Dutch fleet consisted of '95 sail, most of them great ships; three admirals, two vice-admirals, and two rear-admirals. They passed many broadsides upon us very near and yet we had but six men slain and ten wounded.' The 'Letter from the Fleet' gives considerably more detail, as follows: 'Our two ships called the *Vanguard* and the *Victory* (both 2nd Rates) were all the time of the fight (which lasted till moonshine) desperately engaged with 20 of the Dutch ships, two of which were Vice-Admirals, and yet at last they got off well, though much battered in their sails, yards, rigging, and hulls'. Blake, in his flagship the *Triumph* (2nd Rate) says that the *Garland* (3rd Rate) was 'boarded by two of their flags and others and, seconded only by Captain Hoxton, was

---

[9] Op. cit. pp. 89-95, 106-8.

after a hot fight board and board, carried by them, and his second (the armed merchantman *Bonaventure*) with him.' The 'Letter from the Fleet' expands this incident as follows: 'The *Bonaventure* also, a merchant ship which endeavoured her relief, had her captain, by name Captain Hoxton, slain, who cleared his decks many times, and was killed fighting as a private man, but at last his ship was boarded and taken.' Blake, in the *Triumph*, going to their assistance, says, 'Our fore-topmast was shot away, our mainstay being shot before, and our rigging much torn, so that we could not work our ship to go to their relief.' Of the *Triumph's* action, the 'Letter from the Fleet' says, 'General Blake with his own ship, the *Triumph*, bearing up to the relief of these two ships, but too late, was desperately engaged, had his fore-topmast shot down by the board, and his vessel boarded twice, having only the *Vanguard* and the *Sapphire* (4th Rate) standing close by him; yet he got off well out of the crowd of enemies.' An unsigned letter to the Council of State describes the following incident: 'About sunset we saw one ship blown up, as we conceived with powder; for a great smoke rose up of a sudden and continued in one place a good while. At last, when it grew a little dark, we saw it flame out, and another great blast and much smoke arose; but in the end it was quite extinguished.'

Blake says that as soon as it was night they 'made sail towards Dover Road, and came to anchor'. He added, 'In this account I am bound to let your Honours know that there was much baseness of spirit, not among the merchantmen only, but many of the State's ships'. He asked for an enquiry to be held into the behaviour of some of the captains. He believed that a main reason for the shortage of seamen was the great number of privateers, especially out of the Thames. These offered more attractive terms of service, notably in the financial reward from capturing enemy ships.

Finally, Blake asked to be relieved of his command which was too great for him. It is apparent that he was exasperated over Government incompetence which had forced him to fight a Dutch fleet, overwhelmingly stronger than his own.[10]

Blake's letter seems to have stung the Council of State into action. On 2 December 1652 they directed that commissioners were to be sent to the fleet and were, amongst other matters, to inform themselves as to the state and condition of the fleet now with Blake; to acquaint him as to the ships in the Thames that were to be sent to him, and which the commissioners were to hasten; and to examine the conduct of captains in the late fight and remove from command those whom they had found had not done their duty, and replace them.

It is interesting that both English and Dutch commanders complained, frequently, about dereliction of duty by captains of merchant ships taken up for war service, and even sometimes of similar misbehaviour by captains of men-of-war.

It is apparent that the battle was a reverse, though not a decisive one, and that blame must have rested primarily on the Commonwealth Government

---

[10] Op. cit. pp. 92-93.

for failing to make available to Blake the ships and seamen to undertake the task for which they had charged him. It is no wonder that Blake wished to resign.

The Dutch fleet was still a menace, for Blake wrote to the Navy Commissioners on 3 December saying that he understood that the Council of State had instructed them to examine the deportment of several commanders in the recent battle, but regretted that the NC would be wasting their time by coming at this juncture, because the Dutch fleet of over 100 sail was near and he was moving the English fleet the next day to Long Sands Head (the biggest sand bank in the Thames Estuary, with its head about 20 miles NNE of the North Foreland), for it was too dangerous to remain in the Downs in view of the power and experience of the enemy.[11] A report from the fleet at this time said: 'The Butter Boxes (a nickname for the Dutch) appeared again on the Wednesday in a full body in high bravado; but it stood not with the safety or honour of our fleet to re-engage them upon such desperate disadvantage.'[12]

On the same day it was reported from Kent and Sussex that parties from the Dutch fleet had come ashore and plundered houses and driven off flocks of sheep and some cattle before the county militia had arrived to drive them off.

The correspondence cited below shows what a dangerous state of weakness had arisen through the faulty distribution of ships and inadequate provision of seamen to man them — responsibilities that lay with the Admiralty Committee of the COS and the Navy Commissioners.

On 4 December 'News from the Fleet' reported that the Council of State was empowered to requisition ships considered fit for State service. It was noted that the Dutch fleet was lying all along the coast of Sussex and seizing all ships and boats that passed that way. Three English frigates that lay at Portsmouth, the *Hercules*, the *Ruby* (4th Rate), and the *Sapphire* (4th Rate), hearing of Blake's engagement, sailed from Portsmouth to his assistance. On the way they were attacked by de Ruyter, and after an hour's engagement the *Hercules*, in danger of sinking, ran ashore to preserve her men. But the Dutch managed to get her off again. The writer did not know what had happened to the other two, but in fact they got away.[13]

Also on 4 December, Orders of the COS included: 'That the Lord General (i.e. Cromwell) be desired to give an order for the speedy sending down of five hundred foot towards Dover, and also of a regiment of horse towards the coast of Kent and Sussex for the safety and security of those parts.'[14] These orders also gave General Monck 24 hours warning to go to sea and asked Parliament to grant commissions to General Deane and General Monck to exercise the commands at sea to which they had already been appointed.

Blake wrote to the COS on 4 December telling them his reasons for moving the fleet to the Thames Estuary. He wanted 'to have the river to friend if need should require'. With their vastly superior strength, the Dutch would be

---

[11] Op. cit. pp. 105-6.
[12] Op. cit. p. 108.
[13] Op. cit. p.109.
[14] Op. cit. pp. 109-110.

prepared to lose 30 or 40 ships to destroy the principal English men-of-war. He pleaded for rapid reinforcement to enable him to face the enemy again.[15] The tone of Blake's letter is singularly depressed.

Whilst Blake was writing the above letter, Tromp was writing to the Dutch States General giving his account of the battle. At 4.0 a.m. on 29 November he collected his fleet between Calais and Dover, the wind being WSW and WNW. At daybreak they saw the English fleet lying in the Downs. At 11.0 a.m., the tide being slack, they prepared to make sail, as did the English Admiral Blake. The English had 52 ships of the line of which 42 were of middle size.

At 1.0 p.m. the wind was NW by N and began to blow so hard that at about 5.0 p.m. both they and the English anchored; the latter a good two miles (i.e. eight English miles) to the windward of the Dutch fleet. Both fleets were 'close under the high land west of Dover'. It blew a gale during the night. In the morning of 30 November the wind was NNW. Tromp missed some of his ships and fireships. At 11.0 a.m. he made sail 'with the up going tide' as also did the English. At 1.0 p.m. some of his 'best sailers' opened fire. At 3.0 p.m. they were off Dungeness, intending 'to charge the English fleet' there; but Blake succeeded in keeping to windward, so that the two fleets exchanged broadsides as they passed. Tromp's flagship, the *Brederode* rammed the English 44-gun ship *Garland* (3rd Rate). In doing so the *Brederode* broke off her bowsprit and her beak-head, close to the stem. Immediately, the next English ship, the armed merchantman *Bonaventure*, of 36 guns, 'lay us on board' on the other side, so that the *Brederode* lay between the two. The Dutch Vice-Admiral, John Evertsen, then 'ran on board' the *Bonaventure* on the other side, so that all four ships 'lay on board one another'. The *Garland* surrendered after about an hour's hard fighting, and the *Bonaventure* too was taken. Both captains were killed. During this combat other Dutch ships were fighting Blake's remaining ships and Tromp still heard firing till about 9.0 p.m. One of the Dutch ships could be seen on fire. Through the night they were busy repairing their ships.

On the following morning, 1 December, there was a WNW wind and a thick drizzle. At about 1.0 p.m. they weighed anchor, intending to seek out the English in Dover or the Downs. Then the wind shifted to the North and they had to anchor, as darkness came down. Dover was then to the NE of them.

On 2 December they tried to beat up to the Downs, but the heavy ships had difficulty against the contrary wind. The wind on the morning of 3 December was E and NE with a strong gale. They weighed anchor with the flood tide and tried to reach the French coast, anchoring in the evening off Boulogne. But by now Tromp's fleet was so dispersed that he did not know where many of the ships were. He wanted to attack the English again as soon as the greater part of his fleet had assembled — if weather, wind and tide permitted.

From interrogation of his English prisoners of war, Tromp was able to compile a distribution of the English men-of-war. If accurate, it demonstrates

---

[15] Op. cit. pp. 114-5.

the strategic incompetence of the Admiralty Commission. The list was as follows:

In the Downs, ships and frigates	42
Cruising about Ushant	10
Engaged in two voyages to the West Indies, frigates	18
To go to the Mediterranean, frigates	20
To go to the Mediterranean, armed merchantmen	6
Lying up in Portsmouth, ships and frigates	13
Lying up in the Thames near London	12
Lying up in the Thames the 1st Rates *Sovereign* and *Resolution*	2
	123

If, therefore, the available warships had been placed, fully manned, at Blake's disposal, he could have confronted Tromp with a superior force. It was by no means the last time in our history when commanders both ashore and afloat have been ill-served by Parliament.

Tromp wrote again to the States General on 7 December.[16] His ship, the *Brederode*, had, he said, been seriously damaged — 'not a round spur whole in her, her bowsprit and beakhead carried away, and very leaky; hardly a shroud on the masts that I have not had to splice.' But he did not like to send her home as she was one of the best sailers in the fleet, 'and the one that doest best service on the enemy when the weather will but allow us to use the lower deck guns.' He asked that the Rotterdam board be written to 'directing them without loss of time to make new masts and a beak and preparations for putting on a bulge.' (i.e. girdling the ship). He thought this (i.e. by reducing the roll) 'will make her able to use her guns as well as the English ships.' He had been trying unsuccessfully to find the English fleet but had had a report that they had run into the Thames on 5 December.

On this same date of 7 December, there was some more cheering news from the English point of view. Robert Durnford, Captain of the 4th Rate frigate *Portsmouth* wrote to the Council of State relating how he had encountered the *Ruby* (mentioned above in the action in which the *Hercules* was lost) and how the two of them had then met with two 40 gun Dutch men-of-war on 3 December and fought them. They exchanged many broadsides, and shot down the mainmast of one Dutch ship and the mainyard and foreyard of another, besides causing much damage to the rigging and hull of both. They were near to capturing both of them when a shot carried away the *Ruby's* main-stay and fore-stay, and, the sea being very rough, both her masts went by the board, and also the foremast of the *Portsmouth* was so much shot through that they were in danger of losing it. Seeing that the enemy was 'better manned and gunned than we', Durnford was very pleased with the outcome.

---

[16] Op. cit. pp. 137-140.

On 10 December Tromp and his commanders held a Council of War in the light of information received as to the location of the English fleet. A homeward bound Flushing ship had told de Ruyter that a lighter, which had left the Thames on 7 December, had seen the English fleet of 44 ships lying in the Thames. The Dutch had been carrying out a search of the Downs, the two Forelands, and Dover (where they were now lying) without sighting any English ships, nor had their pinks, which had searched the coast as far as Orfordness, found any of the enemy. They therefore believed that the English had indeed retired into the Thames, and the Council of War agreed unanimously to run up the river and attack if possible. The chief pilots of the fleet, who had sailed to London and were perfectly acquainted with the passage, were therefore summoned before the Council.

The pilots, having consulted together, replied that they were perfectly acquainted with the south channel of the river mouth, but from one point up to the buoy of the Nore there was a stretch of shallow water with depths of 8, 9, and 10 feet, which would have to be crossed at high water and in a stiff breeze, for otherwise it would take an hour and a half to two hours to sail through it, and this passage was therefore never or seldom used except by small vessels drawing 9, 10, or 11, or at the outside 12 feet, whilst the majority of the Dutch ships drew 14, 15, 16, 17, and 18 feet. They therefore considered it would be impracticable, except with great risk of losing the ships, for if any of them were becalmed in this stretch they would run aground in the shallow water. If by any chance they had the good fortune to accomplish this and the buoys were afterwards taken up, they would have nothing to guide them out again. As regards the King's Deep, by which the Parliament ships usually sailed in and out, they thought there was water enough for those well acquainted with the channel, but not one of them knew it well enough to find it, especially if the buoys had been taken up. The Council decided reluctantly not to make the attempt.

It would appear that the Dutch pilots saved Tromp and his fleet from probable disaster, and that Blake had chosen his anchorage well.

The difficulty of getting seamen to man Blake's fleet is illustrated by a letter written on 11 December 1652 to the President of the Council of State by Colonel Thomas Kelsey, Governor of Dover Castle. In accordance with his instructions he had sent to all 'maritime places within the Ports' (i.e. the Cinque Ports, which included all the towns and villages between Winchelsea and the North Foreland) to 'cause seamen to be impressed for the State's service'. He could not yet provide information about results in places other than Dover; but in Dover, with the assistance of the Mayor, he had caused about 50 seamen to be 'imprested' and instructed them to come to receive 'conduct money'. Of these only 20 turned up, and, after receiving the money, they refused to report for service. Kelsey gathered that they were more interested in serving in privateers. There were so many of these at Dover that Kelsey thought that as long as they were permitted it was unlikely that any considerable body of seamen would be raised for State service.

Kelsey asked that 'some severe course may be taken for the exemplary punishment of some to deter others from such obstinate courses'.[17]

It is astonishing that impressment was not compulsory and that even after receiving their imprest money (the naval equivalent of the 'King's shilling') men could not be forced to serve.

There was also some trouble over arrears of pay. Captain Thomas Thorowgood, commanding the hired ship *Crescent*, lying at Portsmouth, wrote on 13 December 1652 to Thomas Smith, one of the Navy Commissioners, saying that he had 'tendered our sailors down six months pay, which they refused to take, saying that they would have all or none, and railed upon your worship'. They accused Thorowgood and Smith of cheating them of their wages. The row continued and Thorowgood sent orders through the boatswain for them to be quiet and 'go to their cabins'. As they would not, he went himself and struck one of the leaders. But others laid hold of him 'as though they would have torn me to pieces'. It is probable that the seamen of a hired ship had been serving in her as merchantmen and did not have the discipline of those serving in a man-of-war. However, it seems strange that there were no soldiers at hand to quell the mutiny.

In response to this incident, the Council of State on 15 December directed Captain Francis Willoughby, a Navy Commissioner, to go to Portsmouth and enquire into the mutiny and 'to use his best endeavour for the quieting of them by commitment or otherwise as he shall find the law doth allow in cases of that nature'. It seems a pretty weak reaction against men who had assaulted the captain of their ship!

On 14 December Blake and a number of his captains wrote, in answer to a paper from the Council of State, giving their opinion of the strength needed to undertake successful operations against the Dutch.[18] 'Supposing the enemy to consist of 90 sail of ships of war present', they considered it would be requisite to have a fleet of 60 sail 'all of which we humbly desire to be the State's ships and none under 25 guns, of which 40 sail "should carry from 36 guns upwards".' If it was necessary to have some merchant ships they would not wish them to be more than a third of the above number, and none to carry less than 28 guns, of which the smallest was a 6-pounder. They would also need 6 fireships, and desired that 'the whole fleet be completed with able seamen'. They added that: 'With such a force of ships as above mentioned we shall with all cheerfulness go forth and engage the enemy when God shall call us to it.' If they were to have a lower strength, they would do their best. It is conceivable that the desire for none but State ships had as much to do with the discipline of the ships' companies as with the quality of the ships.

Tromp had written a long and interesting situation report to the States General on 12 December.[19] The convoy of merchant ships, over 200 strong, had sailed on 8 December, leaving him 63 men-of-war and two fireships. Where the rest of the fireships had strayed he did not know. He added: 'They

---

[17] Op. cit. pp. 158-9.
[18] Op. cit. p. 167.
[19] Op. cit. p. 159.

are very urgently needed in the fleet, the more especially as the English are so afraid of them that they will never lie with their fleet where they can come at them'. He mentioned the lack of 'properly skilled and experienced pilots' which had prevented him attacking Blake's fleet in the Thames.

Seeing that the English fleet had retired to the Thames, where he could not get at them, and also that there were 200 merchant ships in Dutch ports that had missed the convoy, he suggested that, instead of his fleet remaining in the Dover Roads for fourteen days after the departure of the convoy and then going to the St. Martin (i.e. the Isle of Ré) to convoy the merchant ships home, the fleet should collect the 200 merchant ships still in Dutch ports and then continue the voyage to St. Martin. This suggestion seems to have been approved. The movement of the convoy to the Isle of Ré is narrated by Captain Peter Florissen, commanding the Dutch man-of-war *Monickendem*.[20] He joined his ship on 12 November and the next day put his whole crew on 'rations for nine weeks, namely, nine pounds of cheese apiece'. (Unless the Dutch pound weighed considerably more than the English pound, there must have been some other food in the ration, for an English pound's weight of cheese would not have sustained a hard-working seaman for a day.) On 14 November the ship's company was increased by 10 musketeers from an infantry company, and were issued with the same ration. 'That evening I received two tons of cheese and one of butter by William van Licten, who was charged with them by my wife.'

On 17 November Admiral Tromp hung out the white flag and Florissen went on board his flagship. On 19 November the NE wind, for which they had waited so long, sprang up, and Admiral Tromp put out the blue flag as a signal to make sail. On 21 November Florissen's ship was run down by 'one of our vice-admirals, carrying away our bowsprit and peak-head, thereby doing us much damage'.

The *Monickendem* took part in the battle of 3 December. Tromp ordered Florissen to take command of the convoy of merchantmen, because his ship had been so badly damaged, instead of the captain previously designated for this duty. He was given 13 men-of-war as escort to the merchantmen and was to remain about Cape Gris Nez to await the various merchant ships that had run for shelter during the gale. About 50 from Zeeland had already arrived. By 6 December all the merchantmen seemed to be present, so Florissen set sail the following morning with the wind SSE. A count of the merchant ships in the convoy on 10 December showed them to amount to something over 220.

On 11 December the coast of Brittany could be seen between Ushant and Roscoff, and those ships for Lisbon, Spain, the Caribbean, and other places left the convoy. On 12 December the captains of two of the escorting men-of-war came on board and requested permission to keep to windward of the fleet, the wind being SW by S, so that the ships in their charge, which were bound for Biscay and Bayonne, might not be hindered in their passage. At sundown the merchantmen bound for Nantes wore to leeward with their

---

[20] Op. cit. pp. 199 f.

escorts. On 13 December the ships bound for Biscay and Bayonne left them, and in the evening others left the convoy for various destinations. On 14 December the ships for Bordeaux left. On 16 December the remainder of the convoy anchored 'inside St. Martin's' (the Isle of Ré). Here Florissen made arrangements to get his ship repaired and for all the warships to be run ashore and cleaned.

The movements of the main Dutch fleet are given in the Journal of Vice-Admiral Johan Evertesen, who commanded the second of Tromp's three squadrons, as follows.[21]

On 11 December, after the pilots had reported their inability to ensure safe passage up the Thames Estuary, Tromp made a signal for all captains to come on board. He was presumably in a bad temper because he lectured them on various faults in navigation and on poor discipline. They were later examined by the Council of War, and those found guilty were fined or given some other punishment, according to the severity of the offence.

The next day the fleet sailed over to the French coast. On 18 December some merchantmen from Dutch ports joined the fleet. Tromp detached a squadron of about twelve men-of-war, with orders to cruise for ten or eleven days outside the Channel, and then to proceed to the rendezvous at Rochelle.

On 19 December the fleet ran into the Straits of Dover to await the Zeeland merchantmen which, about 100 strong, were sighted at midday. The next day the main Dutch fleet, with all the merchantmen, was off the Isle of Wight. It was somewhat scattered by a gale on 24 and 25 December, but by 5 January 1653 all the ships were re-united off the Isle of Ré.

Meanwhile, in England, the Government had been shaken by the defeat off Dungeness and was taking immediate steps for the improvement of the fleet. On Saturday 18 December 1652 the Lord President and some members of the Council of State were appointed as a committee to 'prepare the laws and articles of war for the fleet' and to bring them to the Council on the afternoon of Monday 20 December — a pretty hard weekend's work! In addition, Parliament was to be 'humbly moved' to appoint Tuesday 21 December 'for the taking into consideration what may be done for the encouragement of seamen and also for the making of laws and ordinances of war for the regulating of the fleet.[22]

On 20 December the Admiralty Committee of the COS proposed a list of 'propositions for the encouragement of seamen', relating to wounded and sick men, wages and shares in prizes.[23] On 25 December there were published, with remarkable speed 'Laws of War and Ordinances of the Sea, Ordained and Established by the Commonwealth of England'.[24] By a peculiar coincidence they consisted of 39 articles, which together provided a remarkably comprehensive manual of naval law, considering the rapidity with which they had been drawn up.

---

[21] Op. cit. p. 22 f.
[22] Op. cit. p. 272.
[23] Op. cit. pp. 275-6.
[24] Op. cit. pp. 293-301.

Guidance to enemy shipping was another worry, and instructions were issued in 'Warrants to Light Keepers' showing how lights normally displayed on the coasts were to be altered to mislead an enemy. That addressed to Edward Beane, Light Keeper of the Lights on the South Foreland, directed him to alter the lights of the South Foreland in accordance with directions that would be given to him. When the wind was easterly and any enemy ships likely to be in the neighbourhood he was to light the lights 'dimly in their proper places', and then about 8 or 9 o'clock 'at the furthest' he was to alter them as agreed and 'which you are to keep secret as you can'. He was to do the same when he heard that the enemy was coming from the westward, and at all times when they approached the coast in his area.[25]

On 6 January 1653 interesting reports of an action were submitted by Captain Robert Durnford, commanding the frigate *Portsmouth* and Captain Anthony Houlding commanding the frigate *Ruby*.

Durnford sailed from Portsmouth on 28 December, with orders to cruise westwards, and met the frigate *Diamond*, with which he 'consorted'. They stood over to the French coast, but on account of 'much wind' they lost the *Diamond*. The next day he gave chase to two sails which proved to be the frigate *Ruby* and a prize. 'We stood both out to sea' and then espied a sail standing for the shore 'which proved to be a Holland man-of-war of about 46 or 50 guns'. They both did their best to engage but the weather was so bad they could not use their lower tier of ordnance, whereas the Dutchman, fighting to leeward, could apparently use all his. They fought the Dutchman until 2.0 p.m., but at length the foremast of the *Portsmouth* was shot away and by the time Durnford had carried out the necessary repairs it was nearly dark. Houlding and he decided to lay by the enemy ship all night if possible and fight him the next day. However, owing to the direction of the heavy wind and with a 'lame' mast he was unable to follow the Dutch man-of-war which got away. Houlding's report confirms Durnford's. They kept by the Dutch ship till about 3.0 a.m., when they were between Portland and the Isle of Wight. 'The wind being then very much and a great sea, we were necessitated to leave him lest we should put ourselves to the leeward of the island'. The *Ruby* had received 'some damage to hull, rigging, and sails'. The *Portsmouth* had the same, and also needed a new mast. Durnford added, 'Let me entreat an order from you for a forecastle for this frigate. The ship will be a third better for any service in these times, and not sail any the worse'. He also requested permission to tallow the frigate, which could be done while other work was proceeding: 'She is now very foul'.

Captain Martin, commanding the frigate *Diamond*, reported that he had discovered 'about twelve sail of ships (which he judged to be Dutch men-of-war) that stand to and again in the Channel to the westward'. This was undoubtedly the squadron that Tromp had left to cruise 'outside the Channel'.[26]

---

[25] Op. cit. pp. 303-4.
[26] Op. cit. pp. 349-351, 354.

On 12 January the Council of State issued instructions on the actions to be taken with regard to the captains who were charged with not engaging in the battle of Dungeness. Captain Young and Captain Taylor were to be committed to the Fleet prison to await trial.

On 14 January there were published 'Proposals Concerning Flag Officers'.[27] These are of particular interest because they give the organisation of the English fleet and the distinguishing flags of command.

There were to be 'Three Generals appointed by Parliament', a Vice-Admiral of the whole fleet and a Rear-Admiral of the whole fleet. There were to be two Vice-Admirals, occasional (i.e. acting), of which one might be the Rear-Admiral of the Fleet, and three occasional Rear-Admirals.

The three Generals were 'to wear each of them a standard — the one to have a pennant under the standard and an ensign of red, the second a pennant under the standard and an ensign of blue, the third a pennant under the standard and an ensign of white.'

The Vice-Admiral of the fleet was to 'wear the usual flag in his foretop with a pennant under the flag and a red ensign.' The Rear-Admiral of the fleet to be a Vice-Admiral of a 'grand squadron' and to 'wear the usual flag in his mizzen top and a blue flag in his foretop, with a pennant under it and an ensign of blue.' (The 'usual flag' was that of a flag officer.)

One Vice-Admiral to a grand squadron was to wear a white flag in his foretop and a white pennant and ensign. Of the three other Rear-Admirals, one was to wear a red flag, one a blue, and the other a white in their mizzen-tops with pennants and ensigns of their respective colours.

The rest of the fleet was to be divided into nine parts, and to be put under the nine flags before mentioned, and to wear the colours of the flag they were put under; that is a pennant and ensign of the appropriate colour. All ships were to wear jacks as formerly.

If any of the Generals went out of their ships, that ship was to take down the standard and put up a flag of the colour of the pennant the ship was wearing.

This instruction envisaged a fleet of three 'grand squadrons' each of which was divided into three squadrons (later these became squadrons and divisions respectively). Each grand squadron was to be commanded by a General-at-Sea.

The Vice-Admiral of the Fleet was also Vice-Admiral of the Red Squadron and wore the 'usual flag' (i.e. the Union flag of a flag officer in his foretop). The Rear-Admiral of the Fleet was an 'occasional' Vice-Admiral of the Blue Squadron and wore the Union flag of a flag officer in his mizzen top. The other flag officers were only 'occasional' and so did not wear the Union flag.

In practice the three (more often two) Generals serving with the fleet exercised command jointly in the fleet flagship in the Red Squadron; so that the Vice-Admiral of the Fleet commanded the Blue Squadron as an occasional admiral and the Rear-Admiral of the Fleet commanded the White Squadron in a similar capacity. Eventually, as already stated, the White and Blue Squadrons changed places in order of seniority.

---

[27] Op. cit. pp. 374-5.

On 10 January Captain Henry Hatsell, commanding at Plymouth, reported to the Admiralty Committee on the state of the ships there. His report on the 4th Rate *Expedition* is of particular interest as regards the ship's company. Hatsell writes: 'The *Expedition* is well fitted of those things for the present she stood in need of, and the captain, I observe to be an honest and diligent man, but the company the most unwilling to stay in the Channel with their ship that ever I saw men. They have already been out two and twenty months, that their clothes are all done, which disenables them from doing service, that many of their families are in want at home; but with all they say that, if the State will be pleased to grant them their pay, they will immediately come forth again in their service'. One hopes that the Admiralty Committee responded rapidly and handsomely!

An idea of the work going on in getting the fleet ready for action is given by a 'List of Ships between London and the Hope' which states in detail what each ship needed to be ready for sea and the time it would take.[28] A typical entry reads: 'At Woolwich; *Violet*, 180 men, 38 guns; to be graved (i.e. bottom cleaned and given a coating of pitch), masted, and victualled; will not be ready this three weeks, nor then if men be not sent down in time, having as yet but watermen's boys'.

However, on 10 February 1652 Peter Pett wrote to the Admiralty Committee[29] that on the previous day he had received the enclosed messages from the Generals on board the *Triumph* 'and did well hope to have been their messager myself this day, but meeting with an ill passage (lying upon the hard deck of a nasty sprat boat two nights, which I was forced to accept for carrying me down, the wind blowing extremely hard when I went out of Sheerness), it hath so tired me out that I shall humbly crave to stay at home till Monday next.

'It did much rejoice me to see so gallant a fleet together, being upwards of 50 sail, and truly I think well manned. The Generals told me they resolved to sail this day, which I believe this fair wind will invite them to.'

---

[28] Op. cit. pp. 378-381.
[29] Op. cit. pp. 451-2.

7

The Battle of Portland[1]

On 6 January 1653 Lieutenant-Admiral Marten Harpertszoon Tromp wrote to the States General informing them that he had arrived the previous day at St. Martin's Roads (the Isle of Ré). He had heard that there were about 125 or 130 Dutch merchant ships in the Loire and about the Bay of Biscay, loading with salt and wine. The merchants had asked him to postpone his departure till the middle of February, but he had replied that the ships wanting to sail in the general convoy must join him by the end of January (New Style). He adds that he could not wait any longer because victuals were getting short.

A letter written in Rochelle at this time says: 'The Flemish Admiral Tromp is at Rochelle. I hope you will order it so that he shall be well received at his return. The Flemings here do believe, and make many believe, that the English dare not any more appear since the last defeat; which they report was in such sort and dishonour that it is impossible ever to recover it.'

On 10 February Blake, Deane, and Monck, as Generals-at-Sea, appointed William Penn, Vice-Admiral of the Fleet, to the command of the White Squadron of 31 ships, consisting of two 2nd Rates, two 3rd Rates, nine 4th Rates (including two prizes), one 5th Rate, three 6th Rates, five prizes (unrated), and nine armed merchant ships. At the same time they issued instructions to him (which were presumably repeated to the Rear-Admiral of the Fleet, commanding the Blue Squadron). The main points in these instructions were as follows:

1. Upon the discovery of an unidentified fleet the General (i.e. the fleet flagship) would strike the General's ensign and make a weft in it (i.e. either tying the ensign into a knot, or else gathering it up in the middle). Two already designated frigates in each squadron were to approach these ships and assess their identity, strength, composition, and formation, and then agree on the report to be presented to their respective squadrons. They were not to engage enemy ships which exceeded them in number unless it appeared that they (the frigates) would have the advantage.

---

[1] *Navy Records Society*, Vol. 37, 1910, 'The First Dutch War' Vol. 4, ed. C.T. Atkinson, pp. 23-197.

2. At the sight of the above mentioned fleet the Vice- and Rear-Admirals were to come up with the Admiral (i.e. the Generals' Red Squadron) on each wing, 'giving a competent distance for the Admiral's squadron, if there be sea room' (presumably to form line; if so, this appears to be the first suggestion of such a manoeuvre. It is worth remembering that each of the three Generals had been accustomed to forming their troops in line in a land battle, and they may have decided that the same should be done at sea, in order to bring the maximum fire to bear upon the enemy).

3. The General would give the signal to engage by firing two guns and putting a red flag in the fore-topmast head. Each squadron was then to engage the enemy next unto them. (This certainly sounds as if the whole fleet was to fight in line, and if so it would be the first occasion in naval history.)

4. Any ship in distress was to make a weft in the ensign and jack.

5. It was the duty of all commanders of small frigates, ketches, smacks, etc. to locate the enemy fireships and to do the utmost to cut off their boats (i.e. those used by the crew to escape) or if possible destroy them. For this purpose they were to keep to windward of their squadron. If they were unable to prevent the fireships from approaching the great ships of their squadron, they were to attack and destroy them, using their boats, grapnels and other means to keep them away from the big ships. Such action would be suitably rewarded.

6. The fireships of the squadrons were to try and keep the wind and, with the small frigates, remain as near the great ships as they could, whilst awaiting the signal from the Commander-in-Chief to act.

7. If the engagement should continue into the night and the General decide to anchor, all ships were to anchor on his signal which would be the same as for sailing. If the General should decide to retreat without anchoring, the signal would be the firing of two guns 'so near one after the other as the reports may be distinguished', and within three minutes another two guns.

On 11 February Henry Hatsell, agent for the Admiralty Commissioners at Plymouth, wrote to Robert Blackborne, Secretary to the Navy Commissioners, saying that he had received a letter from the Captain of St. Michael's Mount, reporting that on 8 February 'a very great fleet of ships was seen near the Lizard, and conceived to be Hollanders'. Also there was a letter from St. Ives reporting that a vessel of that town had arrived from Rochelle, the master of which stated that he was preceded from Rochelle and the Isle of Ré by 300 Dutch merchant ships and several men-of-war.

On 17 February Captain Francis Willoughby, a Navy Commissioner, wrote to the Admiralty Committee from Portsmouth to inform them that the English fleet was off the Isle of Wight in expectation of the Dutch but were not sure of their whereabouts. Captain Kendall of the *Sussex* (3rd Rate) was informed by a French vessel that the Dutch fleet was to westward but much scattered. The following day George Strelley wrote to Robert Blackborne from Plymouth reporting that the *Marmaduke* (4th Rate) had arrived at Scilly from Ireland on 15 February and whilst she stayed there the Dutch fleet passed by. It was estimated, added Strelley, that it should now be near the Isle of Wight.

There is a Dutch account (unsigned but obviously written by a captain of one of the ships in this fleet) of the subsequent operations. The weather on the morning of 18 February was rather cold and dirty with the wind NW. They sighted a whole fleet of ships on their lee and when the sun rose they saw that they were English. This unknown captain followed Tromp into action and did his best to fire as much as he could from the windward (i.e. the wind was probably too strong to allow him to use his lower tier of guns). The English, he said, fired always at masts and spars and shot in a hurry. The captain 'made fast with a hawser, and was just going to board an Englishman who was to leeward of me, but he got loose, and I gave him a broadside. Then I ran up to another and gave him as much as I could', and so this action continued. There came up towards the captain from the windward side a Vice-Admiral flying a blue flag, and a Vice-Admiral with a white flag was on his lee. Eventually the captain ran out of ammunition, and his bowsprit was shot to pieces. That night they drifted, it being quite clear with no wind.

The morning of 19 February was calm; the English came up from behind. The captain's ship was a little ahead of the Admiral and he anchored. The Admiral drifted past him flying the white flag so the captain went aboard and Tromp told him to make ready. He replied that everything was in order (so he must have received some ammunition during the night). As he put off from alongside, the English were firing at them again, concentrating on their masts and spars. About noon the Admiral signalled to him with the blue pennon from the mizzen yard. Tromp then called out to him, 'Bear off! Bear off! Sail after the merchantmen and bid them steer E by N and ENE, for they are steering SE, and tell Commandeur de Ruyter to come on my lee.' He passed the message to de Ruyter and, sailing after the merchantmen, set them on their course.

On the morning of 20 February the captain was with the merchantmen and the Admiral to rear of him. The English again bore up from the rear. The captain was urging the merchantmen to make more sail, but they took no notice. The merchant ships were now being harried by English men-of-war (presumably the smaller frigates) and the captain was trying to drive them off. When the sun went down the English drew off.

This account tells us little of the course of the battle, but the general picture is of Tromp beating a fighting retreat and trying to save the merchantmen. The captain's own ship may have been a 2nd or 3rd Rate to chase off the smaller frigates, and he was obviously an officer in whom Tromp had confidence.

An English account of the battle was issued from Whitehall on 20 February, the day the action ended, and must have been prepared from a despatch received from Blake. Its main points were as follows.

On 18 February the Dutch fleet was discovered between Portland and the Isle of Wight, Portland being about seven leagues away N by E and the wind NW. It comprised about 80 men-of-war and some 150 or more merchantmen, all to windward of the English fleet. About 8.0 a.m. Generals Blake and Deane, aboard the Triumph (2nd Rate) engaged the enemy. The Dutch attacked, and initially the Triumph was followed by only three or four of the English fleet, the remainder, being to leeward, had difficulty in getting up. These few had to deal with 30 Dutch men-of-war, of which seven were attacking the *Triumph*. It was not till 10.0 a.m. that any more of the English fleet were engaged, and then only about half, amounting to some 60 sail. The action then became very fierce and continued so for four or five hours, and then moderated till darkness separated the combatants.

During this fight only one English ship was lost, the *Sampson*, a Dutch prize of 26 guns, and she was sunk by her captain, after first sinking the enemy ship that had disabled her. The *Prosperous* (armed merchant ship) was captured, but recaptured by the *Merlin* (6th Rate). The frigate *Advice* (4th Rate) was attacked by four Dutch men-of-war 'which lay aboard of her', but 'she sank one of their Rear-Admirals of 38 guns down by her side and one ship more of 36 guns in the same manner', but her Captain John Day was dangerously wounded; his lieutenant, boatswain, corporal, and 35 more were killed and 40 or 50 wounded. The Dutch boarded her once and got possession of the forecastle but were beaten out again, but the *Advice* was so badly damaged that she went to Portsmouth that night for repair. In the *Triumph* there were between 80 and 100 killed and wounded. A splinter wounded General Blake on the left thigh, but not dangerously, and the same splinter 'tore two pieces of the coat and breeches of General Deane.'

The exact Dutch loss was not known, but one of their Vice-Admirals was taken, a 40-gun ship of 1,200 tons (the *Struisvogel*), and was found to have 100 men killed. She surrendered to Captain Stokes, having been 'much battered' by the *Lion* (3rd Rate). Dutch ships sunk and burnt included one Vice-Admiral, one Rear-Admiral, and nine other men-of-war. In addition seven or eight were so badly damaged that some of them were seen to be towed.

The next day, 19 February, two frigates of the English fleet re-opened the battle at about 10.0 a.m., and then awaited the arrival of the main fleet. By 1.0 p.m. the whole of both fleets were engaged, the English fleet having the wind. During the night the English fleet had been reinforced by some 19 ships from the Downs. Fighting on this day was within four leagues of the Isle of Wight, which was plainly in view. The sea was calm, and the English were pressing the Dutch, who had placed their merchantmen in the van.

It was at about this stage that the account ended, with a brief final note that on 19 and 20 February 'the rest of the Holland fleet were taken, sunk, and totally dispersed'. It is likely that most of it was written on the night 18/19 February. Blake, then had no doubt that he had inflicted a crushing defeat on Tromp.

The Dutch ship *Struisvogel* was brought into Portsmouth, and a letter of 20 February from the small armed merchantman *Martin* said that the Dutch man-of-war was so 'miserably torn' that she and another little armed merchantman, the *Merlin*, had to tow her in.

Some account of the third day of the battle is contained in a letter of 22 February from the armed merchant ship *Waterhound* (32 guns), a prize taken from the Dutch. After heavy fighting the Dutch began to fire out of their stern ports and make off. Several of their merchant vessels were captured. By the evening the English fleet was close to Boulogne and not far from the shore, with a NNW wind, 'which was bad for our fleet to get our own shore ... but in regard many of our ships had their sails and rigging much shattered and torn, we were glad to come to an anchor'. The Dutch prisoners told that their commanders had been very confident of victory, and when the day before the fight they complained that there was nothing to drink except water, the 'captains told them that the next day they should drink good English beer', saying that they would take the whole English fleet.

A letter from the *Eagle* (6th Rate), sent to the Council of State, gives some additional information. The attack on the first day of the battle by General Blake with the Red Squadron was supported by General Monck in the *Vanguard* (2nd Rate) 'and others' (presumably the White Squadron, which Monck was commanding).

'News from the Fleet' of 22 February says something of how the Dutch managed to get away on the night following the third day's fighting. The Dutch Admiral a little before it was dark, the wind being NW, 'bore directly in for the French shore, so near that we durst not follow, it being nigh a lee-shore, and most of the great ships had their masts, yards and sails in such a condition as they were ready to fall down every hour. We thought it the best way to come to an anchor, the tide being the leewardly, and the Dutch fleet between the French shore and us at anchor. Also, as we suppose, this night they stole away from us, notwithstanding our pilots and seamen best acquainted with the coast said, that as the wind was they could not weather the French shore to get home.'

And so a great chance of destroying the whole of Tromp's fleet was missed. Blake must have cursed the pilots, for it would have been worth the risk of losing some of his ships for such a great prize.

On 22 February Tromp wrote his official account of the battle to the States General, though he said that it was not a full report as he was awaiting the detailed statements of his captains.

He said that the fight opened with he and Rear-Admiral Florissen attacking the enemy van, where Admiral Blake and the largest ships were, whilst Vice-Admiral Evertsen was in the centre. The fighting was sharp but during this time no ship was taken or sunk on either side. At 4.0 p.m. on this first day they were obliged to bear away from the enemy because seven or eight fast sailing English frigates were bearing down on the merchant ships and it seemed as if the whole convoy would be cut to pieces unless the men-of-war protected them.

In the evening he took counsel with Evertsen and de Ruyter as to whether they should attack the enemy again and let the merchant ships drift, or cease fighting and protect the merchantmen, because they were not strong enough to do both. It was decided to do the latter and to fire as little as possible because ammunition was running low.

In the morning at about 10 o'clock the enemy started to assail them vigorously, five or six English frigates sailing on either side of the Dutch fleet to try and cut off some of the merchant ships. As far as Tromp could find out, a few small merchantmen were cut off. In the evening several ships came up to him saying that they had little or no powder or balls left. As there was still a quantity of eight-pound balls in the storeship, Tromp ordered that these should be distributed to ships having guns of the calibre.

In the morning of 20 February the wind was NW and at about 9 o'clock the enemy renewed the attack with great vigour, and before they had fought more than two hours he calculated that half his ships must have exhausted their ammunition. Several made sail and took to flight and he fired several shots after them to come back, which they did. With about 25 or 30 ships which still had ammunition they defended the merchantmen from noon until evening.

About two hours before sunset Blake collected the greater part of his fleet out of range of the Dutch guns and made the signal to attack. Seeing this, the Dutch struck their topsails and awaited the attack for about an hour, Vice-Admiral Evertsen and the ships around having exhausted their ammunition. 'But to our great good fortune, the English ships veered off, for if we had fought for half an hour longer we should have exhausted all the ammunition we had still left, and must inevitably have fallen into the enemy's hands.'

When it was dark the Dutch proceeded NNE with shortened sail, to keep the fleet together, the wind being NW and Gris Nez lying NE of them. At daybreak on 21 February they saw Calais S by W of them and no Englishman in sight.

Tromp added: 'We have seen in this engagement that divers of our captains are not as staunch as they ought to be; they did not second myself and their other honest comrades as the English did, for I observed in attacking Blake that, before I could get at him, I had such a welcome from three or four of his ships that everything on board us was on fire and Blake was still unhurt.'

On 27 February Blake, Monck, and Deane sent their official report on the battle to the Speaker, of which the main points are as follows.

On 15 and 16 February they had plied across the Channel between Seine Head and Beachy. Foreign ships they encountered reported the Dutch fleet to be 30 or 40 leagues to the West. On 16 February there was a fog so thick that they could not see 'half a musket shot' and feared the Dutch might have passed unobserved. On 17 February the wind came to the NW and the fleet got some four or five leagues to the west of the Isle of Wight. In the afternoon, standing over to the French shore in sight of Alderney, they encountered a Spanish man-of-war commanded by an English captain who informed them that Tromp with his fleet was some 20 leagues to the west. On 18 February in the morning, being some five leagues distant from the English shore, they descried the Dutch fleet, a league and a half to windward 'of the weathermost' of our ships and two to three leagues of most of the remainder. The *Triumph* (2nd Rate), flag of Blake and Deane, *Fairfax* (2nd Rate), flag of Vice-Admiral Lawson, *Speaker* (2nd Rate), flag of Admiral Penn commanding the Blue Squadron, and about 20 others, were the only ships near to the Dutch fleet, and Tromp, who had the wind, might have got away with his whole fleet; but as soon as he discovered the English fleet, he put all his merchant ships to windward, and attacked the *Triumph* and the other nearest ships with superior numbers. This minor portion of the English fleet had to withstand the attack most of the day until 4.0 p.m., by which time a considerable number of English 'ships and frigates' had got so far ahead that by tacking they could weather the greatest part of the Dutch fleet. As soon as Tromp saw this he, with the main part of his fleet, tacked as well and drew away. Blake says that they spent the remainder of the day and night repairing rigging, masts, and sails, and replacing casualties in the bigger ships by drawing men from the smaller ones (which did not fight in the line of battle). He adds that they took and destroyed seven or eight men-of-war.

During the night the Dutch steered directly up the Channel, with their merchantmen ahead and the men-of-war in the rear. In the morning the English fleet was three to four leagues south of the Isle of Wight, and as soon as it was light it sailed after the Dutch, but being calm it was noon before any ships were within range and the main body did not engage till 2.0 p.m. Fighting was then fierce until dark. Some five Dutch men-of-war were taken and destroyed.

That night the Dutch fleet continued up the Channel followed by the English, the wind WNW and 'a fine little gale all night'.

On the next day, 20 February, Blake attacked at 9.0 a.m. 'with some five great ships and all the frigates of strength'; many of the other ships could not get up that day. Seeing the Dutch men-of-war somewhat weakened, Blake sent smaller frigates and 'ships of lesser force' to get amongst the Dutch merchantmen 'which put their whole body to a very great deal of trouble'. But Blake did not allow any ships powerful enough to tackle the bigger Dutch men-of-war to take part in harrying the merchant ships. Fighting continued till dark, by which time the English ships were some three and a half leagues from Cape Gris Nez, the wind being NW and the Dutch fleet to leeward.

The Generals consulted with the pilots, as well as with men who knew the coast, and they gave it as their opinion that the Dutch fleet could not weather the French coast and get home in that state of wind and tide, and that the English fleet should anchor. It was a very dark night with a strong wind, but the Dutch got away, and in the morning there was not one of their ships in sight. Tromp was a sailor; the Generals-at-Sea were not.

The fruits of the battle were some 17 or 18 Dutch men-of-war captured or sunk (without the loss of any English ship except that *Sampson*), 'besides merchantmen whose number we know not, they being scattered in many parts'.

A letter from the frigate *Nonsuch* (4th Rate) said: 'We can tell you no news of the Hollander, but believe he is gone home to recruit his forces, and then to try another bout, which if he do we shall be ready for him. Their gallant Mr. Tromp when he was in France (we understand) wore a broom, and being demanded what he meant by it, replied that he was going to sweep the narrow seas of all Englishmen.'

The English flag officers and their ships during the battle were as follows:

Robert Blake and Richard Deane, Generals-at-Sea and Admirals of the Red, *Triumph* (2nd Rate), fleet flagship.

Sir John Lawson, Vice-Admiral of the Red, *Fairfax* (2nd Rate).

Samuel Howett, Rear-Admiral of the Red, *Laurel* (3rd Rate).

George Monck, General-at-Sea and Admiral of the White, *Vanguard* (2nd Rate).

James Peacock, Vice-Admiral of the White, *Rainbow* (2nd Rate).

Roger Martin, Rear-Admiral of the White, *Diamond* (4th Rate).

Sir William Penn, Vice-Admiral of the Fleet and Admiral of the Blue, *Speaker* (2nd Rate).

Lionel Lane, Vice-Admiral of the Blue, *Victory* (2nd Rate).

John Bourne, Rear-Admiral of the Blue, *Assistance* (4th Rate).

It is time now to assess the strategy and tactics of this remarkable battle.

Tromp had given himself two objectives (a) the destruction of Blake's fleet and (b) the safe conduct home of the big convoy of Dutch merchant ships. It will be remembered that he had protested at being given two separate objectives on the outward passage; but he had brought both off successfully and perhaps now (if the story of the broom at his masthead is true) was over confident of his ability to do it again. He made masterly use of the NW wind to bring his whole fleet to the windward of the English fleet, with his merchantmen to windward again of his men-of-war, and concentrated.

Blake was worried in case the Dutch fleet were able to slip past him, which, as he says, they could have done. It would seem that he had his squadrons well separated, to prevent this, each squadron in line ahead formation (if the interpretation of his operational instructions is correct). The Red Squadron, under Blake himself and Deane was on the northern flank, to intercept Tromp should he elect to keep to the English side of the Channel, the White Squadron under Monck, the other General, was on the southern flank in case Tromp should choose to keep closer to the French coast, whilst in the centre was the Blue Squadron under Penn, ready to support either Blake or Monck. Inevitably, therefore, either the Red or the White Squadrons would have to face attack, initially, by superior numbers. When the action opened it was the Red Squadron which was attacked. The report says that Penn's ship was already there when the attack took place, which shows that the Blue Squadron was already moving in support. In fact Penn's manoeuvre of the Blue Squadron was decisive, for, by tacking to windward, he managed to bring it to windward of Tromp's battle fleet. The two squadrons, probably fighting in line, would have been able to bear against the Dutch ships the massive weight of broadsides from all the ships in the battle lines of both squadrons. (One may suppose that such a concentration of fire could have been planned by Deane, Fairfax's chief of artillery at the battle of Naseby.) It would be dangerous to pay too much attention to apparently conflicting reports of detail, because personal memories of battle can be notoriously inaccurate.

Held in front by the Red Squadron, with the Blue to his windward and approaching his merchant ships and the White Squadron rapidly approaching, Tromp had been out-generalled. Defeated in battle, he pursued his second objective, the safety of his merchant convoy, and in this he largely succeeded. He had lost some 60 of them, but the States General were so relieved that they gave appropriate awards to Tromp and all his flag officers.

8

After Portland[1]

On 8 March 1653 the Council of State issued an order stating the action to be taken in the light of the situation at sea following the battle of Portland. It directed the Commissioners for the Admiralty to take various actions, including the following.

1. That to the ships already at sea were to be added enough to make them up to 50 sail, which were to be under the command of Vice-Admiral Penn until the Generals joined him with the remainder of the fleet, at present refitting at Portsmouth.

2. That as quickly as possible the main body of the fleet should be increased to 100 sail.

3. That in addition to the above another 20 sail should be prepared for despatch to the Straits of Gibraltar, and that, in addition to the ships' companies, they should carry 600 soldiers and as many marines who could be got up to a maximum of 400.

4. Out of the ships remaining, the Generals were to supply the guards for the coasts of Scotland and Ireland and 'other northern parts', which were to replace ships already on those duties.

5. That Captain John Lawson be appointed Rear-Admiral to the Fleet.

It was all a bit optimistic, for Penn was not able to sail before the end of March, and even then only 40 ships could be got ready for him.

On 16 March the Commissioners for the Admiralty presented to the Council of State, for approval, the names for five new frigates that were to be launched shortly; they were *Bristol*, *Portland*, *Essex*, *Hampshire*, and *Newcastle*. All these were 4th Rates, except for the *Essex* which was a 3rd Rate, and is referred to as the 'great frigate'.

On the same day the COS directed that a letter be written to 'the Generals of the Fleet' informing them that they had put a stop to the granting of any further commissions for privateers until they were certified that the men

---

[1] *Navy Records Society*, Vol. 37, 1910 'The First Dutch War' Vol. 4, ed. C.T. Atkinson, pp. 211 ff.

required by the fleet had been supplied, and they also empowered the Generals to take men from any privateers they encountered if they should need them.

'News from London' dated 25 March to 4 April 1653 is of interest in showing the difficulties facing the preparation of the fleet for sea. 'Our wants of pitch, tar, cordage, &c, are so great, that we shall be forced to leave fifteen of our best ships in harbour, that were somewhat shattered in the last engagement.' The writer goes on to say that 26 ships were ready to go out of the Thames, and adds, 'We had pressed a great many more, but our want of men is such that we shall have much ado to get out these. We have sent into Scotland, Ireland, Wales, and the remotest parts of England to press men.'

On 21 March 1653 there is an interesting example of the arrangements for hiring a merchant ship for State service. On this date 'Articles of Agreement' were concluded between the Commissioners of the Navy 'and James Talbot, Commander and part owner of the good ship called the Samuel, burthen of three hundred tons or thereabout'. The ship was being hired to the Commissioners of the Navy for the service of Parliament for one voyage only. Talbot was responsible for seeing that the ship was 'completely apparelled, rigged, fitted, and furnished with ground tackle, and sea stores . . . in warlike equipage, according to the schedule endorsed, as is usual for ships employed as men-of-war, in the service of the State, as a ship of her rank and burthen.' The length of service was for 'six months certain, or eight months if required'. If she was 'lost honourably in fight', then the State would pay. The owners would provide 20 guns and the State would supply the rest if more were 'thought fit'. The State would supply any 'surplus' ammunition judged necessary and 'bear the charge of all such powder and shot as shall be expended in fight or by command'. The victuals and wages of the 'mariners and seamen' would be the responsibility of the State.

On 24 March Major N. Bourne and Captain (Rear-Admiral of the Fleet) J. Lawson submitted a report to the Admiralty Commissioners, following an inspection they had been ordered to make of the 2nd Rate *Fairfax*, which had been destroyed by fire. As far as they had been able to find out, it had been caused by the accidental 'setting on fire some loose powder that was scattered in the powder room by the fall of a candle'. They considered that neglect of duty as a cause for the disaster could not be excluded. Borne upon the ship's book were 30 men, but only 12 were on board. They added that the 'principal officer of trust (who was yeoman to the boatswain) was absent, and the gunner's mate and yeoman of the powder room, who were on board, we conceive will appear most deeply chargeable. We found by examination that no watch was kept on board.' They would submit another report after examination.

The *Fairfax* was one of the most valuable ships in the fleet and had been the flagship of Lawson (as occasional Vice-Admiral) at the battle of Portland.

On 28 March the Generals of the Fleet (Blake, Deane, and Monck) issued instructions to 'Captain William Penn, Vice-Admiral of the Fleet' regarding the action he was to take with his squadron in escorting to safety such prizes and merchantmen 'as are without in the Road', as well as securing the safety of vessels bound for Dunkirk and escorting such vessels as were in the Downs 'or ports adjacent' and 'bound to the westward'. He was then to detail 'five or more of the best and nimblest sailers' to ply between the North Foreland and Calais. Finally, he was to carry out a general reconnaissance, capturing or destroying any ships belonging to the 'United Provinces of the Low Countries'. After completing these tasks he was to return to Portsmouth as quickly as possible.

The following day, 24 March, the Generals issued their very important 'Instructions for the better ordering of the Fleet in Fighting', which presumably embraced some of the lessons learned at the battle of Portland, and were amendments to the instructions issued on 10 February and quoted above. The principal amendment was that at the end of paragraph 3, after 'engage with the enemy next unto them', there was inserted, 'and in order thereunto all the ships of every squadron shall endeavour to keep in a line with their chief, unless the chief of his squadron shall be either lamed or otherwise disabled (which God forbid), whereby the said ship that wears the flag shall not come in to do that service which is requisite, then every ship of the said squadron shall endeavour to get into line with the Admiral or he that commands in chief next to him and nearest the enemy'.

From this it would appear that squadrons fighting in line had been tried at the battle of Portland and proved successful. It was therefore embodied in these instructions. At the battle of Portland fighting of the whole fleet in line would not have been practicable owing to the disposition of the fleet adopted before the battle to avoid Tromp being able to slip past unseen, but that such was envisaged would appear from the wording of the proviso as regards action to be taken if a squadron flagship were disabled. This is a most important milestone in naval tactics.

On the same day the Generals issued 'Instructions for the fleet at sea but not in contact with the enemy'. These are mainly procedural and need not detain us here; but there were some points of unusual interest. There were various signals displayed by the General to summon on board all captains in the fleet, another to summon all masters of ships, a third for flag officers only. Others required the flag officers and captains of a particular squadron, or the Vice-Admiral and Rear-Admiral of the Fleet only. Then 'if a white flag on the ensign staff, then all captains of frigates that carry 30 guns and upwards'; 'if a blue flag on the ensign staff, then all captains of frigates both great and small;' 'if the jack colours on the ensign staff, the captains of ships that are not frigates.' It is this differentiation of vessels that is interesting. Frigates of 30 guns and over were probably 3rd and 4th Rates — frigates capable of fighting for information and classified as 'great frigates'. Ships 'that are not frigates' probably refers to 1st and 2nd Rates and those 3rd Rates which were not built as frigates. The small frigates would be 5th and 6th Rates, suitable for reconnaissance but not expected to fight to get their information.

The distinction between ships and frigates appears again in an order to all captains from the Generals-at-Sea on 29 March, headed 'Instructions to be put into execution by the respective captains of, and belonging to, the ships and frigates of the Commonwealth of England.' These laid down general duties at sea and administrative matters on board ship.

On 5 April the Council of State wrote to Penn saying that they had received letters of 31 March from the captain of the collier convoy at Newcastle, reporting that he intended to take the first opportunity of wind to come away with the collier fleet of about 300 sail; and that because of the importance to the Commonwealth of the safety of this fleet, Penn (then with his squadron in the Swinn — a channel SE of Foulness) was directed to sail immediately to some place between Harwich and Yarmouth, which was most convenient for his fleet to lie, in order to form a junction with Rear-Admiral Lawson and such ships as should be sent with him from the Thames. He was also directed to send out scouts to keep a watch on the enemy and so to be ready to move for the security of the collier fleet. To make up shortages of men, there were 270 soldiers of Colonel Ingoldsby's Regiment at Dover ready to come on board if he should require them.

This instruction shows the Council of State's fear that the Dutch might try to intercept and destroy the valuable convoy carrying the coal which was so badly needed in London.

On 6 April Captain P. Motham of the 3rd Rate *Bear* and commanding the escort to the collier fleet wrote to the COS that he had been trying without success to discover de With's fleet, and that as he was ready and the wind and weather satisfactory, he had set sail from Tynemouth Bar on 4 April with near 500 sail. On 5th April he had been between Robin Hood's Bay and Scarborough, when at about 3.0 p.m. he was informed that there had been discovered approaching Flamborough Head 19 or 20 sail of about 30 or 40 guns apiece and apparently Flemish (i.e. Dutch) vessels. He ordered all the colliers into Scarborough, the smaller into the pier and the larger as they could get under cover of the Castle guns. He with the rest of the men-of-war remained 'on the off gage'. At 6.0 p.m. the Deputy Governor of the Castle came out to confer with him as to the best means of securing the fleet. He pointed out that the place was very dangerous in bad weather. He also complained of some of the colliers' masters being refractory and stealing away in the night.

On 7 April Deane and Monck, Generals-at-Sea, wrote what sounds like a furious complaint to the Admiralty Committee about the lack of support provided for Penn, saying that, after directing Penn to sail to a convenient rendezvous between Harwich and Yarmouth, the only reinforcements they had sent him were the *Heartsease* (4th Rate) and the *George* (2nd Rate). They commented caustically: 'We perceive that it is far more difficult to get ships ready to sail than to design'. They also included a recommendation as regards medical supplies. On board the Admiral, they wrote, there should be two chests, one with medicines and the other with plasters, ointments and other things necessary for surgery, which should be a reserve to issue as needed, and that there should be a qualified man to take charge of them.

Meanwhile, to return to the troubles of the collier fleet, Major (and occasional Rear-Admiral) Nehemiah Bourne wrote on 7 April to the Naval

Commissioners that he had just returned from the Vice-Admiral (Penn), who with his squadron of 41 sail was at anchor off the North Foreland, and bound for Solebay, where he was to be joined by the Rear-Admiral (i.e. Lawson) and the ships with him. From intelligence gathered by scouts and interrogations, he added, it seemed probable that de With with over 40 sail had been seen about 10 leagues WNW of Texel on 1 April and moving northwards.

On 8 April Captain Robert Woodward, who was on board the *Bear*, wrote (in accordance with their instructions) to the Navy Commissioners, describing the encounter with de With. On 5 April, when they were between Robin Hood's Bay and Scarborough, they were informed by a coble (a small single-masted flat-bottomed fishing boat) that a fleet of ships had appeared off Flamborough Head of about 20 sail, which was believed to be de With's squadron. On this information the Captain commanding the escort (Motham) ordered the fleet of colliers to get under the command of Scarborough Castle. To assist in securing the fleet, the Governor of the Castle positioned some guns on the pier-head and about six to the south of it. On the morning of 6 April the Dutch fleet was in sight, consisting of 18 ships and two galliots (shallow draught ketches), all with considerable armament and five or six having two tiers of ordnance. The wind being off shore they did not come within range. About 8.0 a.m. they weighed and stood in. Their Admiral, on weighing, put out a blue ensign, on the next tack he put out an orange, and then, within range, a red. He then fired a broadside, followed by the rest of his fleet.

Both sides continued firing for about two hours, and then their Admiral fired one gun, put out a white ensign and 'lay with his sails a backstays, and so did the rest of the fleet, driving off to sea'. The successive ensigns of different colours displayed by the flagship from approach to action until withdrawal are interesting.

Similar accounts are written by Motham and by Captain Henry Southward (commanding the armed merchant ship *Violet*) to Robert Blackbourne, Secretary to the Naval Commissioners, and by Motham on 8 April to the Admiralty Committee. It is apparant that Captain Motham fought a very able action in saving his valuable collier fleet.

On 9 April Penn wrote to the Admiralty Committee acknowledging their letter of 5 April, as well as one from the COS directing him to hasten with part of his fleet to Scarborough to help secure the collier fleet, and saying that he would sail without waiting for the Rear-Admiral. Penn wrote from Solebay, where he had arrived the previous day.

On 10 April de With wrote to the States General giving his account of the affair. On 31 March he left the Shallows with 18 ships and three galliots (two-masted craft with gaff-rigged mainmast and short lateen mizzen). On 4 April they were between Flamborough and Scarborough. On 5 April one of the leading ships reported a large fleet of ships coming from NNW, and in the evening he sighted them standing close in to the shore. On 7 April, 'after doing all we could by tacking and working with the tide, we came off Scarborough, and there we saw the said fleet lying close in shore under the castle.'

However, his attempts to attack were prevented by 'the rocks, the narrowness of the channels, the shoals, and strong winds'. His next intention was to reconnoitre off the Thames and in the Downs.

However, this intention by de With was also frustrated. On 11 April Penn wrote to the Admiralty Commissioners, reporting that he had sailed north the previous day, after being delayed by the late arrival of the pilots. At about 6.0 p.m. three of his scouts returned with the report that they had encountered 18 Dutch men-of-war 12 leagues from Solebay, of which they reckoned that the smallest had 30 guns; they also had two galliots with them. The Dutch warships pursued the English frigates but could not catch them. De With obviously appreciated that he was steering into Penn's much stronger squadron, for he made for home!

On 16 April Captain Francis Allen, commanding the hired ship *Recovery*, submitted a report to the Admiralty Commissioners that on 14 April at about 9.0 a.m. that the colliers (his ship being one of the escorts) had entered the Thames. And so this valuable convoy reached London, thanks mainly to the ability of Captain Motham, and despite the insubordinate behaviour of many of the colliers' masters.

On 25 April Tromp wrote a very depressed letter to the States General. He had just received news that 'Vice-Admiral de With is come off the Meuse with the forty weak and crazy ships of which he writes; and I am going thither in person to-day in the utmost dejection, because a great number of our large ships have been burnt, sunk and taken, and those that are left we shall be forced to leave lying at home'. This is a most revealing statement of the extent of the Dutch losses at the battle of Portland.

Tromp went on to complain that if the refitting and repair of ships had been taken in hand promptly, they would have been fit to put to sea two or three weeks ago. 'Nevertheless', he added, 'I shall, although unwillingly, obey your H.M.'s commands, unless your H.M. should be pleased to give me leave to retire'. This seems to have triggered their 'High and Mighty Lordships' into some sort of action; for on 30 April Tromp reported to them that he had sailed out of the Meuse in the frigate *Gelderlant* and 'at eight o'clock in the evening we came up with our fleet consisting of fifty-six warships, five fire-ships and seven advice-boats'. He was going to make every effort to bring this fleet off Texel and join the warships and merchantmen that might be lying there.

'News from London' reported on 29 April that 'Eighty sail of our fleet now lie in the Downs, thirty more are to be with them on Monday from Portsmouth and twenty more (as soon as they can be ready) out of this river, so that we shall by the middle of next month be at sea with 130 sail. Our colliers came in very seasonably for the helping forth of our fleet, which is believed could not have gone out had we not had them, most of our men being both unskilful and unwilling'. That is, the seamen manning the colliers were drafted into the fleet; and it is interesting that the arrival of the collier fleet was not only welcome for its coal but also for its seamen! The report continues: 'Blake is outed of his command, and is come to London highly discontented; he is much for Parliament'. What this means is that Oliver Cromwell had disbanded Parliament and had installed himself as 'Protector' and head of the executive power. Blake was an ardent Parliamentarian and was furious at Cromwell's seizure of power. Cromwell disliked Blake but respected his ability. It is unlikely that Blake was 'outed'. He had been badly wounded at the battle of Portland and was quite unfit for active service. He returned to his command on 5 June, but was still not fully recovered.

Deane and Monck were left in command of the fleet and on that same date of 29 April they reported to the Admiralty Committee that they were at sea with the fleet, had joined Penn, and were riding off the North Foreland. They reported that Penn's ships were deficient in victuals and asked for three ships of about 300 tons each to carry fresh water 'without which we shall not be able to keep the sea any considerable time'. They also wanted hammocks, for about 3,000 men were lying on the decks for want of them.

9

The Battle of the Gabbard[1]

The fleet which eventually assembled under Deane and Monck consisted of 105 ships and was manned by 16,269 men; the total number of guns being 3,850. It was organised into three squadrons, each of three divisions as follows:

First Squadron (Red)
Admirals' Division (Deane and Monck) one 1st Rate, one 3rd Rate, five 4th Rates, one 5th Rate, one 6th Rate, three hired ships, one prize, and three fireships.
Vice-Admiral's Division (Peacock) one 2nd Rate, three 3rd Rates, two 4th Rates, five hired ships, and one prize.
Rear-Admiral's Division (Howett) one 2nd Rate, one 3rd Rate, three 4th Rates, three hired ships, and two prizes.

Second Squadron (White)
Admirals' Division (Penn) one 2nd Rate, one 3rd Rate, four 4th Rates, one 6th Rate, five hired ships, one prize, and one fireship.
Vice-Admiral's Division (Lane) one 2nd Rate, three 4th Rates, four hired ships, and two prizes.
Rear-Admiral's Division (Graves) one 2nd Rate, two 3rd Rates, one 4th Rate, one 5th Rate, two hired ships, and two prizes.

Third Squadron (Blue)
Admirals' Division (Lawson) one 2nd Rate, two 3rd Rates, three 4th Rates, four hired ships, one prize, and one fireship.
Vice-Admiral's Division (Jordan) one 2nd Rate, one 3rd Rate, two 4th Rates, four hired ships, one prize and two fireships.
Rear-Admiral's Division (Goodson) one 2nd Rate, one 3rd Rate, two 4th Rates, six hired ships, and one prize.

The armament of most of the hired ships and prizes was approximately

---

[1] *Navy Records Society*, Vol. 41, 1912, 'The First Dutch War', Vol. 5, ed. C.T. Atkinson, pp. 16-146.

equivalent to that of a 4th Rate, that is 30 to 40 guns. On 2 June Blake rejoined the fleet with another 20 or 30 ships.

John Poortmans (presumably on the staff of the Navy Commissioners) wrote on 2 May to Robert Blackborne, Secretary to the Navy Commissioners, from the Fleet flagship, the 1st Rate *Resolution*. He reported the 'unexpected sailing' to the Texel 'with the whole body of the fleet being about eighty sail fighting ships'. The term 'fighting ships' probably designates all those fit to lie in the line of battle, that is 4th Rates and above and the more powerfully armed hired ships and Dutch prizes. The reason for the move to the Texel was due to information imparted by some Hamburg merchantmen that on 30 April they had seen about 12 leagues from the Texel some 70 Dutch men-of-war under Tromp, who was expecting another 30 or 40 from the Vlie, where de With had been sent to fetch them. The Generals called a Council-of-War at which it was decided to go and fight the Dutch on their own coast.

Two days later Tromp was writing to the States General from the Dutch fleet off the Texel, reporting that he had 80 ships of war and that reinforcements were still arriving. But out of the twenty-four fireships with which their lordships had decided that he should be equipped, he only had five, of which one was so bad that it 'will go to the bottom'. Over 200 merchantmen had come to him, 'all bound for the West and South, the long way round'; i.e. round the north of Scotland. He had had conflicting reports of the movements of the English fleet and did not know what to make of them. He was expecting every hour a richly laden fleet coming the long way round. He had therefore decided to conduct the large fleet of merchantmen with him northwards, along the course which the incoming merchant ships would have to sail if the convoy commander carried out the orders sent to him. If he met them, or the English, he would let the merchantmen with him proceed on their voyage, and convoy the expected fleet to safety.

When the English fleet arrived off the Texel, Tromp had gone. Poortmans, writing again to Blackborne on 5 May, said that Dutch fishermen had informed them that Tromp had gone northward with about 80 men-of-war and some 200 merchant ships. He added, 'We are making all the sail we can after him and hope to overtake at Shetland or thereabouts.'

An interesting note from the Admiralty Committee to the Generals-at-Sea of 9 May details the logistic help which has to be available to the fleet on its way north. 'We have obtained my Lords' warrant for 140 barrels of powder from Hull, which we have appointed Captain Strong to take in there and to call at Yarmouth for the powder that came from Scarborough, and for the 120 barrels of powder that was to be supplied from Harwich and Yarmouth which, with the 200 barrels that were sent by the *Sapphire* and we hope is with you and 500 more that Colonel Lilburne by my Lords' direction is to furnish you with in Scotland will, we conceive, be a competent proportion to answer the present occasion.' They had also written to Hull and Newcastle and the Commissioners at Leith to impress as many men as they could, to put on board such ships as should touch at any of those places. In addition Colonel Lilburne had been ordered to have a regiment of land soldiers in readiness upon the coast of Scotland to supply any further men that the fleet needed. Also the victuallers had ordered a man at Leith to supply the fleet with water, and the Commissioners there were to try and get some ketches to ascertain the needs of the fleet and to obtain information as to the movements of the enemy. In a few days time there should be another 20 ships ready to sail and they would like to have instructions from the Generals as to their disposal. This helpful letter was signed by the following members of the Admiralty Committee: Major Richard Salwey, John Carew, and John Langley.

Tromp would have envied the administrative support thus supplied to his English opponents. On 17 May he wrote to the States General giving a report of his movements. He was joined, he says, on 4 May by de With from the Texel with two warships and six or seven merchantmen. He had left 18 warships in the Texel, still not ready. Tromp immediately weighed anchor and got under sail, steering into the channel between Texel and the Maze and thence along the coast of Norway, past the point of Bergen as far as the north point of the Shetland Isles, where they parted company with the merchant fleet on the afternoon of 11 May, they taking their course to the West. Tromp had 77 warships left and with these he sailed East towards Norway, following the course along which the homeward bound merchant fleet should come. He had sent Commandeur de Wilde to 'the Vlie and Texel in order, with the assistance of the Deputies of your HM and of the respective admiralties or Chambers of Directors and, in their absence, of the Commissaries, who ought to be authorised to hurry out the above-mentioned eighteen ships of war' as well as the rest of the fireships, water ships, and small vessels. It sounds like an organisational nightmare!

Tromp continued that, if the merchant fleet had not arrived, he would continue cruising between the Doggerbank and Texel until they arrived; particularly as he had no information of the enemy's position, much less of their designs. In a postscript to this letter he reported meeting a Norwegian ship which had left Texel on 14 May and told him that Blake had been off the Texel on 10 or 11 May with 80 ships. Also four merchantmen had just arrived, belonging to the expected fleet from which they had parted company on 15 May off Bergen. So if the wind held he expected this fleet within 24 hours.

On 21 May Tromp was able to report to the States General that on 19 May he had been joined by the incoming merchant fleet of about 100 vessels. Eighteen ships had parted company from them off the Naze in Norway, but the rest of the fleet of about 50 sail, bound for the Meuse and the Wielings, had now joined. The last report he had had about the movements of the English was that their Vice-Admiral had been seen off the south point of the Shetlands and Fair Isle with 80 ships. Seeing that there were over 500 Dutch merchant ships lying in the Vlie bound for the Baltic and Norway, together with three East Indiamen and a number of other vessels bound for the West the long way round, he recommended that his fleet should escort them to, respectively, the neighbourhood of Skagen and the Shetlands, and then cruise in search of the English fleet, with a view to attacking it.

In his own fleet there were 92 warships, five fireships, and six small vessels. He was vexed that, in spite of repeated requests, he was still so short of fireships, for, because of the terror with which they filled the enemy, a good number of them would enable him to win the battle, and if he did not get them he would probably lose it. The number of these vessels that had been voted was 24, but only six had put in an appearance and one had already foundered in fine weather. This letter was written from on board the de Vreede off Goree.

Four days later Tromp was in Dover Road. From the English side his arrival was reported by Robert Clarke, Captain of the 6th Rate frigate *Drake*, on 25 May to the Admiralty Committee. He had come from Dunkirk, escorting some merchantmen, when he encountered a French man-of-war which he chased; but the French ship 'made a running fight of it' till he got under the safety of Calais Castle, which fired many shots at the *Drake*, forcing Clarke to withdraw. He came to anchor in Dover Road, and about two hours later the whole Dutch fleet of 114 sail came in through the Downs. Clarke was forced to cut his cables and run ashore, his little frigate receiving some damage from Dutch broadsides. The Dutch then fired many broadsides into the town of Dover and captured two English merchant ships. With the help of boats from the shore, Clarke got his ship into Dover pier for repair. He said that the Dutch were now at anchor in Dover Road.

Poortmans, from on board the fleet flagship off the Texel, wrote a report to Blackborne on 26 May giving information about the fleet's movements. Since they had returned from the Shetlands they had been plying about the Texel and the Vlie to stop Tromp joining with such men-of-war as were at either of these places. The next day he wrote again saying that it had just been decided to sail for the English coast and come to anchor off Yarmouth.

Tromp gave his own narrative of these recent events to the States General on 28 May, being then in his flagship *Brederode* off Dover. At about 10.0 p.m. on 24 May they got under sail and sailed W by S for the mouth of the Thames. At 9.0 a.m. the next day he made a signal for all commanding officers to come on board. They decided to sail in the evening to a point just out of sight of the North Foreland, so that their movements would not be discovered and that, if the wind held, Commandeur de Ruyter and Rear-Admiral Peter Florissen would get outside the Goodwins on the morning tide with their squadrons of 35 warships and two fireships, so as to tack into the Downs from the South and cut off the enemy who might be lying there; whilst Tromp and Vice-Admirals Evertsen and de With with three squadrons, totalling 63 ships of war and four fireships, would enter the Downs from the North.

That evening the Dutch fleet was joined by the *Brederode* (Tromp's flagship) and the *Prins*, which had been under repair since the last battle. Tromp transferred himself and his entire crew to the *Brederode*, which he found had become very stiff after girdling, but sailed as well as ever she did.

On the morning of 25 May, at 6 o'clock, the Dutch sighted the North Foreland and at 2.0 p.m. passed the 'castles in the Downs', and right up against the landing stage and on a lee shore, were two little merchant ships'.

They exchanged several shots with the shore guns. At 3.0 p.m. Tromp was reunited with the two squadrons of his fleet, which had previously separated, as planned, in the manoeuvre to cut off any English ships lying in the Downs. The fleet anchored whilst Tromp sent four or five of his lightest frigates towards the shore. A small Parliamentary frigate was lying there with two or three merchant ships. The frigate ran for the shore and they captured the merchant ships. The next day they tacked towards Calais and at 11.0 a.m. anchored 'between Calais cliffs'.

Tromp added a postscript to the above letter at 9 o'clock that night giving information he had received from a Dutch privateer which had encountered the English fleet, 114 ships strong, at 10.0 p.m. on 24 May, and on the following morning had been fired on by their frigates some 15 miles outside the Vlie. He had promptly notified all the captains of the fleet and was continuing on his course to meet the enemy. This information had been supplemented by that from the mate of a Dutch fishing pink which had been in the midst of the English fleet that morning.

On 31 May Deane and Monck wrote to the Admiralty Committee to say that they, being at anchor off Yarmouth, there arrived the *Unicorn* and the *Portland* frigates (the former being a 2nd Rate and the latter a 3rd Rate, so that the term 'frigate' could only have applied to the *Portland*, as no 2nd Rates were built as frigates). They were accompanying six 'merchant ships of war' and nine or ten victualling and waterships, which were no doubt very welcome. A ketch had informed them that Tromp and the Dutch fleet had been the previous night off the Long Sand Head (about 18 miles NNE of the North Foreland). Since both fleets were anxious to fight a conflict could not long be delayed.

On 1 June William Cullen, Mayor of Dover, wrote to Lieutenant-Colonel Thomas Kelsey, commanding at Dover Castle, informing him that the Dutch fleet was approaching 'with a fair gale on the back of the sands and may be here suddenly.' The troops had marched out of the town when the enemy had previously left the vicinity, and he was now requesting their return. There was obviously considerable anxiety about the possibility of a Dutch landing. The next day Captain William Wilding wrote from Gravesend to the Admiralty Committee, and from his letter it is apparent that Blake had set sail in the 3rd Rate *Essex* with several other ships to join the fleet which they had heard had been off Harwich that morning. Of the Dutch fleet, which the previous day had been riding off the Longsands Head, there was no news.

But battle had now been joined. Tromp wrote to the States General on 3 June reporting that the previous day they had come upon the enemy 'in about the height of Nieuport'. His fleet numbered 98 warships and six fireships, whilst the English had 95 or 100 sail, 75 or 80 of which were 'big', well-armed ships and frigates'. He began to engage them about 8.0 a.m. and the fight lasted till 9.0 p.m., when the two fleets separated. On the morning of 3 June he summoned on board all flag officers and captains, and found that most of them were so short of ammunition as to be unable to continue the fight. He proposed, therefore, to make one more sharp, attack after which he would be forced to retire.

Monck also submitted a report on 3 June, addressed to the Admiralty Committee. On the morning of 2 June the fleet had been at anchor 'some two miles within the south head' of the Gabbard Shoal (a sandbank about 40 miles east of Harwich and about NE by N of the North Foreland). Early in the morning they discovered the Dutch fleet about six miles to leeward and made sail towards them. Between 11.0 a.m. and 12.0 noon the action began and was very sharp for about three hours — from 3.0 p.m. to 6.0 p.m. — at which time the enemy bore right away before the wind. There was little further action, though the frigates gave chase as long as it was light enough to distinguish friend from foe. One of the Dutch admirals was blown up and Monck had been informed that three or four more Dutch ships had been sunk. He did not believe that any English ship had been sunk. Major-General Deane had been killed by a cannon ball. Most of the ammunition had been expended in the battle and he asked that 'a considerable portion may be suddenly provided and sent with such victualling and water ships as are yet behind, to be ready in Yarmouth Road upon all occasions.' He had asked the Lord General (i.e. Cromwell) that Vice-Admiral Penn might be promoted General-at-Sea 'to make up our number' (i.e. on account of Deane's death).

Tromp's report on 4 June to the States General seems to have been an endeavour to conceal something of a disaster. He had intended to get as much as possible to windward of the enemy, and then to attack them in the centre of their fleet. But when they had tacked about the wind dropped and the enemy, having the wind, seized this advantage and themselves came down to attack. Then 'through the carelessness or lack of experience in naval warfare of several of the captains and their officers, several of us ran into one another and were thrown into confusion, and were also surrounded by some of the quickest sailing of the enemy's frigates and captured.' From reports submitted to him by the captains, it appeared that seven Dutch warships had either been taken or sunk. As his ships were very much shattered, as well as being very short of ammunition, and the enemy still in sight with more than a hundred large ships, Tromp had decided, with the advice of the chief officers of the fleet, to run 'with the ships now with us' just inside the sand banks of the Wielings. His own ship, the Brederode had received several shots below the water-line, which they had stopped as well as they could, but she was still very leaky during the night, and was kept afloat with difficulty.

It is apparent from the phrasing of his report that Tromp had suffered a very considerable defeat.

By the second day of the battle Blake had rejoined the fleet, for on 4 June a report was sent to Cromwell signed by both him and Monck. As an account of the first day of the battle had already been sent, they confined themselves to the fighting on 3 June. There had been little wind that morning; the English fleet had had what there was, but it was about noon before they were able to get into action. After four hours fighting, the Dutch fleet tried to get away, but by then there was 'a pretty fresh gale of wind', which enabled them to press the enemy hard and they 'sunk or took many of them'. They thought that if it had not been for the approach of darkness and their nearness to

Ostend and among the sands, they would have destroyed most of the Dutch fleet. As it was they anchored about 10.0 p.m. The following morning some of their ships saw the enemy far off, steering towards the Wielings and the Dutch coast. They decided to pursue as far as with safety they could, and to 'range along the coast' till they came to the Texel.

On the same day Richard Lyons, Captain of the *Resolution*, the fleet flagship (the flag captain in modern terms) sent a rather more detailed account to the President of the Council of State. On 1 June, the English fleet being at Solebay, they saw at about noon 'two galliot-hoys' which were enemy scouts. Several frigates chased them and came very close to the whole Dutch fleet. The alarm being signalled, the English fleet stood towards them, but the weather was hazy and they lost sight of the enemy. At dawn the following morning, 2 June, they saw the enemy fleet to leeward, but the wind failed. Lawson and his squadron, however, were hotly engaged with the enemy for some hours. Tromp, declining engagement with the main body of the English fleet, bore up to relieve de Ruyter's squadron which was fighting Lawson's Blue Squadron. The wind now veered to the East, and the Dutch took advantage of this to bring their whole fleet into sharp action for two hours, after which the English recovered the weather gage. Tromp then tried to keep all his ships close together in order to withdraw without loss, and in fear of the English great ships. Lyons made the interesting comment that 'Our fleet did work in better order than heretofore and seconded one another'.

Lyons continues that the Dutch fleet fled from before them on 3 July and on 4 July till noon, by which time the English were in sight of Calais cliffs and Dunkirk. Here the Dutch tried to destroy the English great ships by engaging them upon the sands and in shoal water. In this attempt they failed. 'The enemy will go where we cannot follow him, like the Highlanders to the mountains'.

As regards Dutch losses, Lyons wrote: 'The first day, the greatest execution was done but not visible to us, further than the blowing up of one great ship of theirs and the sinking of another; but the second day we had the harvest and gleaning of the vintage, and with less loss than heretofore; not one ship, not one commander of note, save our thrice worthy General Deane, who was shot into the body with a great shot the first broadside. . . . The enemy lost that were sunk, taken and destroyed, both days service, about twenty of his fleet, of whom were two vice-admirals and three rear-admirals.'

A list of Dutch losses (contained in 'Several Proceedings June 9th') listed 1,350 prisoners, including 6 captains; 11 men-of-war taken, including one vice-admiral of 1,200 tons and 14 guns in each tier, and two rear-admirals; 6 men-of-war sunk, of which one was a rear-admiral; 2 hoys taken; 2 men-of-war blown up 'among their own fleet', and one man-of-war sunk that was near them 'by means of that accident'; 2 men-of-war fired 'but were not spoiled'; and one fly-boat taken. 'Not one ship of the English lost in all the fight in any one of the days'.

Blake and Monck reported to the Navy Commissioners on 6 June that the enemy had gone into the Wielings, 'where the water is so shoal that we durst not venture after them'. They were (i.e. the English fleet), they said, between the Goree and the Meuse refitting and disposing of 'lame ships and prizes' and also sending away the wounded and prisoners to the ports most convenient or most easily reached according to wind and weather.

Ammunition was now low, the average remaining in the whole fleet was not more than 16 rounds per gun. They reckoned that their requirement was not less than 6,000 or 7,000 barrels of powder with proportionate amount of shot, and they asked that 1,000 barrels with shot in proportion should be sent by the fastest frigates available as soon as possible. Their greatest want was for shot.

On 10 June there was a most interesting 'letter of intelligence from The Hague to my Lord Wentworth at Copenhagen' which appears to provide the only direct information as to the tactical formation of the English fleet. On 2 June the English found the Dutch fleet and when they approached them 'they stayed upon a tack, having the wind, within twice cannon shot about half an hour, to put themselves in their order they intended to fight in, which was in file (i.e. line ahead) at half cannon shot, from whence they battered the Hollanders furiously all that day, the success whereof was the sinking of two Holland ships. Towards night Tromp got the wind, but soon lost it again, and never recovered it the two following days during which the fight continued, the Dutch steering with a slow sail towards their own coast. The second day the English still battered them in file, and refusing to board them upon equal terms kept them at bay but half cannon distance, until they found some of them disordered and foul one against another, whom they presently boarded with their frigates (appointed to watch that opportunity) and took; and this they continued to do until the Holland fleet approached the Wielings, when they left them (by reason of those sands) upon Saturday night. Tromp brought hither only seventy-four of a hundred and two he set out with, besides fire ships and small ketches. Eight of the other ships (the residue of the hundred and two) are come safe but much battered to the Goree and the Texel, and the rest with two of their fireships are (for ought I can find by all the inquiry I can make) sunk and in English hands.'

It would appear from this account that, whether or not fighting in line had been introduced on a squadron basis earlier, the battle of the Gabbard, at any rate, had established it as the tactical formation by which the maximum weight of gunfire could be brought to bear upon a hostile fleet — a formation that was to last until, at any rate, the battle of Jutland in the First World War; and it was a soldier, Monck, who had demonstrated so dramatically its effectiveness.

Lord Wentworth was a Royalist who had served as a cavalry officer during the Civil War, and who was to serve in England again after the Restoration as Colonel of the First Guards. It is interesting to see in this letter from an officer, who had taken refuge in Holland after the Royalist defeat, the half-suppressed admiration for the performance of the English fleet. From the technical detail given, he must have obtained his information from one or more officers of the Dutch fleet.

Tromp's own final account of the battle was given in a despatch of 11 June, and, though very lengthy, it is not as candid as that given to Wentworth and says nothing about the formation of the English fleet. He says that they had 'sought for the enemy upon different rumours,' and at last on 2 June they caught sight of them 'about 100 big warships, more or less right in the wind which was N by E'. The English fleet 'for a long time drove down apon us, we doing our best to beat up towards them'. Finally they separated with three squadrons, a centre and two wings. They then approached within range at 11 a.m. 'General Deane then prepared to attack us, which he did furiously.' In the middle of this encounter the wind dropped. The English Blue Squadron was somewhat separated from the main body, and, the wind having changed a little, Tromp's ships endeavoured to cut off this squadron, and attacked it before the other two English squadrons could assist. The attempt obviously failed because Tromp writes that, 'Whilst we were fighting we fell off into the middle of their main body and passed through it so that both fleets were fighting very hard.'

After sunset the two fleets separated to repair damage. About an hour after sunset one of the Dutch ships blew up 'with most of its crew', owing to the carelessness, Tromp thought, of those responsible for looking after the powder.

On the following morning the English had the wind and about 8.0 a.m. their leading ships opened fire. But by 10.0 a.m. Tromp's fleet seemed to be to the windward of most of the English ships and in a position to cut off a large number of them. Accordingly the Dutch tacked towards them and were beginning to engage when the wind dropped and the English had the advantage of it. About 11.0 a.m. the English fleet was reinforced and attacked fiercely. This forced the Dutch to close up on their main body. 'But our ships being for the most part very small and light, the greater number, crowding upon one another, gave way before the enemy's attack.'

Towards evening, Tromp says, the enemy was again reinforced by several ships of war, amongst which was a fourth Admiral, said to be Blake. Being thus strengthened the English fleet attacked 'most furiously'. The Dutch ships closed in on each other and four of them collided. They were immediately surrounded by English ships and, though one broke loose, the others were captured. After sunset one ship, having tacked in the enemy's direction, came within short range of them and surrendered without resistance. One fireship was set on fire needlessly and let drift; another was also let drift as she had 'received shots under water'. About an hour after sunset the English began to draw off.

On the morning of 4 June, when the Dutch captains came aboard the flagship, it was found that, besides the vessels sunk, takem and blown up, there were still a number missing. Also many ships were disabled and the greater number had run out of ammunition. It was decided, therefore, 'to betake ourselves within the banks of the Wielings'. That night the water in Tromp's flagship the *Brederode* rose to such a height that she was in danger of sinking, despite pumping and bailing.

This defeat must have been the bitterest moment in the career of the gallant Tromp. He had set out to find the English fleet, confident of beating it.

As an appendix to accounts of the battle, an Intelligence Letter from Holland of 10 June has some interest. There is a mention that in Tromp's fleet it was 'muttered there was no great store of powder, which it seems they spent all too liberally at the Downs and Dover to no other purpose but in braving.' And there is a technical criticism about 'the gunport holes in the English ships, that they are too narrow, by which their ordnance cannot play but forth outright: whereas on the contrary those of the Hollanders are wide and large, by which means their guns have liberty to turn more ways than one.' This may be correct, but, as the Dutch enjoyment of that liberty did not save them from defeat, it is difficult to assess its importance.

The extent and implications of the Dutch defeat are shown by the following anguished plea of 9 June 1653 from the States of Zeeland to the States General:

'High and Mighty Lords, — It is with sincere sorrow that we have to report that the great fleet of this State, under the flag of Lieutenant-Admiral Tromp, after an engagement with the ships of the English Government, has been obliged by various occurrences to withdraw here, and retire inside the sand-banks of the Wielings, having been cut off from a great part of the rest of the ships. And although we feel confident that your H.M. will not omit to provide with your accustomed vigilance, against all the inconveniences and dangers that may arise therefrom, and will be required to be warded off, by taking such measures as shall seem most practicable; nevertheless we beg your H.M. to give effect to our recommendation for the prompt protection and preservation of the ships which are expected in these Provinces within a very few days north about both from the East Indies and Guinea, and from the Straits and other parts; submitting to your H.M.'s consideration whether in this great and unavoidable need, the Directors of the East India Company ought not to be induced, or otherwise under some pressure be brought to bear upon them to place at the disposal of the country, as a loan, all such ships, as they may have lying ready under the control of their several Chambers, bound for the said Indies. . . . And if this cannot be done, it would be advisable to send several advice boats secretly to the North at the earliest possible moment to warn the expected ships, as they come up, of what they must do, and to see they take the safest means of retreat in case of necessity.'

10

The First Battle of the Texel[1]

In a letter to the Navy Commissioners of 12 June 1653, Blake and Monck asked for reinforcements because they had information about 'eleven or twelve great frigates nearly launched at Amsterdam, Enchuysen, and thereabouts, which carry 50 guns apiece besides the ten men-of-war which came home with the French fleet'. They had a well-justified respect for the speed with which the Dutch Navy, under the drive of Tromp, was able to re-equip!

Dutch anxiety about the English blockade, on the other hand, is expressed in a letter from Holland of 16 June, as follows: 'By reason the English fleet doth hinder all manner of trade and navigation for East and North, and especially the herring fishery, it seemeth that the commonality who thereby get their livelihood and subsistence are much discontented and it hath been the occasion of a tumult at Enchuysen, where the house of one of the Admiralty hath been plundered.'

With astounding energy, the redoubtable Tromp was already planning a 'come-back'. On 17 June, only a fortnight after his defeat, he was writing from Flushing to the States General: 'Noble and powerful Lords, we are lying here with seventy-seven ships of war, and hope to be reinforced by three or four others from Goree.' He hoped to be able to put to sea with them in 12 or 14 days and would then take the first favourable opportunity of wind and weather to join the warships lying off Texel. He asked that these, together with fireships and other craft should be kept in readiness.

Blake and Monck wrote to the Admiralty Committee on 28 June complaining of 'the defectiveness of victuals, especially beer, bread, butter and cheese'. A hoy called the *David*, loaded with bread, butter and cheese, had been separated from the fleet by a storm and they had no news of what had become of her. They also wanted paper and canvas for cartridges. They reported an encounter with eleven Dutch merchant ships, intercepted by English frigates. The merchant ships were heavily armed but four were captured, one sunk, and one burnt; the remaining five escaping. But 'Captain

---

[1] *Navy Records Society*, Vol. 41, 1912, 'The First Dutch War' Vol. 5, ed. C.T. Atkinson, pp. 183-429.

Vesey, commander of the *Martin* (6th Rate) was slain, whom we understand has left a poor widow with a great charge of children whose condition we leave to your consideration.' Some other English frigates met with about 30 more sail north of the Vlie, but these, being unarmed, attempted to escape. Eleven were captured, some of the remainder scattered, and the rest got into port.

On 4 July 1653 Blake and Monck reported to the Admiralty Committee that there was much sickness in the fleet. 'Our men fall sick very fast every day, having at present on board this ship (the *Resolution*) upwards of eighty sick men and some of them very dangerously, which we hear is generally through the whole fleet alike proportionable to the number of men on board, so we that we shall be constrained to send a considerable number into Ipswich for their recovery.' This was the usual scourge of scurvy, which followed prolonged service at sea without access to fresh fruit and vegetables.

Poor Blake, who had never really recovered from his wound, had at last to leave the fleet and go ashore sick. Robert Blackborne, Secretary to the Navy Commissioners, reported on 4 July to the Admiralty Committee: 'It was late this evening ere I could aback Walderswick, where on my passage I heard Captain Blake was and that he came on shore the last night. Whereupon Captain Limbrey and I repaired to his quarters, where we found him in a very weak condition, full of pain both in his head and left side, which had put him into a fever, beside the anguish he endures by the gravel in his kidneys, insomuch as he takes no rest night or day but continues groaning very sadly.' Blake, of course, recovered and in 1657 achieved the greatest feat of his naval career in the destruction of the Spanish fleet at Santa Cruz. He died of fever on the way home.

Ranks used of officers are interesting. Officers of the Navy are often designated as 'Captain', even if they have the permanent rank of 'Admiral'. Blake was sometimes referred to as 'Colonel', a normal permanent rank in the Army, though he was more often described as 'General' in its application to both land and sea. And, as previously mentioned, we have Nehemiah Bourne, who was a Captain at sea and an 'occasional' Rear-Admiral, but who held the permanent rank of Major in the Army, and which he always used in describing himself.

And so George Monck, soldier of Parliament, Colonel of the Coldstream Regiment (later the Second Regiment of Foot Guards), and prime instrument in the Restoration of the Monarchy, became Commander-in-Chief of the Navy of the Protectorate.

The increasing effect of the English blockade is described in a letter from J. Petersen in Holland of 8 July. He writes: 'The English fleet lie so along our coast that we can get no ships out nor very few in, only such as can outsail the English who now begin to be foul, having been so long at sea. . . . In the meantime we are fain to eat old pickled herring instead of new, for which the English are cursed by the commons with bell, book and candle, for indeed they are a people impatient to be abridged of their wont, which let them but enjoy, and they care not who are their masters.'

There is an interesting letter from The Hague of 22 July, giving intelligence of Dutch intentions and movements, which must have been written by an agent of the English Government. He says that the great anxiety of the Dutch is to how they are to effect a junction of their fleets. Tromp, with Evertsen, intended to engage the attention of the English fleet so that de With might slip out from the Texel and join them. The united fleet would then consist of about 125 sail. But the best ships were in the Texel and without them Tromp could do nothing. The writer adds that if the English fleet could prevent this junction Holland would not be able to hold out for long because their trade was nearly gone and the banks 'begin to go blank'.

Monck, on 23 July, wrote to the Admiralty Committee saying that they intended 'to hinder the enemy's conjunction so far as lies in us'. It is unlikely that he could have received the contents of the above letter, but he was no doubt well aware of the importance of preventing de With from joining Tromp.

On the same day Tromp had written to the States General acknowledging their order to put to sea with the fleet under his command 'as soon as wind and weather and other circumstances allow,' and to carry out the junction with de With's squadron. Tromp was well aware of the economic crisis which had prompted the urgency of the Government's order, and he was determined to put to sea that day. At about 3.0 p.m., therefore, the fleet weighed anchor and were standing by to sail out, when they were prevented by a sudden squall. However, he had just received a despatch from the Texel which showed that orders had not yet been given to the ships there to sail. This seems to have been another example of the administrative incompetence that so frequently frustrated Dutch operations. Tromp requested the States General to give them the requisite instructions, adding that in the meantime he would make his way along the coast towards them.

On 24 July the States General, to 'animate and encourage soldiers at sea', offered rewards. Those that boarded and took the ship 'of the chief Admiral' should, besides the ship 'with all appertaining to it', receive 10,000 guilders. For ships of other admirals the sum would be 6,000 guilders, and 4,000 guilders for any other 'chief officers' ships'. In addition there were awards for flags. Anyone who captured the flag of the 'chief Admiral' would receive 1,000 guilders, and for the flag of any other admiral he would get 500 guilders. There would be 250 guilders for colours on the bowsprit, 1540 for colours on the mizzen mast and 50 guilders for colours on the stern. (It is not clear why the mizzen mast alone was selected.) However, there was a sting in the tail to this order, for it warned 'all the captains and other officers of ships, that in case any shall with the ship under his command leave the standard, without the consent and order of the Lieutenant-Admiral of the Fleet of this State, he shall be punished with death without mercy.' The old principle of carrot and stick!

Of some interest is the conclusion of a letter from Tromp to the Delegates of the States General which says that his flagship can be recognised by carrying, in addition to the 'Prince' flag aloft (that is, the orange, white and blue flag of the Prince of Orange, and not the red, white and blue which later replaced it), a blue flag aft of the quarter-deck.

With Tromp at sea and looking for the opportunity to join de With's squadron from Texel before engaging the English fleet, action could not long be delayed. On 28 July Tromp wrote to the States General acknowledging their letter of 26 July, which said that the ships in the Texel were still prevented by the enemy from putting out, and stressing that all possible means must be taken to get them out to sea. If they should be out and if the wind held, he did not doubt that early the next day he would break through the enemy and join them.

The following day he wrote again to the States General to relate what had happened. With the wind SW they had sailed all night along the coast and at 8.0 a.m. that day, 29 July, they were close to Egmont, and shortly afterwards the captain of the look-out ships in the van came on board to report that they had sighted the enemy's fleet lying off the Texel. The Dutch fleet held its course on towards the enemy. About 11.0 a.m. the wind veered to the NW, giving the English the advantage of it. Tromp decided to wear off from them with the intention of bringing them off from the Texel shallows and so allow the Dutch warships lying there the opportunity to come out and join him, as wind and weather would permit. He would then attack the enemy with his united forces. But as there were some slow sailing ships in the Dutch fleet, the English fast frigates came up with these latter at about 4.30 p.m. and opened fire. The English were about 120 sail strong, large and small. Tromp with the rest of the fleet waited for them to come up and a general engagement ensued which lasted till about 8.30 p.m. As far as he could see, the English did not gain any sensible advantage, and were remaining close to the Dutch. De With had obviously not yet been able to effect a junction, for he added: 'If we had had the succours from the Texel in the fleet, humanly speaking the probabilities are that we should be able to drive them gloriously from the coast.'

Monck (writing on 31 July to the Lord President of the Council of State, i.e. Cromwell) now takes up the story from the English standpoint. On 29 July, at about 9.0 a.m., his scouts discovered a fleet ahead which, within two hours, was seen to be Dutch, coming from the Wielings and of about 97 sail, of which 90 appeared to be men-of-war. Monck's ships made sail towards them, at the same time getting ready for action. But the enemy stood away when they identified the English ships and it was 5.0 p.m. before any of the English frigates could get close enough to engage. About 7.0 p.m. Monck's flagship, the *Resolution*, together with about 30 ships and frigates, got into action; the rest of the fleet being astern and unable to get up in time. They fought till about 9.0 p.m. when darkness separated the opposing fleets.

During the night the enemy got the weather gage by standing to the North, whilst Monck's fleet stood to the South, thinking they were 'under our lee'.

The following day there was little fighting, both fleets finding it difficult enough to get off from the lee shore, the wind being WNW, blowing hard, 'with thick and dirty weather'.

The next morning (31 July and the date of Monck's letter) the weather was fair with little wind, and both fleets prepared to renew the battle. The Dutch had what wind there was and bore down on the English fleet. About 7.0 a.m. (the 25 'great ships' from the Texel having joined Tromp the previous day) there began a very fierce engagement which lasted until 1.0 p.m., when the enemy began to bear away, making all the sail they could with the remainder of their fleet which numbered no more than 60. As far as Monck could gather there could not have been less than 30 or 40 sunk, taken, or destroyed.

Some of the best sailing English frigates were now pursuing the enemy, who, of the nine flagships when the battle began, had only one remaining.

Monck saw two English ships fired by the enemy's fireships, one of which was the *Oak* (a Dutch prize) and the other a fireship.

During the battle the *Resolution* (1st Rate and Monck's flagship) and the *Worcester* (3rd Rate frigate) led the English fleet 'in a desperate and gallent charge through the whole Dutch fleet. Tromp's mast was shot down, which he would have set up again but could not, and so was fain to put his flag upon his near masts. Those of the Dutch that got into the Texel are much shattered: Tromp's Vice-Admiral sunk down by his side.'

On 1 August de With wrote to the States General reporting the loss of the battle and the death of Admiral Tromp. 'I have also', he wrote, 'to report the fact to your H.M. that twenty-four or twenty-six of our captains have behaved in a very villanous way, and kept out of range of the enemy's guns and suffered a number of honourable men to be killed.' He finished: 'I hope to give a faithful account of this disaster on my arrival. . . . We have not more than ninety ships now in the fleet, including yachts and service craft.'

In a longer report of the same date de With made the unconsciously humorous comment: 'We saw, to our sorrow, the former practice of several of the captains, who betook themselves a good way out of the range of the enemy's guns; if they had been hanged on a previous occasion for similar offences, they would not have done the same again now.'

Joseph Cubitt, Captain of the *Tulip* (4th Rate), gave some interesting comments on the battle in a letter to Blackborne of 2 August. He says that in the first day's fighting they 'tacked upon' the Dutch and 'went right through their fleet, leaving part on one side and part on the other.' It would appear from this that the English fleet was in line and broke through the Dutch centre, or thereabouts. Cubitt adds that they 'lamed them several ships and sunk some; as soon as we had passed them we tacked upon them again and they on us, passed by each other very near; we did very good execution on him, some of their ships which had all their masts gone struck their colours and put out a white handkerchief on a staff and hauled in all their guns.' The fighting continued hard and at such close range that Cubitt called it 'almost at push of pike.' He added that 'A Flushinger was sunk close by the *Victory*' (2nd Rate), which the former had been attempting to board and 'had entered three or four of its men with their pole-axes but the *Victory*'s carpenter's axe cut them down on the side of the ship'. He described conditions in this fierce action as: 'The very heavens were obscured by smoke, the air rent with the thundering noise, the sea all in a breach with the shot that fell, the ship even trembling and we hearing everywhere messengers of death flying.' Cubitt

94

could not tell how many ships the Dutch lost but he heard of 14 certainly 'sunk and burnt', but at that time all the captains had not yet reported. The English losses were the *Oak* and a fireship, and 'some speak of another ship of ours fired by them'. They were pleased at recovering the *Garland* (3rd Rate) (captured by the Dutch at the battle of Dungeness), though she was so badly damaged that they fired her. He had only one man killed in his ship and some six slightly wounded, but the ship herself had been so badly damaged that she was 'no longer fit to keep sea'.

On 3 August Monck asked the Admiralty Committee for 900 men (of which 500 must be seamen), boats to take off 600 wounded, and a considerable quantity of beer, 'and that special regard be had to the goodness of it'. He also wanted ammunition, canvas for cartridges, and canvas to make sails, as it was his intention to despatch as many frigates as possible upon the coast of Holland 'very speedily to stop up their trade'.

Replacing the casualties incurred during the battle seems to have presented some difficulties; for Captain William Kendall of the *Success* frigate (4th Rate) has a complaint about soldiers which is redolent of Shakespeare's Falstaff. Writing to the Admiralty Committee on 3 August he complained that Captain Henry Hatsell (one of their agents) 'sent me aboard fifty men which came under the notion of soldiers, but they are not, for they are boys and decrepit old men, and some fitter for hospital than to be sent upon present service, for I have exercised them already and I cannot find six in the fifty which is able to fire a musket'.

11

The End of the First Dutch War[1]

After the battle of the Texel, de With was placed in command of the Dutch fleet, and was soon striving to get a sufficiently powerful squadron together to escort the large outgoing convoy of Dutch merchantmen which was waiting to sail. The English fleet had been temporarily withdrawn from the Dutch coast but Rear-Admiral Lawson was being despatched with a squadron to resume the blockade. In a letter to the States General, de With reported that all possible efforts were being made to get the fleet ready for sea, but he added that 'the said fleet has suffered considerably more damage than reported by some people'. He was probably referring to over-optimistic reports by Vice-Admiral Evertsen and Commandeur de Ruyter, who exaggerated English losses and under-estimated those of the Dutch, both of whom (according to a 'Letter from The Hague' of 11 August) 'had no inclination to serve' under de With, and complained of 'the slight usage they received' of him. They claimed that only eight or nine Dutch ships were missing after the battle (which was obviously untrue) and that of the English 'a great many were shattered and made unserviceable, and that eighteen or nineteen of them sunk, burnt or blown up' which was just as wide of the mark. Indeed, the Dutch Ambassadors in England, Beverling and Paulus van der Perre wrote from Westminster to the States General on 26 August: 'High and Mighty Lords, — The commissioners who have been with the fleet from the Council of State, do affirm as yet that there was but one frigate and one fireship lost in the last engagement and that the whole fleet will be out again very suddenly under the command of General Monck and that 46 or 48 are already gone for the coast of Holland under the command of Rear-Admiral Lawson.' (The gentlemanly arrangement, in these wars, by which ambassadors of the opposing countries remained at their posts, will be noted.)

Lawson wrote a report on 27 August to Monck about his activities. He had been plagued with bad weather with consequent damage to some of his ships, 'some in masts, some in hull, some their sails blown away'. His

---

[1] *Navy Records Society*, Vol. 66 1930, 'The First Dutch War' Vol. 6, ed. C.T. Atkinson, pp. 23-260.

squadron was somewhat scattered and: 'Yesternight I sent the *Ruby* and *Pelican* to ply to the north eastward to look for the rest of the ships and frigates' to tell them that he intended to be ten leagues west of the Texel on 30 August to effect a junction with Monck. He had learned that five Dutch East India ships that had been at Bergen were near Copenhagen, waiting till Dutch men-of-war arrived to convoy them.

On 4 September de With informed the States General that he had sailed from the Texel on 1 September with 43 warships and about 40 merchantmen. In the afternoon of that day they met off the Vlie over 300 merchant ships which had joined the convoy. He was then between the coast of Norway and Jutland but had seen nothing of the enemy. It seems that he had managed to slip past Lawson.

Thomas Pointer (probably a NC representative), who was on board the *Resolution*, wrote to the Navy Commissioners on 8 September telling them that on 29 August Monck had sailed out of Aldbrough Bay with about 18 men-of-war and that the following morning they had joined Lawson. On 31 August they had stood for the Texel till towards the evening. They must have just missed de With who left the Texel the next morning. A frigate brought information (false) that de With had sailed towards Norway the previous day, 30 August. In fact he was still at the Texel. In the light of this news, a council of the flag officers decided to leave some frigates to scout along the Dutch coast, whilst the rest of the fleet should return to the coast of England.

De With, on 9 September, informed the States General that on 7 September, when near the Skagen Reef, the merchantmen for the North left him. Hereabouts he was given information as to the location of various homeward bound merchantmen and issued instructions for them to join him near the Hook of Skagen (the Skaw). De With was alarmed, however, at the weakness of his   force, and on 19 September he wrote to the States General reminding them that he had asked that the warships in the Texel, which had not been ready when he sailed, should be sent to him as quickly as possible, 'with a view of better securing the safety of the rich treasure which we were sent out to fetch.' He had learned that on 6 September 100 ships had sailed from London for the coast of Holland to blockade the rivers.

On 16 October de With wrote a rather exasperated letter to the States General. He was short of provisions, for the ration 'has been diminished by a good third'. Commanders of the ships despatched to him had not been 'victualled for longer than the middle of November' and he was 'very much astonished to think that such a body of ships should be sent out with such small supplies of provisions at this season of the year, when storms and unfavourable weather may be looked for every day.' Nor had either of the commandeurs despatched to him been able to furnish the 'slightest news of the enemy, which causes us the greatest surprise, for the enemy's fleet to be kept so secret'. He also thought it was his duty to state that none of the ships under his command 'have careened or been cleaned for a considerable time, as your lordships are aware, and we have not therefore a single quick-sailing ship in the whole fleet'. In another letter of 26 October, de With said that his wife was 'lying sick to death, that I have moreover a family of ten children living, and for eighteen months I have not slept soundly at home for more than four nights, and during the last seven months I have been on board eight different ships, going straight from one to another, to promote the service of this country; and I therefore once more humbly make my request, on account of the sad news of my wife's illness, that permission may be sent without delay to go home at once.'

It appears that their 'Noble and Powerful Lords' did accede to de With's request, for on 3 December de Ruyter wrote to them acknowledging his appointment as Vice-Admiral.

Meanwhile, on 3 November, de With had written to them an account of the terrible storm to which his ships had been subjected. On 26 October he had received a letter informing him that 20 of his ships were to victual off the Texel shallows. He accordingly asked for instructions from the States General as to how close inshore he should anchor, as he would not on his own responsibility bring the fleet 'so close inshore as is necessary to enable us to victual at sea'. On the morning of 27 October he made every effort to get a 'little nearer inshore' and several victualling ships came out, but he had to put back again on account of the rough weather. In the afternoon it became so rough that they were obliged to anchor. That night it blew a strong gale from the west, and this increased to 'an extraordinary severe gale' over the next four days. Several ships dragged their anchors and 'cut their masts overboard'. During the night of 28 October his own ship lost two anchors and several cables and they 'were obliged to cut our mast overboard also'. On the morning of 1 November he says: 'We counted twenty-six ships lying there unshattered, twenty-three had cut their masts away, and one had lost all her masts. The rest to the number of seventy, were missing; I am afraid they will have suffered terrible damage.'

On 10 November a list of 15 ships that were lost in the storm was given: *Liberty* (all the men lost), *Prince William* (all the men saved), *Gouda* (half the men saved), *Moerian* (half the men saved), *King David* (all the men drowned), *Amsterdam* (all the men drowned except 14), *Der Gais* (a flute with provisions), *Golden Lyon*, *Flushing*, *Crowned Love*, *St. Vincent*, *Graef Hendrick* (the ship commanded by Captain John Rootjes), *Justice* (all the men drowned).

De With said that there was not one of the ships but had suffered severe damage. It is clear that, as an effective fighting force, the Dutch fleet for the moment had ceased to exist.

Nehemiah Bourne, writing from Harwich to the Admiralty Committee, reported the arrival of the *Greyhound* (6th Rate) whose captain had 'met with extraordinary bad weather, and forced to Yarmouth Roads (that being the first place they could recover) which I am apt to believe, for we had about a week since the sorest storms at NW and NNW for 3 or 4 days here that hath been known for many years.'

The Dutch were still determined to renew the struggle against England, according to a letter from Holland of 18 November, in which the writer said that 30 new frigates had been built and 30 other new ships had been ordered, with the intention of having ready by February or March a 100 sail of ships of war, besides two squadrons to convoy their merchantmen.

Monck, obviously irritated about the lack of drive by the Admiralty Committee, wrote to them on 28 November as follows: 'I understand that you are in some dispute amongst yourselves whether or no you shall fit out the great ships presently, or towards the spring. I shall make bold to offer my thoughts concerning it. In case you are not assured that we shall have a speedy peace with the Dutch I conceive the service will suffer very much unless they be expedited out for these reasons. First, because you will not get them manned; second, that then the Dutch will get their summer fleet ready before yours, which in case they should, instead of blocking them up in their harbour we shall be by then blocked up in ours.'

On 2 December the Council of State commissioned Blake (who was once more fit — or nearly fit — for active service) and Monck as 'Generals-of-the-Fleet'. In addition, Major-General Disbrowe and Vice-Admiral Penn were appointed Generals of the Fleet, and Rear-Admiral Lawson was appointed Vice-Admiral of the Fleet in succession to Penn. Also, Blake, Monck, Disbrowe, Penn and John Carew were appointed 'Commissioners for the Admiralty and Navy'; that is, they became members of the Admiralty Committee. It is interesting that, as an example of the confusion of ranks, that as General of the Fleet, Blake and Monck were referred to as 'Generals', yet in their appointments as Admiralty Commissioners, their designations were: 'Colonel Rob. Blake, Colonel George Monck, Maj. Genl. Disbrowe, Vice-Admiral William Penn, and John Carew, Esq^{rs}.' The two former were apparently referred to by their permanent ranks, and the other two officers by ranks related to the appointments they then held. Disbrowe had commanded Cromwell's Regiment of Horse as a Colonel and had by 1650 been seconded from his regiment on being given a Major-General's appointment as Governor of Yarmouth, where, through his association with maritime affairs, he had presumably become suitable as a General-at-Sea.

On 5 December 1653 de Ruyter acknowledged the receipt of the letter appointing him Vice-Admiral, but begged to be excused from accepting.

There is an interesting (undated) letter addressed to the Admiralty Committee from Thomas Taylor, Gunner of the Sovereign (1st Rate), petitioning on account of charges made against him that he was responsible for the lack of powder during the recent battle and for the failure of the Sovereign's guns to equal the range of those of the Dutch. He claimed that he was as well provided with the materials of his office as any ship in the fleet, having 2,000 to 3,000 cartridges filled and fitted for the different calibres of the ship's guns. He stated that the failure of sufficient cartridges to reach the guns was due to his yeomen, who feared the danger of carrying canvas and paper cartridges in a hurry amongst so many lighted matches. He was not able to oversee them directly because he was busy in directing the fire of a 7-inch gun, whereby the mainmast of the Dutch Rear-Admiral was 'shot by the board' and the ship consequently captured.

As regards the range; some guns did shoot further than those of the *Sovereign* because they allowed a greater quantity of powder, and also because they usually carried 'in their quarter one of their best long guns, whereas ours are our chase pieces.' But the main reason for the greater apparent range of other ships' guns was that at this time the *Sovereign* 'was at least a mile and a half to leeward, and therefore had not the advantage to carry a shot by a quarter part of the way with that to the windward.' One hopes that Gunner Taylor was 'restored to his employment', as he petitioned.

It is conceivable that de With's departure from command was due as much to his knowledge that there was no longer any prospect of being able to engage the English fleet with success, as to his domestic anxieties.

Tentative negotiations had been opened, for on 4 February 1654, Blake and Penn wrote from the *Swiftsure* (2nd Rate) at Spithead to the Admiralty Committee, 'We are sorry to hear that the treaty between the Dutch and the Commonwealth is come to no certain resolution, their delay portends no great hope of agreement, the consideration thereof doth quicken our former endeavours that such of the fleet now here may be ready for service upon all commands.'

On 4 March Blake and Penn wrote again that they had received 'intelligence that the Dutch intend to be at sea with a considerable fleet very speedily', and they would have the fleet 'in such a posture as may answer the service', but they wondered why they were not being reinforced by ships lying in the Thames.

However, on 18 March Blake and Penn expressed their pleasure to the Admiralty Committee 'that the treaty with the Dutch is likely to produce the expected and desired end'.

The Dutch, indeed, had had enough and on 21 April the 'Proceedings of the Council of State' announced that 'The Articles of Peace Union and Confederation betwixt His Highness the Lord Protector and the States General of the United Provinces of the Low Countries, together with the ratification thereof by His Highness were this day read (the same being signed by His Highness and passed under the great seal of England), and consented to by the Council, and it was ordered that it be offered to His Highness as the advice of the Council that the same be delivered as His Highness' ratification of the said articles to the Lords Ambassadors of the said States General.'

1 A Battle in the First Dutch War by Pieter Coopse.

2 A Dutch Ship before the Wind, c.1650 by W. Hollar.

3 An English 4th Rate in the Second or Third Dutch Wars by Van de Velde the Elder.

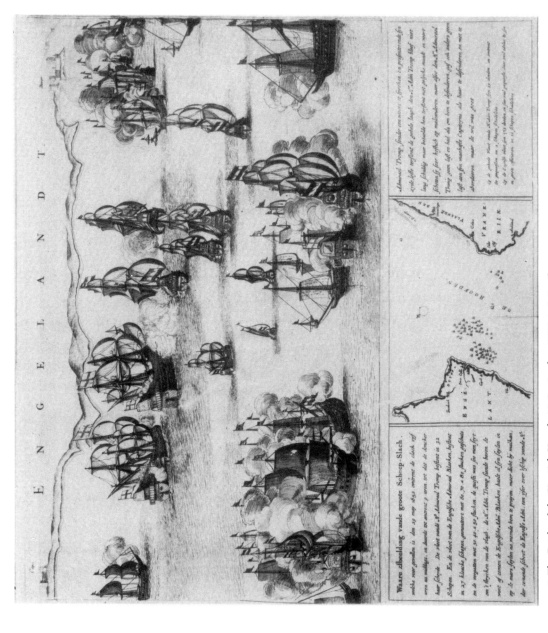

4 The Battle of the Kentish Knock, 28 September 1652 Artist unknown.

Engagement between the English and Dutch Fleets off the North Foreland, Sep.t 28.1652.

5 The Battle of the Kentish Knock by J. Pass.

6 The Battle of Dungeness (the date shown is New Style) by C. Jannson.

7 The First Battle of the Texel, 31 July 1653 Artist unknown.

8 An English 5th Rate about 1654 by W. Hollar.

9 The 2nd Rate Royal Katherine in 1664 by I. Sailmaker.

10 The Four Days Battle, 1 to 4 June 1666 by Soest.

11 The Four Days Battle by A. Storck.

12 The Surrender of the 1st Rate *Royal Prince*, aground on the Galloper, in the Four Days Battle by Wetterwinkel, after Van de Velde.

13 The Four Days Battle by A. Storck.

14 Dutch Flagships *Eendracht* and *Zeven Provincien* (the latter being de Ruyter's) with other Dutch Men-of-War, c.1666 by C. Van Mooy.

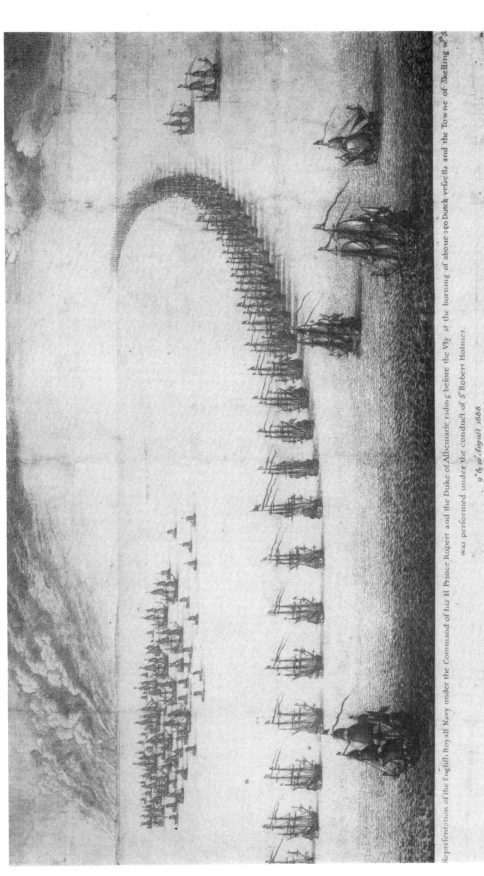

Reprefentation of the English Royall Navy under the Command of his H. Prince Rupert and the Duke of Albemarle riding before the Vly at the burning of about 150 Dutch veſſells and the Towne of Skelling wᶜᴴ ꜱ... was performed under the conduct of Sʳ Robert Holmes.

9ᵗ & 10ᵗ Auguſt 1666

The Frigatts ordred to attend Sʳ Robert Holmes

The Fire shipes ordered to attend Sʳ Robert Holmes

| The Drragon Vyper | Aduice Sweepstake | Fountaine Pembrooke | The Eryer Prichard | Samuell Lezard | Foxe |

Thatt was the Fanfan which carried the Flag with 15 Ketches & 16 boates None of the Frigatts befides the Pembroke could get into the Harbour by reafon of the ſhallowneſs of the Water

15 The English Fleet riding before Vlie Island at the burning of 150 Dutch merchant ships by Sir
Robert Holmes on 9 August 1666 by W. Hollar.

16 The 3rd Rate *Resolution* (built 1667) in a gale during that year by Van de Velde the Younger.

17 An action in the Second Dutch War by Renier Zeernam.

18 The Dutch Fleet off Sheerness during the attack on the Medway, June 1667 by Van de Velde the Elder.

19 The Dutch attack on the Medway by Jan Peeters.

20 An action in the Second Dutch War by A. Willaerts.

21 The 1st Rate *St. Andrew*, built 1670 by Van de Velde the Younger.

22 The Battle of Sole Bay, 28 May 1672 by P. Monamey.

23 The Battle of Sole Bay by Van de Velde the Younger.

24 The Burning of the Earl of Sandwich's flagship, the 1st Rate *Royal James*, at the Battle of Sole Bay by Van de Velde the Elder.

25 The Second Battle of the Texel, 11 August 1673 by Van de Velde the Younger.

26 The Second Battle of the Texel — the defence of the new 1st Rate *Royal Prince* (centre) (built 1670) by Van de Velde the Younger.

27 Cornelis Tromp's flagship, *Gouden Leeuw*, at the Second Battle of the Texel by Van de Velde the Younger.

28 The *Royal Prince* in 1679 by Jan K.D. Beech.

12

The Restoration

September 1658 marked the end of am era, for in that month Oliver Cromwell died. Like most dictators he left nobody of comparable status to take his place. A great man, certainly; a good man, doubtfully; but the head of a ruthless military form of government that was loved by few. Edward Mountagu, one of his more prominent adherents, had supported proposals to make the Protectorate, he had established, hereditary, and even convert it into a monarchy. But Oliver's son, Richard, was not the stuff of which leaders are made, and in April 1659 he was removed from power. A month previously Mountagu had been despatched with the fleet to the Baltic to mediate in the war between Sweden and Denmark. He had been made a Councillor of State in Cromwell's Protectorate in 1653 and a General-at-Sea in 1656. But he could now see no stable future for the government of England other than a restoration of the monarchy. Accordingly, whilst still on his mission of mediation, he made contact with agents of exiled Charles II, and, when he brought the fleet home in August 1659, he was under suspicion of sympathising with Royalist risings which had been suppressed that month. Officially in disgrace, he retired to his family estates.

The country was now governed by the Parliament known as the 'Rump'; that is, by the 50 members who remained of the Civil War Parliament, which had been in session since Richard's fall the previous April. In October the generals of the army, under the leadership of Lambert, one of the most distinguished of Cromwell's commanders, took over the Government and dismissed the members of the Rump. However, because it was some months since the disgruntled soldiers had received any pay, Lambert no longer had an effective army behind him; indeed, hundreds of men were deserting the Colours.

In Scotland Monck commanded the strongest reliable body of troops. He denounced Lambert's seizure of power and marched south towards the border at the village of Coldstream. His force included his own regiment, which was destined to acquire the name of that village as its permanent title.

In December Lambert's military government collapsed, and the fleet, under Admiral John Lawson, declared for a free Parliament. On Boxing Day the Rump re-assembled and on 1 January 1660 Monck crossed the Tweed and began his march towards London.

As this book deals with naval operations, it is not concerned with the details of the political events which followed. However, the 'secluded Members of Parliament', that is 154 political 'moderates' who had been expelled in the 'Purge' carried out by Colonel Pride (which preceded the execution of Charles I in 1649), were re-admitted on 21 February. Parliament now could muster sufficient strength to pass the legislation for its dissolution and for the election of the free Parliament which was being demanded. Writs for the elections were issued on 16 March and the new Parliament met on 25 April.

On 2 March, before the dissolution, Monck and Mountagu had been voted Generals-at-Sea by a Parliament reinforced by the 'Secluded' members. Four days later Mountagu invited Samuel Pepys to go to sea with him as his Secretary. He also told him that he believed 'the King would come in'.[1] It was apparent to Pepys that Mountagu was to command the fleet which would sail to fetch home Charles II if Parliament voted for the restoration of the monarchy.

On 23 March Pepys accompanied Mountagu to the Tower of London, where they embarked in barges to take them to the Long Reach (a little below Gravesend) where the 2nd Rate *Swiftsure* lay at anchor. On the morning of 26 March Pepys rose early and prepared a list of all the ships in the fleet, giving in respect of each the number of men and the armament.

On 30 March the fleet flagship, the 1st Rate *Naseby* (a new ship, only built in 1655), came to anchor close to the *Swiftsure*, and Mountagu, accompanied by Pepys, went on board her.

On 5 April the *Naseby* sailed at about noon and anchored in the evening in Lee Road (bordering Canvey Island). On Sunday 8 April the ship sailed to join the fleet, coming in sight of the North and South Forelands the following morning. At about 5.0 p.m. they were off Deal, where the fleet lay, and salutes were fired by all the ships and by the guns in the Deal castles. Here the *Naseby* anchored.

On 2 May news reached the fleet that a letter from Charles II had been read in the House, and that a notice had been received in the Commons from the Lords asking them to join in a vote for a constitution of King, Lords, and Commons. The Commons agreed and voted unanimously in favour — after all, that was the constitution for which they had originally fought in the Civil War! The result of the vote had been welcomed with great joy in London, where there had been bonfires, the ringing of bells, and, wrote Pepys, 'drinking of the King's health upon their knees in the streets.'

On 6 May Mountagu gave Pepys a letter he had written to the King which Pepys was to deliver to Sir William Compton, Master of the Ordnance, who was on board the 4th Rate *Assistance* and was to carry the letter to Breda, in

---

[1] *The Diary of Samuel Pepys*, ed. Robert Latham and William Matthews, Vols. I to IX (London, Bell & Hyman, 1970 to 1978).

the Netherlands, and present it to the King. Pepys delivered the letter and joined in drinking a health to the King on board the *Assistance*. As soon as he had left the ship she sailed immediately to Breda.

On 10 May Mountagu told Pepys that he had been commanded to set sail and bring back the King. The next day a start was made in pulling down the old State Arms from the sterns of ships throughout the fleet, and painters were ordered from Dover to set up the Royal Arms. On 13 May Pepys saw, on the quarter deck, tailors and painters cutting yellow cloth to produce the letters 'CR' with crown above, and mounting them 'upon a fine sheet, and that on to the flag instead of the State's arms'. This 'sheet' was presumably red and would obscure the red cross and harp borne upon the State standard flown by a general-at-sea. The result was shown to Mountagu, who was so pleased with it that he rewarded the tailors. The new flag was then hoisted at the main masthead.

The fleet was now under sail and the next day, 14 May, Pepys saw the Dutch shore and soon The Hague. Pepys and others in due course went ashore, and he got the opportunity to kiss the hands of the King, the Duke of York, and the Princess Royal (wife of William of Orange and the future Queen of England). Mountagu told Pepys that the Duke of York had been made Lord High Admiral of England.

On 22 May the Duke of York and the Duke of Gloucester came on board the *Naseby* and were greeted by the guns of the fleet firing a salute; and the following day the King himself came on board, to be received by a Royal salute fired by all the ships of his fleet. After dinner he and the Duke of York altered the names of some of the ships. The *Naseby* became the *Royal Charles*. (To Mountagu there may well have been a recollection of that battle in which he had commanded his own regiment of foot in the army which destroyed that of the new King's father.)

The same day they set sail for England. Pepys records that the King related on the quarter deck an account of his escape after the battle of Worcester, and how he had travelled for four days and three nights on foot, 'every step up to the knees in dirt'. At an inn, as the weary King was standing by the fireside with his hands on the back of a chair, the master of the house 'kneeled down and kissed his hand privately, saying that he would not ask who he was, but God bless him whither that he was going'.

On 25 May the King landed at Dover where General Monck was waiting to receive him. And so the Navy's part in the Restoration of the Monarchy was over. Monck became Duke of Albemarle and Mountagu Earl of Sandwich, the relative seniority of their peerages presumably reflecting the King's assessment of their respective contributions to the return to his Kingdom.

13

The Second Dutch War

Before discussing the outbreak of hostilities against the Dutch, it will be appropriate to describe, in brief, the organisation of the body which had so much to do with the government and efficiency of the Navy. This body, the Navy Board, had, under the authority of the Lord High Admiral, charge of the civil administration of the Navy, a responsibility that included the building and repair of ships and the management of the dockyards.[1]

The Navy Board had been set up over 100 years previously, and in 1546 had consisted of a Treasurer, a Comptroller, a Surveyor, and a Clerk of the Navy — this last appointment often being given the title of Clerk of the Acts. During the Civil and First Dutch Wars the Board had been replaced by Commissions; ultimately the Admiralty Committee and Navy Commissioners, already mentioned. After the Restoration of the Monarchy the Navy Board was again formed. Former Commissioners carried on for a short time whilst the new Board members were selected. These being appointed, they took up their duties on 4 July 1660. They consisted of four Principal Officers — Sir George Cartaret as Treasurer; Sir Robert Slingsby as Comptroller; Sir William Batten as Surveyor; and Samuel Pepys as Clerk of the Acts. There were also three Commissioners; Sir William Penn and Lord Berkeley of Stratton as full Commissioners, and Peter Pett as a local Commissioner with responsibility for the Chatham Dockyard.

The most important of these appointments was that of Treasurer. Sir George Cartaret, of an old Jersey family, had been a Captain in the Navy under Charles I and was appointed Comptroller of the Navy in 1639. He adhered to the Royalist side in the Civil War. In 1643 the King sent him to Jersey and, having secured it, he was appointed Governor. He was created a baronet in 1646, and remained as Governor until forced to surrender to Commonwealth forces in 1651. He then joined the French Navy and became a Vice-Admiral. However, in 1657 he was banished from France for some

---

[1] *The Diary of Samuel Pepys*, ed. Robert Latham, Vol. X, *Companion*, 'The Navy Board', by Andrew Turnbull (London, Bell & Hyman, 1983).

reason and lived in Venice until the Restoration. As Treasurer his prime responsibility was to see that the money allocated to the Navy was provided by the national treasury and to oversee the payment from it authorised by the Board. He was also responsible for preparing the naval estimates for the Board and subsequent submission to the Lord High Admiral.

Sir Robert Slingsby was another Royalist who had commanded a squadron in the Channel in 1640-42, and was imprisoned as a Royalist in the latter year. However, two years later he undertook a mission to Paris and Amsterdam. At the Restoration he was created a baronet. As Comptroller he was responsible for auditing the various accounts and presenting the annual audit to the Navy Board and the Lord High Admiral.

The Surveyor, Sir William Batten, we have already met and the Queen Mother could hardly have happy memories of him! He was responsible for the design, building, and repair of His Majesty's ships; satisfying himself that the requisite materials were provided, and supervising generally the work in the dockyards.

As Clerk of the Acts, Samuel Pepys was Secretary to the Board. He had to record all their decisions, deal with correspondence, and prepare letters for signature and despatch. Actually, however, he gradually expanded these duties and, with his enthusiasm for all aspects of the Navy, took over many of the responsibilities of other more idle members of the Board (who were only too glad to be relieved of them), and became the first equivalent of a present day Permanent Secretary of a Government department.

Of the Commissioners, Sir William Penn had, as we have seen, a distinguished career as a flag officer in the Parliamentary Navy. After his success in the capture of Jamaica in 1654, he was committed to the Tower for returning from the West Indies without leave. After his release he retired in indignation to his estates in Munster and opened a secret correspondence with the Royalists. On the Restoration he was knighted. Pepys did not like him, but he was to serve again with distinction as an Admiral in the Second Dutch War. His son, William, who became, to the annoyance of his father, a Quaker, and therefore a pacifist, became the founder and first Governor of the State of Pennsylvania.

Lord Berkeley of Stratton had been the outstanding Royalist commander of the Cornish infantry during the Civil War, and his title reflected his victory in the battle of that name. He had no knowledge or experience of the Navy, however, and took little interest in the proceedings of the Board.

Peter Pett was Commissioner of Chatham from 1648 to 1667 and was largely responsible for the men-of-war during that period — he being one of the few who held the same high position during the Parliamentary, Protectorate, and Royalist regimes. Nevertheless, he was held primarily to blame for the River Medway disaster when the Dutch succeeded in the destruction or removal of some of the Navy's finest 1st and 2nd Rates.

Sir William Coventry later became a Commissioner. He had been a Captain in the Royalist infantry in the Civil War, and went to France after Parliament's victory. He became Secretary to the Duke of York when he was appointed Lord High Admiral at the Restoration and held that post till 1667. In 1662 he replaced Lord Berkeley, his Commissionership being a logical extension of his duties with the Duke of York. He was knighted in that same year. He became a great friend of Pepys, whose ability and energy he appreciated.

Relations with the Dutch, owing to trade rivalry, started to deteriorate soon after the Restoration. On 28 June 1662 Samuel Pepys recorded in his Diary that there was fear of war with the Dutch and that orders had been given for 29 warships to be got ready. However, there must have been a sad deterioration in the state of the Navy for Pepys added that the King would not be able to get five ships to sea because there was no money, no credit, and no stores! Luckily, fears of war then seem to have subsided for over a year. On 1 October 1663 Pepys was told in a Coffee House (the approximate seventeenth century equivalent of the London club of today) that a war with Holland was very likely. On 9 February 1664 there was talk of the Dutch excluding any ships but their own from the Indian trade, with the threat of confiscation; and that they had proclaimed themselves in India as 'Lords of the Southern Seas'.

That matters were getting serious became apparent to Pepys when six days later Sir Thomas Chamberlain, Governor of the East India Company, came to his office with letters from the East Indies which stated that the Dutch had been molesting English traders, even in the sole English factory at Surat. The letters said that the Dutchmen had beaten several men of the English East India Company and had even, in derision, hoisted the St. George's Cross flag of England under the Dutch flag. All during April there were talks of conflicts between English and Dutch ships on the Guinea coast of Africa. On 23 April, St. George's Day, Coventry discussed with Pepys the possibility of war with Holland. The Lords had concurred with a Commons vote on precautionary measures, and Coventry, as Secretary to the Lord High Admiral, was anxious that the Navy Board should ascertain what stores were lacking and buy what they could.

Two days later Pepys went with Sir William Penn to see the Duke of York to consider the prospect of war with Holland and the immediate preparatory steps needed to be taken by the Navy Board. One of the matters of concern to the Duke was the establishment of a proper discipline in the fleet.

On 18 May Penn was directed to go to Portsmouth and look into the business of new ships. Four days afterwards the Duke of York asked Pepys if he intended to accompany him on a visit to Chatham, to which Pepys replied that if he commanded him he would, but he believed there would be business for him in London. The Duke said that in that case he had better stay.

A month later, on 20 June, the Duke of York told Pepys that the Dutch had written to the King assuring him that their setting out of ships was only to defend their fishing trade and not to annoy the King's subjects, and hoped he would do the same with his ships. The King had laughed at this, but was vexed that they should think him such a child as to believe that excuse for bringing home their East India Company's big ships, adding, 'and then they will not care a fart for us'. On 23 August Pepys was sorry to learn that the Dutch East India fleet had got home safely. The big and heavily armed East Indiamen would, of course, be a valuable addition to the Dutch naval strength. Relations between the two countries were deteriorating and both English and Dutch fleets were hastening to the Guinea coast of West Africa for the protection of their rival commercial interests.

On 6 September Coventry told Pepys that the Duke of York had that day received the Dutch Ambassador and had told him that if they were under the impression that the English were not serious about naval preparations, he believed that Prince Rupert, who was going with the English fleet to Guinea, would show them that they were in earnest, and that he himself would do the same as commander of the home fleet. The Dutch Ambassador had the temerity to remind the Duke of the Puritan fanatics in England who would profit by the King being at war. The Duke replied coldly that 'The English have ever united in all their private differences to attend Foreign', and that Cromwell never found that the Cavaliers did ever try to disrupt his foreign affairs.[2]

The normal courtesies nevertheless continued. On 16 September 1664 Thomas Allin arrived in the Bay of Gibraltar with a squadron from England[3] and saluted Sir John Lawson, who was there with a squadron, giving him eleven guns and was answered with eleven (they being of equal rank and status). The *Bristol*, a 4th Rate, saluted Allin with seven guns and was answered with five. Five other 4th Rates, of lower seniority in their squadron, saluted him with five guns, and were answered with three. (The naval saluting conventions of the period were of some complexity!)

In June Captain Thomas Allin had been appointed to the 3rd Rate *Plymouth* and made Vice-Admiral of a small fleet commanded by the Earl of Sandwich. It was the middle of July before the fleet had assembled in the Downs and then, a little over a month later, this squadron (owing to the development of the political situation) left for the Mediterranean under the command of Allin, who was to take over from Sir John Lawson. The squadron consisted of the 3rd Rates *Plymouth* (Flag) and *Essex*; the 4th Rates *Leopard*, *Antelope*, *Bonaventure*, *Advice*, *Portsmouth*, *Phoenix*, *Crown*, and *Nonsuch*; and the 5th Rates *Milford* and *Oxford*.

On 25 September, when Lawson and Allin were off Cadiz, de Ruyter and his fleet arrived, de Ruyter striking his flag and saluting Lawson with nine guns. Lawson answered with nine and de Ruyter thanked him with five. (Lawson having recognised him as of equal rank and status). When de Ruyter came under Allin's stern he asked how Allin did, gave him a seven gun salute and drank his health. Allin, in return, drank to de Ruyter and answered his salute with seven guns, for which de Ruyter thanked him with three. (The decrease by four in the number of guns when expressing thanks will be noted.)

These courtesies, however, did nothing to mitigate the mutual feelings of hostility, and on 27 September Allin persuaded Lawson to write to the Duke

---

[2] *The Diary of Samuel Pepys*, op. cit. 6 September 1664.
[3] *The Navy Records Society*, Vol. 79, 'The Journals of Sir Thomas Allin, Vol. 1,' ed. R.C. Anderson, 1939, pp. 141 f.

of York informing him that de Ruyter had taken in large stocks of provisions and that they suspected him of being on his way to Guinea. Allin was right, for de Ruyter was indeed going to the Guinea coast with orders to restore the Dutch position there after the damage done to the settlements by an English squadron under Sir Robert Holmes and to inflict similar damage, in retaliation, to the English settlements.

On 3 October 1664 the Duke of York told Pepys and others that he had decided to go to sea himself, in the preparations against the Dutch, and would take Penn with him. Pepys knew that matters were now 'past a retreat'.

The first act of war, or the first known in London, was the capture by Captain Teddiman of some 20 Dutch merchantmen of their Bordeaux fleet, together with their escort of two men-of-war. Pepys heard the news on 21 November and commented sadly, 'So that the war is begun: God give a good end to it.'

Allin's suspicions that de Ruyter was on his way to Guinea had been only too well justified, for on 23 December Pepys heard that the English squadron there had been defeated. In the coffee house the following day he was told that Captain Reynolds, commanding the King's ships had promptly yielded to de Ruyter and that the King and the Duke of York were very annoyed about it.

Meanwhile Allin and his squadron had been in action with the Dutch at about the time that Pepys was learning of the Guinea reverse. On 6 November he had arrived at Iviza, south of Valencia. There he was rejoined by one of his ships, the *Phoenix*, which had been at Alicante, and her Captain brought Allin 'letters of concernment'. In the light of what followed later these must have been orders to commence hostilities. On 2 December he had a near disaster. About 2.0 a.m. on a dark night, stormy and rainy, navigational errors led to five of his ships running ashore to the east of Gibraltar. Three got off, but the *Nonsuch* and *Phoenix* sank and the *Bonaventure* was damaged.

On 12 December, back in Gibraltar Road, a small ship arrived and reported 33 Dutch ships in Malaga Road. On 14 December Allin and his ships arrived in the Bay of Bulls, hoping to obtain victuals and get the *Bonaventure*, which was leaking, repaired in Cadiz. The English Consul there came aboard and by arrangement with him an officer was sent ashore to get provisions.

On the morning of 19 December 12 or 14 of the great armed merchantmen of the Dutch East Indies fleet suddenly appeared at about 7.0 a.m. Allin ordered the cables of his ships to be cut, but before they could set their sails six of the Dutch ships were close to the rocks on the south side of the entrance to Cadiz, where the English ships could not get at them. Allin, however, encountered one of the Dutch great ships and 'lamed him'. Captain Clarke in the *Antelope* went alongside and captured it. In rear of the merchantmen came the Dutch escort men-of-war. As the Dutch 'Admiral' entered he fired a salute of five guns (obviously unaware that hostilities had begun), but the small 5th Rate, *Milford*, commanded by Captain Seale, gave him 'what guns he could', and Captain Mohun, in the other 5th Rate, *Oxford*, also engaged him, both ships being to leeward. Allin, in the *Plymouth*, got to windward and 'gave him all my upper tier and 2 demi-cannon in the gun room' and then went on to tackle the other two men-of-war (called 'Vice-Admiral' and 'Rear-Admiral', i.e. in their order of seniority and not denoting the ranks of their captains). Allin says that he 'gave them all they could', but his 'ship was lying down-side so much' that he could not open any more ports, that is, being to windward and the ship heeling over so much that those in the lower tier could not be opened. The *Portsmouth* and *Leopard* were also engaged on the windward side, whilst the two small frigates were to leeward of the enemy. Allin took on another of the great ships and Captain Seale in the *Milford* boarded and captured her, but she had been so badly mauled by the *Plymouth's* broadsides that she sank.

Allin had hoped to renew the conflict in the morning, but during the night the Dutch ships had managed to get into Cadiz, which was, of course, a neutral port.

It was not till 23 January that Pepys received a letter from Allin reporting the loss of the *Nonsuch* and *Phoenix* and (what Pepys called the 'great news') the account of the fight in the Bay of Cadiz, and of his sinking of the very rich *King Solomon* and another ship, and of the taking of three other merchant ships.

Allin says that on 20 December Don Paulus, the Vice-Admiral of the Spanish fleet came aboard to welcome him and 'wished that it had been better weather the day of our engagement', and added that he could have anything he needed from the King's stores. It was apparent which side Spain favoured in the coming struggle! Before Allin's squadron left, the Governor of Cadiz came aboard to inform him that some Dutch ships were coming from Naples 'with soldiers for His Catholic Majesty's service and desired his favour of their passing'.

War with Holland was not officially declared until 4 March 1665, and on 22 April Coventry told Pepys that the fleet had sailed the day before from Harwich to the Dutch coast.

14

The Battle of Lowestoft and After

Allin, now back in home waters, was with the fleet and in command of the *Plymouth*.[1] On 5 May 1665 he recorded that, 'The General put the Standard in the mizzen shrouds and fired his gun about ten o'clock for the Flag Officers who consulted fore noon. About one o'clock the Union Flag was put in the mizzen shrouds for all Captains.' On 14 May, in accordance with an instruction he had received from the Duke of Albemarle, Pepys took a boat about midnight and went down to the Hope, where he called on every one of the victualling ships to get them away to the fleet. He visited Albemarle the following morning to report on his night's activities. Albemarle explained the urgency by showing Pepys letters he had had from Sir George Downing, the English Ambassador to Holland, dated four days previously, reporting that the Dutch fleet had set out with the object of boarding the best English ships and certainly intended to fight.[2]

On 1 June, writes Allin, they spied the Dutch fleet. It was the prelude to the battle of Lowestoft. The fleet weighed and stood off SE, the weather being fair and the wind ENE. They 'anchored upon the flood, thinking the Dutch would keep under way and drift to leeward, but they held their ground.' The following day the fleet made sail towards the Dutch, but there was very little wind in the forenoon and the only incident was a Dutch fireship blowing up.

On Saturday 3 June they came within range and opened fire, starting with Myngs, Vice-Admiral of the White, who was leading the van. However, the range was great and the fire had little effect. The wind at this time was SW.

Captain A.T. Mahan gives a brief description of the battle which ensued in his book *The Influence of Sea Power on History*.[3] The Dutch commander, Jacob van Wassenaer, Earl of Opdam, was a cavalry officer. He had been given positive orders to fight and this gallant soldier did so. But able though he may have been as a higher commander in the field, he does not appear to

---

[1] 'The Journals of Sir Thomas Allin', op. cit. pp. 227 f.
[2] *The Diary of Samuel Pepys, op. cit.*
[3] *Captain A.T. Mahan, The Influence of Sea Power upon History 1660-1783* (London, Sampson Low, Marston, & Co, 1890) pp. 108-9.

have been very competent in chief command at sea. Mahan says that the Dutch van gave way in the battle, and a little later one of the flag officers in Opdam's own squadron was killed, resulting in his crew panicking and carrying the ship out of action. This caused some thirteen other ships (presumably in that division) to follow the flag away from the battle, leaving a great gap in the line of the centre squadron. Opdam, apparently in despair at this occurrence, tried to grapple the flagship of the Duke of York, commanding the English fleet, and failed, and in the heavy close fighting Opdam's flagship was blown up and he was killed. Shortly afterwards three or four Dutch ships ran foul of one another, and this group was burnt by the successful attack of an English fireship. Before long the same fate befell three or four others singly. The greater part of the Dutch fleet was now in disorder and it retreated under cover of the rear squadron commanded by Tromp (son of the great admiral of the First Dutch War) who kept his ships in fighting order.

Allin's description of the battle is confined mostly to the action of his own ship, which was in the Red Squadron, directly under command of the Duke of York. The opening range being too great, Allin received orders from the Duke of York to stand in towards the enemy. Allin did so, and for the next two hours the *Plymouth* was hotly engaged with Opdam's flagship and several other Dutch men-of-war. The *Plymouth* suffered heavy damage, 'masts, yard, sail and hull very much torn and rigging ropes'. He had to withdraw to repair what he could but it was not till 3.0 p.m. that his ship was ready to fight again. During the time he was absent Opdam's ship blew up. On his return into action, he says: 'I went aboard his Royal Highness who thanked me for my adventure'. Allin told him that he would continue it, and was soon hotly engaged again, and saw the burning of the second lot of Dutch ships. The fleet followed the Dutch all night. The next day he overhauled and captured the Dutch 54-gun ship *Carolus Quintas*. They made Camperdown by 9.0 a.m. and saw many of the Dutch ships at anchor, and he commented that: 'Had we had many fireships and gone upon them shooting, we had destroyed many of them'.

On 9 June the Duke of York ordered Allin to take command of the *Old James* (2nd Rate); her Captain, the Duke of Marlborough, had been killed in the battle. Although it was promotion to a larger ship, in recognition of his distinguished service in the battle of Lowestoft, Allin left the *Plymouth* with reluctance.

The previous day Pepys had seen the Duke of York's report on how the fleet under his command had totally defeated the Dutch in the battle of 3 June, and how the Dutch had neglected the advantage they had of the wind, so losing the benefit of their fireships. The Earl of Falmouth and two others were killed on board the Duke's flagship, the *Royal Charles*, 'their blood and brains flying in the Duke's face'. It was believed that 24 of their best ships were taken or sunk, and Dutch losses in men were thought to have been between 8,000 and 10,000, as against not more than 700 English. The remains of the Dutch fleet were being pursued. It was stated that Sir William Penn had played a distinguished part in the battle.

On 11 June Allin went aboard the *Old James* to see what repairs were needed and 'found her much torn, her great cabin lying all open to the deck and state-room much torn also'. Although the *Old James* was a 2nd Rate, with 70 guns, as compared with the 58 of the *Plymouth*, she was a much older ship. The *Plymouth* had been built in 1653, whereas the *Old James* dated from 1634. She had originally been called the *James*. In 1658 a new ship was built called the *Richard*, after the Protector's son. On the Restoration she was re-named the *Royal James*, and to avoid confusion the *James* became the *Old James*.

On 13 June Allin wrote that 'Captain Harman made Rear-Admiral of the White, upon which Major Holmes laid down his commission and Capt. Lawson took his ship'. The irascible Irishman had felt that this appointment should have gone to him. (The seniority of the army rank of major over the naval rank of captain will again be noted.)

On 16 June when Pepys went to his office, he was told that the Duke of York had returned from the fleet. He hurried off to Whitehall and 'kissed his hands'. Later Coventry, who had attended to the Duke during the battle, spoke to Pepys about the action. The Earl of Sandwich, he said, had done very well; Sir John Lawson had been badly wounded in the knee; Jonas Poole, commanding the *Vanguard*, 'did basely' and would be 'turned out of his ship'; Captain Holmes, on the death of Robert Sansum, Rear-Admiral in Prince Rupert's squadron, had expected to be promoted Rear-Admiral in his place, but the appointment had been given to Sir John Harman and Holmes had resigned his commission. In the battle the great ships (that is, the 1st and 2nd Rates) had proved the ships to 'do the business', they 'quite deadening the enemy'. The Duke said that Captain Grove had 'done the basest thing' in that, though hearing the guns, he could not be got to leave Lowestoft, and he was to be tried.

Allin's performance in the battle was soon to be rewarded. On 2 July he was given his commission as Rear-Admiral of the Fleet and Admiral of the Blue. Sir William Penn was Vice-Admiral of the Fleet and Admiral of the White. The Earl of Sandwich was now to command the fleet. On 17 July the fleet was assembled in Sole Bay with the 1st Rate *Royal Prince* as fleet flagship. Sandwich ordered Allin to move from the *Old James* to the more modern 2nd Rate *Royal James*.

The objective of the fleet was to intercept de Ruyter on his return, or the homeward bound Dutch East India fleet, or both. On 21 July information was received from a passing vessel that de Ruyter had been in Bergen twelve days previously with about 60 sail.

During the night of 25 July Allin's squadron got separated from the rest of the fleet. He says 'The fleet tacked to the WSW and Mate Lestock, a heavy moulded dotard, never saw them, and so we stood in to the NNE until daylight, having lost sight of the fleet'. The squadron regained contact at about 3.0 a.m.

On 26 July Sandwich held a Council of War and it was decided to send a detachment under Sir Thomas Teddiman into Bergen. This detachment was to consist of '8 merchant men-of-war, 5 4-rates, 4 5-rates and 2 fireships'.

Supplies were now running short. On 30 July, at another Council of War, William Penn (the wind being now NW) said that God had sent them a wind to make use of and they should go homeward and lie before the Texel to meet the Dutch fleet and await supplies from England. However, this would be contrary to Sandwich's instructions which were to 'follow the East India fleet or de Ruyter into Norway and to take or destroy them'. During the discussions the Captain of the *Sapphire* brought information from an Ostend ship that some 50 Dutch ships were in and around Bergen. Upon this news Teddiman's detachment of 20 ships was increased by the addition of the *Revenge* (3rd Rate) and *Sapphire* (4th Rate). At about 8.0 a.m. the next day Teddiman's little fleet departed on its expedition.

In the event the expedition was a failure. On 14 August Pepys wrote that a letter had been received by Albemarle from Sandwich. The latter had been told that the Governor of Bergen would not oppose an attack on the Dutch ships. Only eight or nine of Teddiman's ships could get into action, but the Governor stipulated that not more than five ships should enter the harbour and also requested time to think about it. But the Governor was in league with the Dutch, and the guns of the town and castle opened fire on the five ships, which, because the wind was off the land, had to withdraw.

At Greenwich Pepys heard much criticism of Teddiman's handling of the Bergen affair. It was said that he had spent too long in negotiations whilst the Dutch and the Norwegians (Norway being then under Danish rule) were getting a defence ready; and that if he had sailed in immediately he could have taken every Dutch ship. On 9 September it was reported in London that all the Dutch East India fleet and their escorting warships had got home from Bergen on 3 September, 'which' thought Pepys, 'will make us all ridiculous'. However, on 10 September he had much better news, for a letter arrived from Coventry to say that Sandwich had intercepted part of the Dutch fleet and had taken two of the East India ships and six or seven others. The only English loss was the hired ship *Hector* (about which Pepys commented, 'Poor Captain Cuttle'). Even more Dutch ships were taken, for on 14 September Albemarle showed Pepys a letter from Sandwich, written at Sole Bay on 12 September, saying that they had met 18 of the Dutch fleet and had taken most of them. The messenger who brought the letter added that they had taken three more after the letter was written. Pepys calculated that the total number of ships captured was now 35. He had been worrying that if the fleet returned without encountering the Dutch, Parliament might be less inclined to provide more money for the Navy.

This more or less ended the naval operations of 1665. On 25 October Pepys complained that lack of victuals had been 'the whole overthrow this year'.

In November Sandwich was replaced as General-at-Sea by Monck (the Duke of Albemarle) and Prince Rupert as joint Generals-at-Sea. In January 1666 France and Denmark sided with the Dutch in the war against England, and on 23 April (St. George's Day) Monck and Rupert assumed command of the fleet at the Nore in the 2nd Rate *Royal Charles*. Monck was the foremost naval commander in England, with an impressive record in the First Dutch

War. Rupert, during the Civil War, had proved very able as commander of a cavalry regiment, but that was his limit. As a higher commander, his brilliant leadership did not compensate for his tactical incompetence; for it was the wild and uncontrolled charge with which he led his cavalry right off the battlefield that deprived the King of victory at Edgehill and of his kingdom at Naseby. At sea he showed the same characteristics. He would probably have done well as the junior flag officer in a squadron: in supreme command he was no match for the great Dutch Admiral de Ruyter.

Much valuable information relating to naval operations and administration of this period is contained in the Navy Records Society's 'Rupert and Monck Letter Book'[4] In statements of the needs of the fleet, we detect the experienced hand of the Duke of Albemarle. For example, there is a letter to Sir William Coventry, the day following the assumption of command, containing a request for those useful little vessels, ketches. Ten of them were wanted for each squadron, in addition to those already allowed to the fleet flagship. The immediate need for them arose because as long as the fleet lay at the Nore, it would be necessary to have sufficient ketches to send to Gravesend for water. But the letter also looked ahead to their permanent duty with the fleet, carrying letters, for instance, between ships, and supplementing the small frigates in scouting for, 'they be good sailers and able to defend themselves from a privateer'.

There was also concern about the scale of ammunition, and on the same date a letter was sent to the Commissioners of Ordnance on the subject as follows: 'Gentlemen: Since we come to the Hope we have made an enquiry into all the ships here and do find they are generally supplied with no more than 40 rounds of powder, shot, tho' they could receive more, we suppose we shall find the like proportion in the ships in the Buoy of the Nore'. They went on to request that all, except fireships, should be supplied with 50 rounds each. Though some could not take 50 rounds, other ships could take more, so that ammunition surplus to capacity could be disposed to other ships in the same squadron.

On 28 April the Generals-at-Sea wrote again to the Commissioners of the Ordnance on the same subject; for the increase above the '40 rounds of powder and shot' had not yet been received. In addition they wanted more canvas for making cartridges as paper cartridges were unsatisfactory. 'We find that if we fill paper cartridges with powder, that the saltpetre will make them moist, and so, when we come to charge our guns, they will be apt to break and be something dangerous at such a time when there are so many lighted matches about the ships.' Returning to the need for extra ammunition, they pointed out that, 'There is nothing that can endanger the losing of the victory more than the want of powder or shot.'

The flag officers of the fleet that was soon to go into battle against the Dutch were as follows. The Red Squadron was under the direct command of

---

[4] *The Navy Records Society*, Vol. 112, 'The Rupert and Monck Letter Book' 1666, ed. J.R. Powell and E.K. Timings (The Navy Records Society, 1969).

Albemarle and Rupert, the White Squadron was commanded by Sir Thomas Allin, and the Blue Squadron by Sir George Ayscue. The Vice-Admirals of the three squadrons were, respectively, Christopher Myngs, Sir Jeremy Smith, and Sir William Berkeley; and the Rear-Admirals Sir Joseph Jordan, Sir Thomas Teddiman, and John Harman.

15

The Four Days Battle[1]

We now come to a division of the fleet which led to Albemarle becoming engaged with inferior strength against the Dutch fleet at the start of the contest known as the Four Days Battle. On 31 May Pepys recorded news of the French fleet coming to Rochelle and the English fleet divided, Prince Rupert having gone with about 30 ships to the westward to meet the French and hinder them from joining the Dutch. Albemarle remained in the Downs with the rest of the English fleet and was intending to sail to the Gunfleet.[2] This was a pretty accurate assessment of the situation of the English fleet, but quite erroneous as regards the French.

Sir William Coventry wrote his own recollections as to how the fleet came to be divided. About 13 May 1666 he was commanded to attend the King. After several matters had been discussed by those present at the conference, the movements of the French fleet were considered. Sir Edward Spragge had arrived with information from a correspondent in France that the French fleet was assembling about Brest or Belle Isle. It was concluded that it was desirable to deal with the French before their preparations were complete, but that nothing should be done before consulting Prince Rupert and the Duke of Albemarle. The Vice-Chamberlain (Sir George Cartaret) and Coventry were to accompany Spragge back to the fleet for this purpose. Albemarle liked the idea of an expedition against the French, but Cartaret and Coventry doubted whether sufficient force could be spared from the fleet for such a task. Albemarle replied, 'Leave us 60 sail and we shall do well enough'. Looking at the list of ships, it was found that there were 80 and Albemarle agreed that 20 could go. After some discussion, Albemarle asked who was to command the 20 ships. They replied that the King had given them no instructions about that; indeed, pending the result of their discussions with Albemarle, he had not even decided whether any force should be sent against the French. Rupert interjected that the King had promised the command of any such detachment to him. Coventry and Cartaret

---

[1] 'The Rupert and Monck Letter Book', op. cit.
[2] *The Diary of Samuel Pepys*, op. cit.

thereupon returned to the King, conveying the approval of the Generals-at-Sea, and carrying with them the names of the ships proposed, and also the proposal that the whole fleet should sail to the Downs and the detachment depart from there. The King approved the plan.

It will be noted that nothing has been mentioned in the above discussions about the readiness of the Dutch fleet, and therein lies an argument which has not been resolved yet. It is inconceivable, however, that an Admiral with Albemarle's experience would have agreed to such a detachment without some reassurance as to the possibility of a Dutch attack whilst the fleet was split. Lord Arlington, Secretary of State, is stated to have received information that the Dutch fleet was not ready, though Secretary Morrice had been assured that it would be ready to sail in a few days. Long afterwards, Pepys (in support of Coventry) says in his Diary on 1 November 1667 that Albemarle told Coventry that it was he that had informed him that the Dutch would not be out for six weeks. Coventry hotly denied this. It seems probable that Albemarle had indeed been so informed but made a mistake in thinking he had got it from Coventry. However, whoever told Albemarle this story was wrong: the French fleet was not ready to move but the Dutch fleet was.

Albemarle, in the *Royal Charles* and commanding the main fleet, wrote to Coventry at 2 o'clock on the morning of 26 May from '3 leagues off the North Foreland' saying that they were going to sail at 7.0 a.m. He had nothing much to report other than the capture of a vessel 'laden with wine and brandy bound for Bordeaux, pretended to be a Hamburger'. Rupert also wrote to Coventry on the same day, before leaving the *Royal Charles*, asking the Duke of York's instructions as to what flags were to be worn in his squadron and the names of the frigates which were to meet him.

Albemarle wrote another letter to Coventry on 26 May, saying that once Prince Rupert's ships had left he would only have 51, which were too few to engage the Dutch, and asking him to hasten away the remaining ships nominated for his command. The following day he reported from the Downs that Rupert would sail the next day 'if the wind serves'. He also reported an apparent breach of security as 'some Gentlemen that came aboard us here told us of the design, though I am sure that there was never a Flag Officer here knew till we sent the order about it'. (That is, the intention to divide the fleet.) 'I know not', added Albemarle, 'how secret you carried the business in London'. He had need to be worried, particularly as the Dutch still had their Embassy in London.

On 28 May Albemarle wrote to Arlington, acknowledging his letter of 24 May 'whereby I understand the Holland fleet will be suddenly out' and hoping the King would hasten away the other ships, for he still had only 56. 'If we could make up 70 sail I should be very confident to meet the Dutch anywhere, and on the other side I should be loathe to retreat from them being it goes agst. my stomach to do it. The Prince I believe will set sail with his squadron this evening'. Having received this information about the Dutch, it seems surprising that nobody — not the King, the Duke of York, Arlington, nor Coventry — seems to have considered cancelling the departure of Rupert; yet Albemarle was plainly uneasy.

On 30 May Albemarle sent to Coventry a report from the captain of his scouts. He had intercepted a ship which reported that 75 sail of the Dutch fleet had left the Texel on 21 May and another 18 from Zeeland. On 31 May the Duke of York wrote to Albemarle saying that the Dutch fleet had left the Texel and Zeeland, and that by the King's direction he had despatched letters to Prince Rupert to return with his squadron, one letter to Portsmouth and another to Plymouth.

On 1 June Albemarle wrote to Coventry, informing him that at about 11.0 a.m. that day they had discovered the Dutch fleet towards the coast of Flanders and that the opposing fleets were sailing towards each other, but that he did not think they would engage that day.

At this stage it is interesting to return to Pepys' Diary, for the reports of the ensuing battle, as they reached London, are somewhat reminiscent of the early reports of the battle of Jutland in 1916.

On 2 June Pepys wrote that a letter dated the previous day at 11 a.m. had been received by the King from the Duke of Albemarle to the effect that they were in sight of the Dutch fleet and were getting ready to fight. Several people had told Pepys that they had heard the guns on the afternoon of 1 June. Pepys soon got orders to send 200 soldiers to the fleet and went down to Greenwich to arrange their transport, sending orders for the soldiers to march to Blackwall. Going ashore at Greenwich, he 'could hear the guns from the Fleete most plainly'. Presently the King and the Duke of York arrived and Pepys gave them a report of his actions. They too went to Greenwich Park to listen to the guns. All were hoping that Prince Rupert, with his squadron, was returning to join Albemarle. The message ordering his return had been despatched on 30 May, and he had replied the same day from off the Isle of Wight that he intended to sail from St. Helen's Point that same day at about 4.0 p.m., and it had been hoped that he would join Albemarle at noon on this 2 June.

On the following day, Whit Sunday 3 June, Pepys went early to Whitehall, meeting Coventry who told him that the only news from the fleet had been brought by Captain Elliot of the 4th Rate *Portland*. His ship had been rammed by the 5th Rate *Guernsey* and had to return for repairs. Elliot had seen one of the Dutch great ships blown up and three on fire. A letter had been received from Captain Harman, commanding the 2nd Rate *Henry*, which had fallen into the main body of the Dutch fleet and was attacked by, one after the other, three fireships. He drove two off and disabled the third, which, however, managed to get his ship on fire. A number of his men leaped into the sea — led by the parson! — and perished. He had got the fire out but had suffered over 100 casualties. He had brought his ship into Aldebugh (Suffolk) for repair.

Pepys went on to see Sir George Cartaret, Treasurer of the Navy, who told him that there had been bad management. The King's orders recalling the Prince had gone out on Wednesday 30 May, but by the ordinary post and had only reached Prince Rupert on Friday 1 June (and not as reported above). And then, instead of sailing immediately, Rupert had waited till 4.0 p.m. and did not reach Dover till 10.0 p.m. on 2 June; though the *Hampshire* (4th Rate), coming from the Straits of Gibraltar with 'merchants money' and sailing just before Rupert's fleet, was in the Downs by 5.0 a.m. on 2 June.

On 4 June Pepys had news of the battle. He was told that a couple of men from the fleet wished to speak to him. One was a naval officer friend, Mr. Daniel, 'all muffled up, and his face as black as the chimney and covered with dirt, pitch and tar, and powder, and muffled with dirty clouts and his right eye stopped with oakum.' Daniel had been serving in the *Royal Charles* and had landed at Harwich that morning with about 20 other wounded at about 2 o'clock. Pepys took Daniel and another officer, who had been wounded in the eye, to Coventry's house. As he was not there, Pepys left the two men at the house and, going into the Park, found the King, whom he told that Prince Rupert had joined the Duke of Albemarle at about 7.0 p.m. the previous day. The King asked that the two seamen should be brought to him to tell him about the battle and they gave him the following account.

The Dutch fleet had been found at anchor on Friday 1 June half way between Dunkirk and Ostend. They numbered about 90 ships against the English fewer than 60. The English fleet attacked and forced the Dutch to withdraw until they were reinforced by about 16 fresh ships, when they bore up again. The fight continued until nightfall and started again at 5.0 the next morning and continued until 7.0 p.m. On 3 June it was again resumed in the early morning and fighting went on until about 4.0 p.m. For most of 2 and 3 June the Dutch were pursuing the retreating English. By and by Prince Rupert's fleet was seen approaching. The Dutch Admiral, de Ruyter, made a signal for a Council of War, and was then seen to divide the fleet into two squadrons, 40 in one and about 30 in the other (the Dutch fleet having been reduced to a strength of about 70 ships). The larger squadron was to follow the Duke of Albemarle and the smaller one was to face Prince Rupert. But Rupert joined Albemarle, and the Dutch reunited their fleet, withdrawing towards their own coasts followed by the English.

Neither Daniel nor his companion knew how the battle had gone after this, as they had been evacuated with other casualties. At the conclusion of this narrative, Pepys says: 'The King did pull out of his pocket about twenty pieces of gold, and did give it to Daniel for himself and his companion'.

By 6 June, as no guns were heard, it was concluded by Pepys and others that the Dutch had been beaten. A report from Captain Hayward of the 3rd Rate *Dunkirk* said that on 4 June the two fleets were fighting all day until 7.0 p.m. and then the whole Dutch fleet fled. It was believed that only about 50 Dutch ships got home and few if any of their flagships. This caused great rejoicing. If this was the view of a captain of one of the bigger ships, it hardly supports the contention that the English fleet had suffered a defeat, as most historians have stated.

Subsequent comments in London suggested, like those in England after the battle of Jutland, that the enemy had gained a victory. Such, indeed, was the opinion that was expressed to Pepys on 7 June. He had expected to hear the victory confirmed, but to his astonishment, Lord Brouncker and Sir

Thomas Harvey, Navy Commissioners, who had come from the Court, said that the English fleet had been beaten, losing many ships and good commanders, and had not taken any enemy ship. The 1st Rate *Prince* had run ashore on the Galloper and stuck; she had been burnt by the Dutch after they had tried unsuccessfully to get her off, and Sir George Ayscue, whose flagship she was, had been taken prisoner. The 1st Rate *Royal Charles*, the fleet flagship, and the 2nd Rate *Royal Katherine* had both grounded on the Galloper but got off. The 3rd Rate *Essex* had been captured, and the 2nd Rate *Swiftsure* and the armed merchantmen *Seven Oaks* and *Loyal George* were missing.

Again, like the battle of Jutland, the results of the battle were assessed in terms of ships lost and the strategic effects were ignored. Yet the Dutch, who had succeeded in catching the English fleet divided, had failed in their objective of decisive victory, by destroying the major part of that fleet, so that the result was a strategic defeat.

Sir George Cartaret told Pepys that the 'management of the late fight was bad from top to bottom', but he added that the fighting on 3 June was a 'very honourable retreat and that the Duke of Albemarle had done well in it, and it could have been well if he had done it sooner'.

Albemarle's own account of the battle paints a rather different picture from that presented by the civilian officials in London. The gist of this was as follows. On 31 May they weighed anchor in the Downs and stood for the Buoy of the Gunfleet. On 1 June at about 10.0 a.m. they sighted the Dutch fleet. Albemarle called a Council of War of flag officers. The Dutch being to leeward (the wind SW) it was decided to attack them. As they drew near the Dutch were found to be at anchor; but on observing that the English were intending to attack, they cut their cables. Albemarle and his officers reckoned them to be about 75 in number. The English, in line, passed down the Dutch fleet, as near as they could, firing; but the ships, heeling before the strong south-west wind, could not get out the lower tier of guns. On the second pass, standing to westward, the sails of his flagship 'were all shot to pieces'. Albemarle adds that 'having got a little ahead of the Dutch, we anchored and brought to a change our foresail, foretopsail, and maintopsail.'

After they had fought all day (that is, from 1.0 or 2.0 p.m.) 'to windward of some and to leeward of others,' they anchored at about 9.0 or 10.0 p.m., as did also the Dutch about 1½ leagues from the English.

On 2 June both fleets weighed anchor in the morning and the English fleet 'bore through them three times, some to windward and some to leeward, several of our ships being much damnified'. At about 6.0 p.m. Albemarle called a Council of War at which it was decided to make for the English coast 'to secure our fleet'. Albemarle directed that fifteen of the best ships should 'keep upon a line to defend the other lame ships which were ahead'. In other words, the fifteen were to fight a rearguard action to cover the withdrawal of the most damaged ships in the fleet. Albemarle says that they had 'burned many of the Dutch fleet (and fired these two days four of them)'. Four English ships had been lost up till this time. The Dutch followed up the withdrawal,

120

but could not get up enough ships to engage the English rearguard. Fighting continued all that night and the following day until at about 5.0 p.m., they sighted Rupert's fleet. Whilst altering course a little to join it, the *Royal Charles, Prince,* and *Royal Katherine* 'fell aground upon the Galloper'. Whilst the others got off, the *Prince* stuck fast; 'so eight Dutch ships came towards her drawing less water to whom she suddenly struck her flag and ensign before 5 frigates which I sent to fetch off her men and set her on fire could come up.' Albemarle was obviously disgusted!

Having joined Rupert, Albemarle went aboard his flagship, the *Royal James*, for consultations. They decided to pursue the Dutch fleet and that night carried out repairs.

The following morning, 4 June, Rupert's squadron, being fresh, was put in the van. At the first encounter the English fleet was to leeward and out of range. At the second 'pass' they got close to the Dutch and a fierce engagement followed. A fireship succeeded in setting two of their ships alight. As soon as they had passed the whole of the Dutch line, the English fleet tacked and split the Dutch into two or three parts; both fleets having suffered much damage.

Towards night the Dutch fleet sailed towards Holland and, finding his ammunition nearly exhausted, Albemarle 'stood homewards'. In his report, Albemarle concluded: 'We burnt of their ships three this day which with those burnt before is 7 in all, being of their best ships some of them Admirals and Vice-Admirals and very few of their men were saved'.

Albemarle's account (and he was not the man to whitewash a catastrophe) was hardly that of a commander reporting a defeat.

Allin got his first news of the division of the fleet on Friday 25 May 1666.[3] The two Generals-at-Sea, Albemarle and Rupert, hoisted a white flag to signal a Council of Flag Officers. Allin went aboard the fleet flagship where he was informed that Prince Rupert would embark in Allin's flagship, the *Royal James*, and take a detachment of the fleet 'to the westward'. On 28 May Prince Rupert came aboard the *Royal James* at 6.0 p.m. and hoisted the Union flag to denote his command of a detached squadron. Allin went aboard the *Royal Charles* to take leave of the Duke of Albemarle.

On Tuesday 29 May the detached squadron weighed at a little after 7.0 a.m., and about midday anchored near Folkestone. On 30 May it anchored between Hastings and Pevensey. On 1 June, at about 10.0 a.m., the squadron anchored at St. Helens, to be met with a packet from the Duke of York ordering their return to the Downs to rejoin the Duke of Albemarle 'for that the Dutch fleet were put out to sea'. They accordingly weighed anchor at 4 p.m. that day. About 1.0 p.m. the following day, 2 June, they 'had the Dungeness lights' and 'got the length of Dover'. The next day at about 4.0 p.m. they came close to the rival fleets and observed 'our fleet standing before the wind making a retreat and the Flemmings following them'. When the Dutch saw Rupert's squadron they detached some twenty ships to attract it towards

---

[3] "The Journals of Sir Thomas Allin" op. cit., pp. 232 f.

them over the Galloper bank, on which they hoped that the English ships would ground. But Allin had sent his ship's 'shallop' to Albemarle to know how affairs stood. He replied that they should bear towards his guns because the *Prince* had grounded on the Galloper and been taken by the Dutch.

Rupert's squadron stood towards the *Charles* and Albemarle came aboard and told them that they had fought three days with 53 or 40 warships against over 80 Dutch. It was decided therefore that the next day Rupert's fresh squadron should lead the fleet.

At daybreak on Monday 4 June the Dutch fleet was out of sight. They were eventually sighted about five leagues away. The wind was SSW and by 8.0 a.m. the English fleet, having the weather gauge, were close to them. The English frigates, ahead of the fleet, had waited for it to come up to them. Sir Christopher Myngs, Vice-Admiral of Rupert's squadron, put his division into line to lead the van, followed by Rupert and Allin with the centre division, and Sir Edward Spragge, Rear-Admiral of the squadron bringing up the rear with his division. The rest of the fleet followed in 'very good order', according to Allin. Rupert 'led the whole line through the middle of the enemy, the General following with the rest of the fleet in good order'. Allin's account of the fighting is hard to follow, but it appears that they were pressing the Dutch hard. Then, 'Just as we thought to break with the Holland fleet we were prevented'. The prevention was the shooting down of much of the *Royal James*'s masts and rigging. But the Dutch, 'seeing the *Charles* and many other ships laying sails aback to stay for them, bore away to leeward and were glad to part'.

Allin, obviously, did not think that the English fleet had been defeated. Certainly some ten English ships had been lost compared with four Dutch, but the Dutch had failed in their strategic objective, and a comparison of respective losses in men and equipment is not a sound way of assessing victory or defeat either at sea or on land — as Jutland, for instance, showed.

Captain A.T. Mahan[4] quotes a French naval writer, Chabault-Arnot, as follows: 'In 1666 as in 1653 the fortune of war seemed to lean to the English. Of the three great battles fought two were decided victories; and the third, though adverse, had increased the glory of her seamen. This was due to the intelligent boldness of Monck and Rupert, the talents of part of the admirals and captains, and the skill of the seamen and soldiers under them.'

On 5 June the fleet anchored off Harwich. On 10 June the Generals-at-Sea asked Sir William Coventry for nine 5th Rate frigates, so that every flagship might have a fireship and a 5th Rate to attend to it. This request to Coventry was amplified on 14 June 1666 as follows: 'If you would spare us 9 5th Rate frigates, one to attend on each Flagship, they would much countenance the fireships to do execution, when they see themselves aided with a small frigate to take up their men. They would also keep off fireships from the greater ships, and be good for scouting some times.' It was an admirable idea, though there does not appear to be any record as to whether Coventry was able to provide the nine frigates.

---

[4] Captain A.T. Maha, *The Influence of Sea Power upon History 1660-1783* (London, Sampson Low, Marston, 1890) pp. 126-7.

The fleet began to assemble at the Nore on 27 June, but lack of men prevented it sailing until 19 July. On 25 June the Generals had written to Coventry requesting that soldiers to help man the fleet should be invited 'in the newsbooks' to come to London 'and to list themselves in the King's, Duke's, and General's Regiments[5] for a speedy way of raising a great number of men'. The soldiers referred to were presumably men discharged from the old Cromwellians regiments.

De Ruyter with the Dutch fleet had sailed on 25 June and by 1 July was at the back of the Long Sand. On 3 July he anchored off the King's Channel with the intention of entering the Thames to attack, presumably hoping to achieve surprise, but he could not find any competent pilots.

According to Allin, a Council of Flag Officers was called on 5 July at which it was determined that the White Squadron 'should go ride fair by the Buoy of the Oase Edge, open to both channels, and that we should send 4 fourth-rate frigates to the Buoy of the Middle Ground, to anchor as near safety as they could, with two fireships and those formerly there, to be commanded by Captain Zachary Browne' (of the 2nd Rate *Loyal London*), 'and to take up the buoy and place it upon the sand, to prejudice the enemy in case they presume to come further up'. It is apparent from these dispositions that the Generals were well aware of the position of the Dutch fleet.

On 18 July Allin sent three fireships from his own White Squadron to the Middle Ground, which were accompanied by fireships from the Red and Blue Squadrons.

On the same day Albemarle and Rupert issued 'Additional Instructions for Fighting in the next engagement'. These dealt with two cases, firstly when the English fleet had the wind on the approach to contact, and secondly when the Dutch had it. 'In case we have the wind of the enemy, and the enemy stands towards us, and we towards them' (that is, the two fleets approaching each other in line ahead formation), 'then the van of our fleet shall keep the wind, and when we' (that is, the van) 'are come up to a convenient distance of the enemy's rear, shall stay' (i.e. the van) 'until the whole line is come up within the same distance of the enemy's van' (that is, until the rear of the English fleet is the same distance from the enemy's van, as its van is from the enemy's rear), 'and then our whole line is to stand along with them the same tacks aboard, and keeping them to leeward, and not suffering them to tack in their van. And in case the enemy tack in their rear first, the he that leads the van of our fleet is to tack first, and the whole line is to follow, standing along with the same tacks aboard as the enemy does.'

'In case the enemy has the wind of us and we have searoom, then we are to keep the wind as close as we can lie until such time as we see an opportunity of gaining the wind to divide their fleet, and if the van of our fleet find they have the wake of any part of them, then they are to tack and stand in to strive to divide the enemy's body; and that squadron shall pass

---

[5] These regiment were the First Guards, the Duke of York's Maritime Regiment of Foot, and Albemarle's Coldstream Regiment.

first, being come to the other side, are to tack again and the middle squadron is to bear up upon that part of the enemy so divided, which the last' (that is, the rear squadron) 'is to second either by bearing down to the enemy, or by endeavouring to keep off those that are to windward, and shall be lost for that service.'

Instructions were given to Mr. Collins, a pilot on board the ketch *Mary*, to see that neither the Admiral's ship nor the whole fleet ran aground. Except when fighting, he was to keep on the lee bow of the fleet flagship and to signal if he met with a depth of less than seven fathoms. He was given various signals to make night and day. If the enemy was engaged 'anywhere amongst the sands' he was to lie well ahead of the fleet and signal whenever the depth was less than seven fathoms. Obviously Monck was determined that there should be no repetition of the diaster to the *Prince*.

On 17 July the Generals-at-Sea had reported to the King that sixteen Dutch ships were in the Gunfleet and that the rest of the Dutch fleet was in the Sledway (off Harwich). They thought that the Dutch intended to sail towards their own coast to draw the English on to the sands. To counter this they would sail towards the Dutch coast and anchor at the back of the Middle Ground before attempting the Narrow Ground.

On 19 July Allin wrote: 'We sailed within a mile of the Buoy on the Middle Ground and all the fleet riding towards the Shoe. It was ordered that Captain Elliott in the *Revenge*' (3rd Rate) 'should command ten frigates and ten fireships' (the organisation recommended by Monck and Rupert) 'to sail ahead of the fleet to force the enemy to give ground; the fleet to follow close after them with rules for their return.'

The manoeuvre agreed on by the Generals was carried out on 22 July, and the fleet passed the Narrow Ground and entered the Gunfleet. Allin with the White Squadron weighed at low water and ran down as low as the buoy of the Middle Ground and kept on. The Red and Blue Squadrons anchored short of that buoy.

This deployment forced the Dutch to withdraw, and at dawn on 23 July the English fleet followed them.

16

The St. James's Day Fight[1]

The two fleets were of practically the same strength, 89 ships in the English fleet and 88 in the Dutch (both figures exclusive of fireships). In the Red Squadron (directly under the Generals) Jordan was Vice-Admiral and Holmes Rear-Admiral; in Allin's White Squadron he had Teddiman and Utber (his brother-in-law) as Vice- and Rear-Admirals respectively; Smith commanded the Blue Squadron with Spragge and Kempthorne as Vice- and Rear-Admirals. In the Dutch fleet the Van Squadron was commanded by Jan Evertsen, the Centre Squadron by de Ruyter personally, and the Rear Squadron by Tromp.

On 20 July Sir Thomas Clifford, writing to the Earl of Arlington (Secretary of State) from the *Royal Charles,* reported, 'Our cabins are all broken down and we are a clear ship.' The next day he wrote again to Arlington, saying, 'Our men are in better heart now than they probably will be after two or three nights without their hammocks, for every ship now is a clear ship'. Clearing a ship for action created some discomfort for everybody, not only in the seventeenth century! On 23 July Clifford wrote, in a further letter to Arlington, 'The Generals were all day on deck, and sometimes a little rough with the pilots'. Tempers were perhaps getting a little brittle on account of the approaching battle.

Silas Taylor, a Navy Commissioner, wrote to Albemarle's Secretary, Joseph Williamson, on 24 July, 'At 4 a.m. the English fleet sailed cheerfully, beating drums.'

The official account of the battle on St. James's Day, as supplied by the Generals, was published in the London Gazette.

On 23 July the fleet set sail from the Gunfleet with a slight easterly and variable wind, the enemy falling back eastward before it. At 8.0 p.m. they anchored, Orfordness being 3½ leagues away W by N, the Dutch fleet 5 leagues distant from them SE by E. During the night there was a thunderstorm and the *Jersey* (4th Rate) lost her mainmast, struck by lightning and destroyed,

---

[1] 'The Rupert and Monck Letter Book', op. cit. pp. 266 f.

so that the ship had to be sent off to Sheerness to be repaired. Anchor was weighed at 6.0 a.m. on 24 July. It was very hazy and there was no sight of the enemy till 4.0 p.m. when the Dutch, who had the wind, were observed standing towards the English fleet. However, the enemy tacked and stood away and both fleets anchored that night.

On the morning of 25 July the English fleet, 11 leagues off Orfordness, weighed anchor with a strong NNE wind and discovered the enemy two hours later. They stood with the intention of engaging them van to van. By 6.0 p.m. the English fleet was within two leagues of the Dutch, the wind N by W. The Dutch then drew up their fleet into a half moon, hoping, it was supposed, to weather all, or a greater part of, the English fleet with either their van or their rear. About 9.30 a.m. both vans were within range and the White Squadron was before long engaged with the Dutch van. Within half an hour the Red Squadron too was in action, and then the Blue; so that by noon the whole of the English fleet had opened fire. At 11.0 a.m. the Dutch van began to give way and by about 1.0 p.m. the whole of it bore away. About half an hour later the *Royal Katherine, St. George*, the *Rupert* and another ship of the White Squadron came out of the line to repair; at which time a ship in the enemy line was seen to blow up. At about 3.0 p.m. Sir Robert Holmes's ship, with topmasts disabled, lay by to repair. Between 2.0 and 3.0 a.m. the *Resolution* was burnt by a fireship, and the *Sovereign* sank a Dutch fireship, whilst the topmast of de Ruyter's flagship was shot down. About 3.0 p.m. the fleet flagship, the *Royal Charles* came out of the line to repair. She had fought de Ruyter's ship for a long time within musket shot. After some half-hour's repair, she stood in again and once more engaged the Dutch flagship to such effect that the latter's tackle was shot away and she had to be towed out of the line by boats. Two more Dutch ships were seen to blow up about the middle of their line, and not long after that another. 'About four de Ruyter made all the sail he could, and ran for it, but made frequent tacks to fetch off his maimed ships'. Their whole van then 'began to give ground and run for it', pursued by the Red and White Squadrons, which followed them till night fell. About 7.0 p.m. the *Royal James* took the *Tholen* of 60 guns, and soon afterwards the *Sneek* of 66 guns, both new ships. Tromp, with the Dutch rear squadron, continued fighting against the Blue Squadron until darkness separated them.

That night the wind veered from NNE to SW, and thus at 4.0 a.m. on 26 July the Dutch had it, but it was very slight. The English ships were not able to keep up with the Dutch, but the little *Fan Fan*, a sloop recently built at Harwich for Prince Rupert, came up with her oars to de Ruyter's flagship and bringing her two little guns to one side, continued for nearly an hour 'plying broadside and broadside, to the great laughter of our men, and the indignation of the Dutch to see their Admiral so soundly chased'. Eventually the Dutch ships managed to hit the *Fan Fan* with 'two or three shot between wind and water, with which she retired'.

The English fleet continued the pursuit over many flats and banks, till it came too near the shore for the great ships to follow, leaving the smaller frigates to continue the chase. These went on till the Dutch got into the Zeeland Durloo Channel. De Ruyter's own ship was so much battered by the frigates, that, if their had been enough wind for the great ships to come up, his ship and most of those with him would have been destroyed.

At 2.0 p.m., the wind veering to NE, the Generals saw Tromp and his squadron being chased by the Blue Squadron. At 8.0 p.m., therefore, the *Royal Charles* tacked to get between Tromp and home, anchoring at midnight with the intention of tracking him the following morning. The rest of the fleet, 'not anchoring so close, fell more to the leeard'.

Early in the morning of 27 July the Dutch appeared to the windward. Sir Jeremy Smith had apparently 'laid by, for fear of shoal ground, the enemy in the meantime stealing away from him'. The Red Squadron could not get up with them, though they gave them a close chase till they had only six fathoms of water off the Isle of Schoowen. At 2.0 p.m. the wind favoured Tromp, who stole into Weiling to join the rest of the fleet.

Sir Robert Holmes, whose ship had been damaged so that he had to pull out of the line to repair, subsequently joined the Blue Squadron. After the battle he called Sir Jeremy Smith a coward, in front of the two Generals, for failing to pursue Tromp. Albemarle wrote to the King defending Smith, whom he said had been falsely accused and had more men killed and wounded in his ship than any other in the fleet, and his ship, so it appeared, had 'received more shot'. Smith was subsequently 'examined' with the result that the King and the Duke of York were fully satisfied of his valour. Smith brought counter-charges against Holmes for cowardice. However, the King, having examined these, 'found' no cause to suspect Sir Robert of cowardice, but 'thinks that on the night of the 26th he yielded to easily to the opinion of his pilot, without consulting those of other ships, muzzled his ship, and thus obliged the squadron to do the same, and so the enemy, which might have been driven into the body of the King's fleet, then returning from the pursuit; was allowed to escape'.

It looks as though Smith got the better of this argument! However, later, as a result of it, they fought a duel. The enmity between these two men may have stemmed from the Civil War, when Smith fought for Parliament and Holmes for the King.

Allin, in his account of the St. James's Day Fight[2], notes the night of 23 July as 'a sad night of thunder, lightning and rain, the wind variable, and very dark. We anchored about 7 o'clock'. On the following day both fleets manoeuvred but there was no contact. On 25 July, the Feast of St. James the Apostle, action began between 9.0 and 10.0 a.m. Allin describes as follows the action of his squadron. 'There were' (of the Dutch) 'two Vice-Admirals with about 5 ships more, then another Admiral. Sir Tho. Teddiman' (in the *Royal Katherine*, 2nd Rate, Vice-Admiral of the White) 'fought bravely upon his party, although the *St. George*' (2nd Rate, John Cappin) 'and *Ann*' (3rd Rate, Robert Moulton) 'did him no service and the *Old James*' (2nd Rate,

---

[2] 'The Journals of Sir Thomas Allin', op. cit. pp. 277 f.

Edmund Seaman) 'did us as little. . . . The Rear-Admiral's' (Richard Utber, Rear-Admiral of the White and Allin's brother-in-law in the *Rupert*, 3rd Rate) 'division did us little help. We fell in close and in 4 hours time put them to bear up from us. We maimed two Admirals, that one bore away to leeward into company of 5 ships to help him, his main topsail yard shot a-pieces. We followed them so close upon the rear, they being come to fire only their stern guns. The *Sneek* of Harlingen yielded; a ship of 66 guns, the first voyage, 320 men, but great store killed and wounded. . . . About 7 Vice-Admiral Bankert forsook his ship in his boat and went aboard another ship . . . and the ship under him . . . the *Tholen*, 60 guns, 270 men, 440 tons, 24 guns brass, yielded, and being much disenabled and much water in her, Sir Tho. Teddiman's boats, the *Warspite*' (3rd Rate) 'and others having rifled her, left her with several Dutchmen in her. My Lieutenant going aboard set her on fire also about 9 o'clock at night, and being dark we tacked to our fleet, being all this day little wind. Our fireships lost very foolishly; they going on without order were torn a-pieces and then forced to burn themselves without doing any execution. Our Admiral division' (i.e. the centre division of the Red Squadron) 'plyed their second squadron' (de Ruyter) 'until his fore topsail yard of the *Charles*' (1st Rate, fleet flagship) 'was shot a-pieces and so fell off to recruit. The *Henry*' (2nd Rate, Sir Robert Holmes) 'much disenabled, that he went out of the fleet. The' (Dutch) 'rear squadron tacked to get the wind of us, but the Blue Squadron tacked with them, that we lost sight of them and did no execution upon the enemy. We had the *Resolution*' (3rd Rate, Blue Squadron) 'burnt by one of their fireships. Captain Hannon saved, but lost part of his hand. A great quarrel arose between Sir Ro. Holmes' (after he repaired the damage to the *Henry* he joined the Blue Squadron) 'and Sir Jeremy Smith' (Admiral of the Blue Squadron) 'for miscarriages that day'.

Coherent narrative is not Allin's strong point, but he does manage to convey a picture of the fighting.

The next day, 26 July, an unlucky shot for Allin hit his 'main topsail halliards block, which strick me with splinters in my cheek, a long rent and thought my jawbone had been broke; another above my elbow, a deep hole and dangerous; another upon the top of my arm, much contused and the skin broke. These put me to great dolour, and a small blow upon my thumb.' However, poor Allin was pretty tough and he recovered quite soon.

They pursued the Dutch fleet on 27 July, but the Dutch got into the shallow waters off their coast and so escaped.

On 28 July Rupert and Albemarle, having to leave the partially disabled *Royal Charles*, transferred to the *Royal James*, much to the annoyance of Allin who himself had to move to the 1st Rate *Sovereign*. At a Council of War it was decided that the fleet would go to the Texel, but that ships with unserviceable masts would return home.

The fleet anchored off the Texel on 7 August after an undisturbed passage. Allin went on board the *Royal James* to attend a Council of War on the action that should be taken next. The plan agreed was that 900 men should be sent to land on Vlie Island under command of Sir Robert Holmes and do what damage they could. Each division of the fleet (there being three divisions in each squadron) was to provide 100 men, and Holmes, with this detachment, went ashore on the island the following day.

Allin records on 9 August that 'We saw divers smokes arise upon the land, which made us judge that Sir Robt Holmes was prosperous, and they continued burning all the night'. Holmes's landing party had, it was reported, burnt 150 ships, many of which were very rich merchantmen. 'Some', wrote Allin 'bound to Archangel, some to Guinea and some to all parts of the East, some come home. So great a loss the Dutch never had. This morning they burnt the town of Schelling, as big as Portsmouth. They burnt two men-of-war 28 guns'.

On 15 August Samuel Pepys received a letter from Sir William Coventry telling him about the above episode. Pepys hurried to St. James's, it being the day for attending the Duke of York. It had been reported that the Dutch ships burnt were generally good merchant ships, some laden and supposed to be rich. Five fireships had been sent amongst them. The Duke of York said that the intention had been only to land and burn some stores, but the ships were seen and the advantage taken.

On 26 August Sir William Penn, who had just come from the fleet, told Pepys that the burning of the ships and town by Holmes was 'a great thing' and a great loss to the enemy.

17

The Medway Raid and the End of the Second Dutch War

As the campaigning season drew to an end, Parliament had had enough. Money for the fleet dried up and ships were laid up. Though the politicians, as so often in our history, were oblivious to the risks, the dangers of leaving the country virtually defenceless were all too obvious in naval circles. On 31 October 1666 Pepys wrote[1] 'Everybody fears an invasion the next year.'

In the spring of 1667, with the Dutch having a fleet in readiness, the threat under which the country lay became apparent even to Parliament — but it was too late. England had ships but not the men to man them. In March preparations were made to fortify Sheerness and the yard at Portsmouth, and there were worries about the landing of Dutch troops on the undefended coasts. The Duke of York expected the Dutch to blockade the English fleet in the Thames and on 18 March he went off to Harwich to prepare fortifications there.

On 23 March Penn returned from Chatham, where he had been considering means of fortifying the River Medway, in which many of the great ships were lying. Penn proposed stakes connected by a chain covered by guns 'to keep the enemy from coming up to burn our ships'. The folly of a Parliament which had thus thrown away the victory gained by English seamen is almost incredible. They had forgotten the King's preamble to the 1662 Articles of War: 'It is upon the navy under the Providence of God that the safety, honour, and welfare of this realm do chiefly attend.'

Yet on 3 April Pepys wrote that every demand for money was met with the answer from Sir George Cartaret, 'No money'. On 5 May Coventry told Pepys that the Dutch had fired 400 or 500 shot into Burntisland on the Forth, but had caused no damage. The Dutch were determined on revenge for the burning of their merchant fleet. Before the end of 1666 the Grand Pensionary of Holland, de Witt, had had soundings made in the Thames, and he now despatched de Ruyter with 60 or 70 ships of the line with orders, says Captain A.T. Mahan[2] to destroy ships at Chatham and in the Medway, and to take possession of Sheerness.

---

[1] *The Diary of Samuel Pepys*, op. cit.
[2] Captain A.T. Mahan *The Influence of Sea Power upon History* op. cit. pp. 131-2.

By 3 June it was reported in London that the Dutch were at sea with a fleet of 80 warships and 20 fireships, 'while', wrote Pepys, 'there is not an English ship at sea to deal with them'. Meanwhile, the English Ambassadors were at Breda negotiating peace terms. Pepys wrote that the Dutch regarded them as coming to beg for peace and were treating them accordingly.

On 8 June the Dutch were reported off Harwich with 80 sail and their guns had been heard the previous day at Bednall Green. On 10 June they had come as high as the Nore and Coventry was pressing for all possible fireships. Albemarle had arrived, and with his usual energy in a crisis he had ordered two frigates to be brought in a line between the block houses at Greenwich, and was arranging the hurried strengthening of the boom and chain across the Medway.

On 11 June news came that the Dutch had captured Sheerness after a two to three hours battle. Fireships were in great demand and an Order in Council authorised the requisitioning of any ships for this purpose. It was far too late. Albemarle had thought that the strengthening of the Medway defences would suffice, but on 12 June the Dutch succeeded in breaking through. The *Royal Charles* was towed away by them (though Pett had been ordered to take her further upstream) and the *Royal James*, *Oak*, and *London* were burnt.

On 13 June the King and the Duke of York arrived to take personal charge and were down the Thames by 4.0 a.m., ordering the sinking of ships at Barking Creek to stop the Dutch coming higher up the river. Pepys was in such a panic that he packed his wife and father off into the country with £1,300 in gold 'in their night-bag'.

Penn told Pepys that even if they had had the money and stores they could not have set out a fleet that year because from 10,000 to 15,000 seamen had been allowed to man the merchant ships which went abroad!

On 21 July peace between England on one hand and the United Provinces, France, and Denmark on the other was concluded by the Treaty of Breda.

Though a humiliation, the Dutch incursion into the Medway had not materially reduced the strength of the Navy. Both nations wanted the war to end, but the Dutch had secured a badly needed bargaining counter at the negotiating table, for they had gained, though temporary, command of the sea. Nevertheless, the terms reflected their relative strengths, should the contest be resumed, for the Dutch relinquished what are now New York and New Jersey to England and confirmed the salutes required to the English flag in the Narrow Seas.

Although peace had been signed on 21 July, de Ruyter had not heard of it. After failing at Harwich on 2 July, he returned to the mouth of the Thames. There he left half of his fleet under the command of Admiral van Maes, and with 29 men-of-war and 5 fireships he was off the Isle of Wight on 13 July. A large fleet of English merchant ships, homeward bound, had passed Plymouth on 7 July. De Ruyter was well placed to capture them, but fortunately Allin, who was then in command at Plymouth, heard of de Ruyter's appearance and sent a ship after the merchantmen, which caught up with them and diverted them into Dartmouth. De Ruyter arrived there on 18 July, but it was too difficult for him to attack the harbour.

Still unaware of the peace, de Ruyter was off Plymouth Sound on 29 July. On 30 July Allin sent off officers under a flag of truce to tell him the war was over. De Ruyter entertained these officers, and in return for his hospitality Allin sent him a supply of fresh meat and appropriate liquid refreshment.

On 16 August 1668 Allin sailed in the new 3rd Rate *Monmouth* in command of a squadron for the Mediterranean consisting of nine men-of-war, one fireship, and a ketch. On 6 September he recorded: 'About noon we saw 6 ships, which proved to be Holland men-of-war. About 4 afternoon there came a Captain of theirs, an Irishman, as it was told me, preferred for coming up the river of Chatham. He was sent by Rear Admiral Van de Zaen to present his respects and service and that he would fold his flag and salute me with 15 guns'.[3]

---

[3] *The Navy Records Society*, Vol. 80. 'The Journal of Sir Thomas Allin', ed. R.C. Anderson, Vol. II p. 40.

18

The Opening of the Third Dutch War[1]

The King and many of his subjects, particularly in the Navy, had been furious at the way in which Parliamentary parsimony had deprived England of a fleet at sea in 1667 and so enabled the Dutch to stage their humiliating raid on the Medway. There was a desire for revenge and it was soon apparent that a third outbreak of war could not be long delayed.

When the war ended in 1667 the United Provinces had France as an ally against England. In the following year, however, France had joined England and Sweden in the Triple Alliance. In 1670 King Charles II, in the secret Treaty of Dover, arranged to join Louis XIV of France in an attack on the Dutch.

France had been recently engaged in constructing a formidable navy. French naval affairs had been in the very capable hands of the great Jean-Baptiste Colbert from about 1660, first in his position as Finance Minister and later as *Intendant de la Marine*. He had set about rebuilding the fleet which he had found in a deplorable condition. Largely owing to his genius at finance France had been able to purchase Dunkirk from England in 1662. With Dunkirk he acquired the yards that built the famous Dunkirk frigates which have already have extensive mention in these pages. Also, Sir Anthony Deane was prominent amongst the foreign experts whom he got to advise him on the design and construction of men-of-war. In a few years Colbert had a fleet of new and well-built ships.

During the Second Dutch War France had been ineffective at sea. Now she had a navy powerful enough to make her a valuable ally of England at sea — that is, if she were determined to use it effectively. Events were to show that there was no such determination, for King Louis did not want his nice new fleet to suffer loss, and could regard with equanimity the mutual battering of English and Dutch warships. So while England, with some French help, engaged the Dutch at sea, the French army would invade the Netherlands.

In the summer of 1671 de Ruyter was at sea in command of a moderate sized fleet of 37 ships, organised into the usual three squadrons. The purpose

---

[1] *Navy Records Society*, Vol. 86, 'Journals and Narratives of the Third Dutch War', ed. R.C. Anderson.

of the fleet was to carry out exercises, primarily to train the flag officers of the three squadrons and also captains of ships. Whilst these exercises were being carried out there occurred an incident which played a part in the outbreak of war. It did provide a nice excuse for the English, but that it arose at all was the fault of the Dutch.

On 14 August 1671 the Dutch fleet lay at anchor about midway between Walcheren and Orfordness. Through the fleet came the English Royal yacht *Mercia* returning from Holland with the wife of the English Ambassador, Lady Temple. As no notice was taken of her, the *Mercia* fired 'several shotted guns'. De Ruyter's ship was careened and unable to reply to what he thought was a salute (apparently not noticing the fall of shot), but van Ghent, second-in-command of the fleet, fired seven guns as a reply and de Ruyter, when he could, added nine more. Van Ghent, a friend of Lady Temple, had found out that she was the important person on board. However, Captain Thomas Crow, commanding the yacht, told him that he had not fired a salute, but live rounds as a demand that he strike his flag and lower his topsail in salute. Van Ghent replied that his orders did not allow him to do so. As we have seen, this recognition of English sovereignty in the Narrow Seas had not been annulled by the Treaty of Breda. However, Crow did not try to enforce the order, and on his return to England he was committed to the Tower for failing to do so. Though what poor Crow was expected to do with his yacht against the Dutch fleet, with the added responsibility of looking after Lady Temple, is far from clear.

Some months later, in January 1672, the King requested a written acknowledgement of his 'Dominion of the Seas' and an undertaking that in future Dutch ships or fleets would strike their flags and lower their topsails to any ship or ships carrying English colours. The Dutch, on weak ground, replied that they considered themselves bound by the Treaty of Breda, in which they had undertaken to render the salute 'as it had always been rendered, but maintained that there had been no suggestion that a whole fleet had to strike to a single yacht (but there had been no suggestion that they should not!). They added that they would investigate the question and would act in accordance with precedent. It would appear that the Dutch had resented this clause in the treaty and had issued orders to minimise it.

The Dutch do not appear to have undertaken much investigation, for on 25 January they mobilised their fleet. This seems to have been understood in England as a declaration of war, for on 4 February Downing, the English Ambassador, left The Hague and a fortnight later orders were sent to English men-of-war in the Mediterranean to take and destroy all Dutch ships.

On 13 March that fiery Irishman Sir Robert Holmes intercepted and attacked the convoy of Dutch merchant ships known as the 'Smyrna Fleet', homeward bound from the Mediterranean. However, warnings had gone out from Holland to commanders overseas of the possibility of war, and the convoy commander had organised the escorting men-of-war and the merchant ships (which were armed) into three squadrons.

Holmes had bitten off more than he could chew. By nightfall two of his men-of-war were disabled and he had not captured or destroyed any of his opponents. He was reinforced during the night and renewed his attack the following morning. He did eventually sink one Dutch warship and capture three merchant ships, but the bulk of the valuable convoy got safely back to Holland.

England's official declaration of war followed on 17 March and France declared war on the United Provinces on 28 March. Plans had already been made for a combined fleet of three squadrons under the command of the Duke of York. The Red and Blue Squadrons were to be English, and the French were to supply the White Squadron. This gave them the second senior squadron and it was also appropriate because the flag of France was white. Count d'Estrées was to command the French squadron and to be second-in-command to the Duke of York. The Red Squadron was, of course, directly under the Duke of York, whilst the Blue Squadron was commanded by the Earl of Sandwich. But if the Duke of York became a casualty, or was otherwise incapacitated, Sandwich, and not d'Estrées, was to take over command of the fleet. It had been agreed that the squadrons were to be ready on 25 April, the English in the Downs and the French at Brest. The French were to sail for Start Point and the junction of the two fleets would be somewhere between there and the Downs.

The Duke of York's flagship was the 1st Rate *Prince*, built in 1670 and commissioned in January 1672. She was commanded by Captain John Cox and, as a principal flagship, she had a second captain. This was Captain John Narbrough who, in this first commission of the ship, was described as 'Captain John Narbrough, First Lieutenant of his Majesty's ship *Prince* under the command of Captain John Cox Esq, Commissioner of his Majesty's Navy'. The *Prince* had been designed by Sir Phineas Pett. She had a narrow hull and Pett aimed to get the centre of gravity as low as possible by mounting as many of the heavy guns as possible below the upper deck. Narbrough called her a 'great and brave-contrived ship', but it was soon apparent that when fully loaded she carried the lowest tier of her guns only 3½ feet from the water and was 'a little tender sided' — in other words, rather unstable. Narbrough considered that if she were girdled she would be one of the finest ships afloat. But with impending war it was too late to have that done. The Duke's temporary remedy was described by Narbrough, by an entry in his Journal on 10 April 1672: 'As the ship carried her guns so near the water and being a little tender-sided, the Duke of York ordered her masts to be shortened'.

On 23 April 1672 Narbrough mentions the King coming on board the *Prince*. The flags 'put aboard' were a silk ensign, silk jack, silk pendant at every yardarm and the topmast head; and at the main-topmast head the 'silk Standard of England'; and at fore-topmast head the 'silk flag red with yellow anchor and cable in the fly'; and at the mizzen-topmast head a Union flag. These were all flying while the King was on board. When the King left the ship, leaving the Duke aboard, the Standard and Union flag were struck, and the red flag, charged with the foul anchor, was transferred to the main-topmast head.

The Dutch had appointed de Ruyter, Lieutenant-Admiral of Holland, commander of the fleet of 72 men-of-war planned for the year 1672. In accordance with the practice of the time, he had direct command of the centre squadron. The Van, or 2nd squadron, was commanded by Bankert, the Lieutenant-Admiral of Zeeland; and Van Ghent, Lieutenant-Admiral of Amsterdam, commanded the Rear, or 3rd squadron. It was the latter who had had the embarrassing interview with the Captain of the *Mercia*. The Vice-Admiral of the Van was Aert Van Nas, Lieutenant-Admiral of the Maas, and he was designated as fleet commander, should de Ruyter be killed or disabled.

On 26 April the *Prince* sailed with some 24 ships of the fleet, with both the King and the Duke of York on board, and at 1.0 p.m. anchored on the Cant, four miles from the buoy of the Nore which bore W by N from the *Prince*. A gun was fired to called the Flag Officers aboard. In the afternoon the King knighted Commissioner John Cox and then left the ship and boarded his yacht.

On 29 April de Ruyter left the Texel with 35 ships. Bankert was due to join him there with his Zeeland Squadron, but the Zeeland authorities had stopped him from sailing until they knew that de Ruyter was at sea. They were presumably nervous in case his squadron should be attacked by superior numbers before the junction had been effected. That information did not arrive until 2 May, so de Ruyter was forced to wait.

Meanwhile, Holmes had been sent by the Duke of York to see d'Estrées and request him to join the English fleet at Portsmouth. On 28 April Holmes met d'Estrées, and the next day the French fleet sailed, arriving at Spithead on 3 May. There they were met on 5 May by the English fleet of 38 ships which had sailed from the Nore on 29 April. On that day de Ruyter was off Dover; but when he learned that he had not been able to attack the English fleet before its junction with the French (the fault of the Zeeland authorities), he decided to return to the Dutch coast and await reinforcements.

The squadron under the command of Vice-Admiral Comte d'Estrées consisted of 30 men-of-war, accompanied by fireships, smaller armed craft and store ships. The organisation of the English fleet by squadrons was as follows. (The name of the ship is followed by the number of its rate or M for armed merchantman; ships are shown in the order of their sailing — flagships, as was normal at the time, being in the centre of their division.)

Red Squadron: Commander, the General (the Duke of York)
    1st Division: Commander, the Vice-Admiral of the Fleet
    Resolution (3) *Bristol* (4) *London* (1) (Vice-Admiral) *Supply* (fireship)
    Algier (M) *Old James* (2) *Sweepstake* (5) *Dunkirk* (3) *Diamond* (4) *Monck* (3).
    2nd Division: Commander, the General (Duke of York)
    Yarmouth (4) *Cambridge* (3) *Fairfax* (3) *Victory* (2) *Prince* (1) (General)
    Katherine (fireship) *Castle* (fireship) *Bantam* (fireship) *Nightingale* (5)
    St. Michael (2) *Monmouth* (3) *Adventure* (4) *Robert* (fireship).

3rd Division: Commander, the Rear-Admiral of the Red Squadron
York (3) Greenwich (4) Charles (1) (Rear-Admiral) Ann (3) Christopher (fireship) Portsmouth (sloop) Rainbow (2) Forester (5) Dover (4) Revenge (3).

Blue Squadron: Commander, the Earl of Sandwich
1st Division: Commander, the Rear-Admiral of the Blue Squadron
Gloucester (3) Bonaventure (4) St. George (2) St. Andrew (1) (Rear-Admiral) Success (fireship) Pearl (5) Spy (M) Warspite (3) Antelope (4) French Ruby (2).
2nd Division: Commander, the Earl of Sandwich
Mountagu (3) Falcon (5) Leopard (4) Rupert (3) Royal James (1) (Admiral) Alice and Francis (fireship) Henry (2) Edgar (3) Crown (4).
3rd Division: Commander, the Vice-Admiral of the Blue Squadron
Mary (3) Ruby (4) Triumph (2) Sovereign (1) (Vice-Admiral) Unicorn (2) Tiger (4) Plymouth (3) Francis (fireship) Emsworth (sloop).

Narbrough says that on 5 May the flagship hoisted the Union flag at the mizzen peak, 'a signal to have all the fleet fall in their stations as is prescribed in their Fighting Instructions, when we fight by a wind with the enemy'. A French ketch arrived with news of the French fleet riding at Spithead. The English fleet stood in for St. Helens and eventually saw 30 sail of the French fleet. The next day news was received that the Dutch fleet, of some 90 sail, was on the back of the Goodwins.

The French squadron joined the English squadrons on 7 May. It consisted of 34 men-of-war 'great and small', 6 fireships, and 6 ketches. The French flag-ships looked very good, about the same size as the smaller English 2nd Rates. Their other ships were equivalent to 3rd, 4th, and 5th Rates. In the evening the Dutch fleet was reported as riding between Folkestone and Fairlight.

On 8 May the Anglo-French fleet sailed in search of the Dutch. On the morning of 12 May the fleet was abreast of Newhaven, about five miles off the shore, and at 8.0 p.m. anchored the same distance abreast of Beachy Head. On 14 May, at 11.0 a.m. they anchored off Dungeness, and received information that the Dutch had lain about the Galloper Sand on 12 May. In fact, on 13 May the enemy, by now reinforced, anchored at the entrance to the King's Channel, south of Harwich.

On 10 May a small English force of six men-of-war had left the Nore and by 13 May were just below the Middle Ground. The next day de Ruyter sent Van Ghent up the Thames Estuary with 12 of his lighter men-of-war. Captain Coleman, commanding the English detachment, fell back before them as far as Sheerness. Van Ghent found the defences too strong for him and had to retreat in his turn, followed by Coleman, until on 16 May he rejoined the main body of the Dutch fleet. In the evening of 15 May the Allies anchored south east of the Goodwin Sands. At a Council of War on 17 May it was decided that, if the fleet were separated by bad weather, the rendezvous should be Sole Bay if the wind were southerly and Portsmouth if it were northerly.

At 8.0 p.m. on 18 May eight sail were spotted to the NE and it was thought they belonged to the Dutch fleet. On the Prince orders were given to knock down all the standing cabins and heave the boards into the sea, and the ship was made clear to fight. However, the ships turned out to be the frigate *Gloucester*, Captain Coleman, and the rest of his small force. Coleman reported that the Dutch lay about the Galloper and Gabbard Sands. In the evening the fleet anchored with the North Foreland bearing SW.

On Sunday 19 May, writes Narbrough, the fleet weighed and at 6.0 a.m. made sail and stood NE. Several sails appeared ENE and the scouts were seen firing their guns and their topgallant sails flying, indicating that they were in sight of the enemy. The fleet made sail towards them and at 9.0 a.m. the whole Dutch fleet was in sight standing SE. At 2.0 p.m. they were within three leagues of the Dutch, and at 5.0 p.m. 'got the length of their whole fleet, our van against their van and our body against their body, within three miles of them on their weather gauge'. The French squadron was in the van and the Blue Squadron brought up the rear, 'our seamen being very desirous to fight them'. Narbrough thought that the Allied fleet had a superiority of at least 16 or 17 sail as he could only count 85 Dutch sail with three masts and 42 galliots and other small craft; whereas in the Allied fleet there were 103 ships and 28 ketches, etc.

By 7.0 p.m. they were within two miles of the Dutch but were running into shallow waters (where the cunning de Ruyter, with his much shallower draught ships, was seeking to entice them). The night passed, therefore, without serious action, though there was some long range gun fire.

At about 2 o'clock in the morning of 20 May it was very foggy. There was also a WSW gale which prevented the lower tier of the *Prince's* guns being 'carried out'. At 9.0 a.m. the fog lifted and Narbrough saw the Dutch fleet astern, about four leagues away and standing NW. The Allied fleet tacked and stood towards them; whereupon the Dutch fleet also tacked and stood towards their own coast. By midday the Allied fleet had got the length of the Dutch (i.e. were sailing in line parallel with the Dutch line) about two miles from them and with the weather gauge. They continued thus till 3.0 p.m., but then it blew hard and the sea became so rough that the lower tier of guns could not be run out, and it was impracticable to fight. That night the Allied fleet anchored about six leagues from the Flanders banks.

The morning of 21 May dawned with heavy weather, a WSW wind, and no Dutch in sight. The Galloper Sand was about one mile ahead NW. The fleet shaped a course for Sole Bay and anchored, remaining there for some days, taking on provisions and heeling ships for cleaning, English and French frigates were sent out to scout and the Duke of York gave orders that no ships should moor in order that they should be ready for action quickly if the Dutch appeared.

19

The Battle of Sole Bay[1]

There are a number of contemporary accounts of the battle of Sole Bay. In his version, Narborough says that the *Prince* had been heeled for cleaning at 2.0 a.m. on 21 May. At 3.30 a.m. on 28 May he heard guns firing to the East; then a French scout was seen standing towards the fleet with topgallant sails flying and guns firing. Astern, and about a league from her, came the Dutch fleet. Narbrough immediately gave orders for the ship to be righted and made clear, and he informed Sir John Cox that the Dutch fleet was standing in with the wind ESE. He then ordered the anchor to be got aboard, and went to inform the Duke of York, who gave orders for the fleet to get under sail. At 5.30 a.m. the *Prince* was under sail in a very smooth sea. They stood off North 'to receive the Dutch Admiral'. The Blue Squadron, commanded by the Earl of Sandwich, which was riding North of the Red Squadron, got away and stood ahead of the Red and 'stood bravely up to the Dutch'. Several of the English large frigates (4th Rates), as well as fireships and ketches, lay close to the shore and, with the lack of wind, had difficulty in getting out.

The fight began at 7.0 a.m., with the *Royal James*, Sandwich's flagship of the Blue Squadron, opening fire. The Blue and Red Squadrons were sailing North on the starboard tack, the former leading; but the French squadron, against the Duke of York's orders, was heading South on the port tack. De Ruyter detached one squadron to engage it.

By 8.0 a.m. the *Prince* was in fierce contest with de Ruyter's flagship and six other Dutch ships, at 'about a musket shot distance'. No other ship of the Red Squadron had yet been able to get up to assist owing to the light wind. The sea, says Narbrough was 'as the saying is, as smooth as a milk bowl'. The Duke of York 'went fore and aft in the ship and cheered up the men to fight, which did encourage them very much'. Between 9.0 and 10.0 a.m. Sir John Cox was killed by a round shot whilst he was standing close to the Duke of York on the poop. Narbrough then took over command of the ship. (He commented on the Duke's bravery and his navigational knowledge; 'he is

---

[1] 'Journals and Narratives of the Third Dutch War', op. cit.

General, soldier, pilot, master, seaman'). Between 11.0 a.m. and noon, the *Prince* suffered much damage to masts and rigging. The main topmast was brought down by a shot, and the mass of rigging brought down with it prevented the upper deck guns being used; nor could the ship be worked to keep the wind. Narbrough had two boats manned to tow the ship's head away from the enemy and towards their own ships 'which they did in time'.

The Duke of York, his flagship disabled, ordered his boat to be got ready, 'with the Standard' and then transferred to the *St. Michael*, commanded by Sir Robert Holmes and in the Duke's own division in the Red Squadron. Narbrough's main object now was to get his ship out of action in order to carry out temporary repairs. He got her on to the other tack with foresail, mizzen, and mizzen topsail.

Sir Edward Spragge, Vice-Admiral of the Red, in his account of the action, says that the Dutch attacked before the Allied fleet could come into line. The Blue and Red Squadrons stood with heads to the North, the French with heads to the South. The Dutch Zeeland Squadron stood with the French, and the English squadrons did not see either of them all day. The first guns were fired by the Blue Squadron at 7.0 a.m. At 8.0 a.m. the fleets on both sides were heavily engaged. At about 9.0 a.m. a Dutch flagship, with fourteen sail and two fireships bore down on Spragge's division against a stout opposition. One of the enemy's great ships sank within musket shot of Spragge's own ship, the *London*. The ships of his division which received the most damage were those in the rear. About 2.0 p.m., when the fighting had died down, Spragge saw the *Prince* and sent his pinnace to see how the Duke had faired, and to ask what he wished Spragge to do; but he had no sooner despatched the pinnace, when he saw the Royal Standard 'spread' in the *St. Michael*, with his head to the South, and with him of his own division the *Victory*, *Fairfax*, *Cambridge* and *Phoenix*.

At 4.30 p.m. Spragge tacked and got ahead of the Duke under his lee, for he had seen that the *St. Michael* was somewhat disabled. At 5.0 p.m. the Duke of York came aboard the *London*. About 40 Dutch were then to windward within gunshot and about the same number to leeward. The Vice-Admiral of the Blue was then to windward of the most weathermost line of the enemy with some ten or twelve sail. De Ruyter's own squadron was that next to the Red Squadron on the weather side, but it was being well repulsed and at about 8.0 p.m. the Dutch bore away. The *Dartmouth* had destroyed one enemy fireship and taken another.

Seeing the 2nd Rate *Royal Katherine* stationary to leeward, Spragge sent an officer to board it and find out what was amiss. He returned with the extraordinary information that she had been taken by the enemy and that the captain and officers had been taken prisoners to Holland, but that the boatswain, gunner, and the people of the gun deck had retaken the ship, forcing some of the Dutch overboard and making prisoners of the rest. They now intended to sail for Harwich to secure the ship.

Spragge disabled a small Dutch frigate on his weather bow by shooting down his main yard, main topsail yard, and spritsail yard.

By about 9.0 p.m. the Duke had about 24 or 25 sail — all the Red Squadron in fact except the *Ruby*. He ordered rigging to be refitted and the squadron to follow the enemy, keeping the weather gauge of them. They kept the wind and stood all night to the eastward within half a league of the enemy till 4 o'clock the next morning. At that time Spragge was summoned by the Duke of York, who ordered a Council of War at 10.0 a.m. The Council decided that, owing to the scarcity of ammunition and the number of ships which had suffered severe damage to masts and sails, they should return to the Thames and refit. However, no sooner had this decision been made than the Dutch were seen approaching. At about 2.0 p.m. the fleet was in line, abreast of the enemy — except for the French, who, wrote Spragge, 'will never be as they ought to be'. Soon there arose a fog, which continued till 5.30 p.m. The Duke then hoisted his red battle flag and Spragge bore down with his division within less than a league of the Dutch. The French now belatedly arrived to rejoin the fleet — Spragge caustically remarking, 'The French were very slack in bearing down and in great disorder; nor do I expect better of them'. This delay caused the Duke to take down his red flag.

A further account of the action by the Red Squadron comes from Sir John Harman, its Rear-Admiral, whose flagship was the new 1st Rate *Royal Charles*. The Duke of York ordered him to lead the van of the Red Squadron, which he obeyed immediately, though he had only three ships of his division with him. De Ruyter with his squadron came directly against the Red Squadron, the Zeeland Squadron opposed the French, and the Holland Squadron attacked the Blue Squadron.

About two hours after the fight began, Harman, in the *Charles*, was standing on the starboard tack, with the wind SE. About noon de Ruyter concentrated on Harman's division, engaging in a fierce contest till around 2.0 p.m. All the ships in his division were disabled except the *Charles*, and her masts were badly damaged. The following morning he tried to take his place in the line of battle, but was unable to do so because hsi main mast was in danger of going overboard. He accordingly sent his flagship back to England and embarked in his ketch to report to the Duke. The Duke of York sent him on board the *Cambridge* of the Admiral's Division of the Red Squadron.

Sir Joseph Jordan was Vice-Admiral of the Blue Squadron, with the 1st Rate *Royal Sovereign* as his flagship. He says that, the Dutch being near, the Duke of York gave the signal for weighing anchor and for the fleet to get into line of battle. Some ships and fireships, which were nearer the shore, could not get out. His ship led the van, standing towards Lowestoft. At about 8.0 a.m. a great part of the Dutch fleet, being then to windward, attacked the Red and Blue Squadrons furiously. The *Sovereign* was attacked by a Rear-Admiral and other ships in a conflict which lasted about an hour, during which a boat came to the *Sovereign* with a message from Lord Sandwich telling him to tack and, if possible, get to windward of the enemy. Jordan says that he had already tried this before the order came. The attempt was ultimately successful and Jordan then engaged an Admiral, a Vice-Admiral and a Rear-Admiral, together with five or six great ships and four or five fireships. This was presumably the bulk of de Ruyter's leading squadron. The *Sovereign* was handicapped because she had no fireships to attend to her (they were presumably amongst those vessels becalmed when the fleet sailed). About noon they espired ships on fire to the leeward but did not know which they were. (One of them was probably Sandwich's flagship the *Royal James*.) At around 2.0 p.m. the *Sovereign* engaged the Dutch squadron at closer range and continued so until 6.0 p.m. Jordan then saw the Duke of York's standard to leeward of the enemy's van and tried to join and assist him.

What happened to the *Royal James* and Sandwich is recounted by her Captain, Richard Haddock. The Blue Squadron had formed line of battle at the start of the action as best as it could, with the Vice-Admiral of the Blue and his squadron ahead, and the Rear-Admiral astern. The Dutch attacked with two fireships, the first of which the *Royal James* set on fire with her shot and disabled the second by shooting down her yards. Haddock mentions the despatch of the ship's barge to Jordan, but gives a slightly different version of Sandwich's order. He says that Jordan was directed to weather the Dutch ships that were attacking Sandwich's division and come to his assistance. Jordan makes no mention of the second part of the instruction. Haddock then sent the pinnace astern to direct the other ships of Sandwich's division to come to the assistance of the flagship. Several tried, but could not manage it.

About one and a half hours later a Dutch ship ran aboard the bows of the *Royal James*. Sandwich suggested that they should board her, but Haddock was opposed to this as he had from 250 to 300 men killed and wounded and would probably lose another hundred in taking the Dutch ship; in addition they would not be able to cut her loose because the flood tide was pressing her against the bows; and another factor was that by taking men away from the guns the ship's fire would be slackened, causing the enemy to believe that she was disabled and more of their ships to board the *Royal James*. Sandwich reluctantly agreed.

Van Ghent's ship was now ranged alongside and raked the *Royal James* with broadside and small arms fire. She replied with the middle and lower tier of guns, the upper guns having been silenced, as nearly all their men had been killed. Sir Joseph Jordan passed by to windward and Haddock commented that this was 'unkindly'. At 12 noon Haddock was shot in the foot and had to go below for it to be dressed. The flood tide was now over and, remembering this, Haddock sent word to Sandwich asking for the ship to be anchored by the stern. This enabled men to cut the Dutch ship loose from entanglement with the rigging and she fell away. Haddock then requested that the cable be cut and the ship brought to sail before the wind and to set the mainsail. All this was done, and whilst he was issuing these suggestions to Sandwich the surgeon was 'cutting off the shattered flesh and tendons of my toe'. Immediately afterwards the *Royal James* was boarded by another fireship and set on fire. Sandwich lost his life, but Haddock was one of those who survived.

In the French squadron under d'Estrées the van was commanded by du Quesne, the centre by d'Estrées himself, and the rear by Rasbesnières. As we have seen, the French set off on the port tack to the south — breaking contact with the English squadrons, either deliberately or through misunderstanding of the Duke of York's orders. This move by the French squadron was so hurried that it was disorganised. The van division was left to leeward and it was some time before du Quesne's ships could get up into line.

Bankert, commanding de Ruyter's Zeeland Squadron, peeled off from the rest of the Dutch fleet and engaged the French at long range. Amongst the French there was much mutual recrimination. Du Quesne accused d'Estrées of having abandoned the English; Rasbesnières was mortally wounded and as he lay dying he accused some of his captains of failing to do their duty; and du Quesne was dismissed from his command by d'Estrées for insubordination.

Narbrough, in the meantime, had passed the *Royal James*, which was on fire, and saw small vessels rescuing some of the crew who were in the water. He managed to get sufficient emergency repairs carried out to sail his ship, got her cleared, and made all sail he could to get up to the Duke, who with 20 English ships was engaged in the middle of the Dutch fleet. The *Sovereign* and six or seven other ships, had got to windward of the Dutch. At 6.0 p.m. Narbrough saw a squadron of 26 Dutch ships, about two leagues away to the SW, which had been fighting the French Squadron and were returning to join de Ruyter. The French were in sight following them.

Between 6.0 and 7.0 p.m. the Duke of York had shifted his flag to the *London*, the *St. Michael being disabled and ready to sink. At 8.0 p.m. Sir John Kempthorne, Rear-Admiral of the Blue, in the St. Andrew, and Sir John Harman, Rear-Admiral of the Red, in the Charles*, with about 30 ships of their respective squadrons (many of which had suffered considerable damage), joined with the *Prince*, as the fleet flagship, and stood North. The Dutch, with about 70 ships, were standing South. The Duke of York was about two leagues to windward of the *Prince* and the ships which had joined her. With the Duke were about 20 ships and also Sir Joseph Jordan, Vice-Admiral of the Blue, with some of his division.

At 9.0 p.m. Narbrough saw the lights of the Duke's flagship and tacked, standing SE to join him; Kempthorne and Harman, with ships of their respective squadrons, followed him. The weather was fair with the wind NE by E. Narbrough saw the Dutch lights until 11.0 p.m., then lost them, but soon afterwards saw the Duke of York's lights again. At midnight Narbrough, having rejoined the Duke, had the red fighting flag taken down from the fore topmast head, the *Prince* reverting to the status of a private ship. (It is apparent that when the commander-in-chief had temporarily abandoned his flagship, his flag captain retained some particular authority and status until re-united with his chief.)

The sea, says Narbrough, had been 'as smooth as a fishpond' and it had been a hot and sunny day. He thought that if the Dutch had had the courage to make use of their initial advantage they might have inflicted as much damage on the English fleet as they had received from it; 'and glad they are so quit of us, as I perceive by their haste in going away from us'.

Narbrough assessed the respective losses as: English the *Royal James* and three fireships; Dutch five warships sunk and one taken, fourteen fireships sunk and one taken. But as so often, both then and now, the enemy's loss was greatly over estimated. The Dutch losses in men-of-war were the *Joshua* sunk and the *Stavoren* captured.

On the following morning, 29 May, the Duke of York returned on board the *Prince* at 7 o'clock, and gave Narbrough a Commission to command her. At about 10 o'clock the French squadron arrived, and soon afterwards the Duke of York summoned a Council of War. At this it was decided to keep the sea with those ships fit enough to fight and to send the rest away for repair. However, at 11.0 a.m. Narbrough saw the Dutch fleet to the SE, some four to five leagues away and standing North, the wind being NE. The Duke promptly ordered the fleet to make sail and stand with the enemy. As soon as the Dutch saw this, they tacked and stood SE towards their own coasts; the Allied fleet following.

The French squadron was in the van and got the length of the Dutch fleet, and the Blue Squadron, bringing up the rear, was up with the rear of the Dutch; so the whole Allied fleet was abreast of, and a mile to the windward of, the Dutch fleet. 'A seaman set at the fore-topmast head with the flag of defiance, loose in his arms and ready to hoist'. At 3.0 p.m., just as the *Prince* was ready to fire and to hoist the red flag, a thick fog came down from the NE — so thick that from the *Prince* they could not see the ship next to them. It kept thick until 5.0 p.m., and then cleared. The Dutch fleet could then be seen 1½ miles to leeward. The Duke decided to fight and, as the Allied fleet bore down on the Dutch, he ordered the red flag to be hoisted. The whole ship's company of the *Prince* gave shouts of joy. But the red flag had not been flying for half an hour when it began to blow so hard that the lower tier of guns could not be carried out. As the weather seemed likely to worsen and night was approaching, the Duke reluctantly ordered the red flag to be lowered, and the only chance of decisive victory in the Third Dutch War was lost. The Dutch fleet, half a mile distant, bore away ESE. The following morning scouts came in to report that the Dutch were within the Oosterbank at anchor among the sands.

This was about the end of active operations in 1672. During June and July the fleet hung about the Dutch coast, but de Ruyter did not come out. On 20 July 'the seamen caught haddocks and whiting with hooks and lines by the ship's side', wrote Narbrough. On 3 August a council of flag officers decided that, having regard to the very leaky condition of several ships, to the loss of anchors and cable by most of them, and to the high proportion of sick, the whole fleet should go to the Nore 'to repair and satisfy their needs'.

The Duke of York struck his flag on 18 September and on 21 September the French squadron sailed back to France.

20

The Two Battles of Schooneveld[1]

For the year 1673 the Duke of York was succeeded as Commander-in-Chief of the Fleet by Prince Rupert — a far less competent commander. Unfortunately, owing to the bigotry of Parliament, the Duke, as a Roman Catholic, was prohibited by the Test Act from exercising command.

De Ruyter planned to attack before the junction had taken place between the English ships, lying in the Thames and at Portsmouth, and the French contingent coming from Camaret Bay, near Brest. He intended to sink ships to block the channel used by the main body of the English fleet as their exit from the Thames, and then operate against the Portsmouth ships and the French. Fortunately, although the Allies were late in their concentration, the Dutch administration was equally bad and de Ruyter's sailing was delayed.

The Dutch fleet sailed on 1 May and reached the exit from the King's Channel of the Thames estuary on 2 May. De Ruyter despatched his 'sinkers' with an escort of six frigates and six fireships, but he was unlucky. A thick fog descended and the progress of the detachment was so slowed down, that it had not reached its objective before the English fleet was seen approaching.

Sir Edward Spragge, Admiral of the Blue, in the *Royal Prince*, takes up the story, with the brief entry under 3 May: 'Fleet sailed and anchored short of the Middle Ground, 27 Dutch sail sighted'. At about 11.0 a.m. the next day there was a council of flag officers: information having been received that 40 Dutch sail had been sighted. It was decided that the smallest of the 4th Rates, together with the 5th and 6th Rates and four fireships should ply East of the Middle Ground with orders not to retire except if forced. By 7 May the enemy was steering away SE. In fact, de Ruyter, having failed to coop up the main body of the English fleet, had sailed for home and to his previous anchorage in the Schooneveld channel, outside Walcheren.

On 11 May the *Royal Charles* and the men-of-war from Portsmouth, about 14 in number, joined the main body of the fleet in Rye Bay. Prince Rupert transferred his flag to the *Royal Charles* the following day.

---

[1] 'Journals and Narratives of the Third Dutch War' op. cit.

The Comte d'Estrées joined the fleet on 16 May, with 24 men-of-war, the least of which, says Spragge, had 50 guns and 300 men. On the same day the King and the Duke of York visited the fleet, and on 17 May a Council of War decided to attack the Dutch if they were still at Schooneveld, where they had last been reported. The order of sailing was to be Rupert with the Red Squadron in the van, the French (or White) Squadron in the centre (instead of the van, which was its proper place), and Spragge with the Blue Squadron bringing up the rear. This was to prevent the French acting as they had done at Sole Bay, though perhaps d'Estrées was told that his squadron was being given the place of honour!

On 22 May the fleet approached the enemy coast, and at about 2.0 p.m. the Dutch fleet was reported as still at Schooneveld. The Allied fleet thereupon anchored for the night. The next day the Allies sailed towards the enemy, the wind being South; but about 2.0 p.m. it changed to the East, and in the evening the Dutch fleet of some 80 sail was seen riding within the banks. The Allied fleet anchored by the Ooster Banks, and remained there until 28 May, held up by heavy wind, rain, and fog.

Spragge commented during this forced immobility that in peacetime able men should be employed to find the truths and dangers of these banks. 'They saved', he says, 'the Dutch fleet from destruction in 1666 when Rupert and Albemarle beat them, and they saved themselves by retiring into Zeeland; and also in 1665 when His Royal Highness won the battle in which Opdam died; their fleet retiring in great disorder into the Texel.' He concluded that no decisive victory could be gained over the Dutch until we were well enough acquainted with their ports to pursue them into them.

On 27 May it was resolved at a council of flag officers to attack the enemy at the first opportunity. The plan decided was to send a force composed of smaller ships into Schooneveld ahead of the main body to prevent the enemy from withdrawing without fighting. This force consisted of 35 ships and frigates (including 9 French) and 13 fireships.

The First Battle of Schooneveld took place on 28 May. Spragge says that at 10.0 a.m., the weather being reasonable, they stood towards the enemy. About 1.0 p.m. the van began to engage, but it was 2.0 p.m. before the Blue Squadron got into action, and this was with the Dutch Zeeland Squadron. By 5.0 p.m. they encountered de Ruyter 'who had tacked from the shore'. Spragge could then see no sign of the Red Squadron. The wind veering NE, he then stood off for half an hour. At 5.30 p.m. he tacked and stood in again just 'aweather' of all the Dutch fleet and receiving most of their broadsides within musket shot, with only the *Cambridge* of his squadron to support him. About 6.0 p.m. he encountered Tromp, who had changed his ship. The Red Squadron then came along at a great distance to windward of the Dutch. Spragge says that if they had borne down and given him the opportunity to have weathered the Dutch, they would have gained a complete victory.

At about 11.0 p.m. Spragge's ship was in a foot less than five fathoms, and he comments. 'It proved a very ill fighting place for so great a number of ships', which must have been one of the classic understatements of naval history! He added that the battle was 'as ill fought on our side as ever yet I saw'.

Another view of the battle is given by George Legge, Captain of the *Royal Katherine*. At 8.0 a.m. the *Katherine* fireship arrived, ordered by Prince Rupert to attend upon the *Royal Katherine*. Legge sent an officer and the Gunner aboard to take a survey of her stores, fireworks and number of men.

At 10.30 a.m. the whole fleet set sail to engage the enemy, the wind being SW. The Red Squadron, to which the *Royal Katherine* belonged, steered E by W, the van towards the North end of the enemy's fleet, which was Tromp's Squadron. It was nearly 1.0 p.m. when the leading ships came within range of the enemy. The Red Squadron hauled away NE on the port tack till about 3.0 p.m. Then, being near Tromp's Vice-Admiral, Legge sent his fireship to 'clap him aboard', but a 50-gun man-of-war came between the fireship and its prey, but then started to sink by the side of the fireship. Legge immediately sent men to take the Dutch ship, but her rigging, masts and sails were so much shot to pieces and there was seven foot of water in he hold, that the English sailors abandoned her. The *Royal Katherine* was then within a cable's length of the Banjaard Sands, so Legge put his ship about and fought on the starboard tack till 6.0 p.m. Fighting went on till 10.0 p.m.

The strategy of sending in a light squadron to draw the Dutch out had been a waste of time, for de Ruyter was only too anxious to fight in the shoal waters which he knew so well. His fleet weighed with surprising speed and were attacking the light squadron before it had managed to rejoin the main body of the Allied fleet. In the French Squadron, de Grancey, seeing a chance to do so, led his division in an effort to cut off the rear Dutch squadron under Bankert; but the French were not experienced in fighting in line, and the attempt failed.

The battle was indecisive; de Ruyter had hoped to lure the Allied ships on to the sand banks and thus win a decisive victory. But those same sand banks deprived Rupert of a chance of victory because English knowledge of the banks was so slight that it limited his scope for manoeuvre. As Legge said, 'The place where we fought was very dangerous, for we feared more the losing of our ships upon the sands than we did losing our ships and lives in fight with the enemy'.

The Allied fleet anchored the next morning at 5 o'clock on the Ooster Banks. Rupert transferred his flag to the *Royal Sovereign* as the new *Royal Charles*, in fighting to windward, was too 'crank' to use her lower tier of guns.

From 29 to 31 May the fleet was at anchor, fitting and repairing sails and rigging, ready for another engagement. Prince Rupert sent a fresh fireship, the *Truelove*, to 'wait upon' the *Royal Katherine*. Legge was not impressed; he says that she was in poor condition, having neither foremast nor foretopmast, most of her fireworks 'damnified' with water and she had no boat. This last was essential, because without it the crew could not evacuate the ship after they had set her on fire. Legge went on board her himself to inspect her condition. As a result he ordered his carpenter to make a foremast and foretopmast out of the *Royal Katherine's* studding sail booms and directed his gunner to go aboard and get the fireworks in as good an order as possible.

On 1 June Legge noted that several of the Dutch fleet were under sail and the Allied fleet got ready to fight; 'but the Dutch anchored again'. On 4 June, at about 10.0 a.m., Spragge left his ship to go on board the fleet flagship, the *Royal Sovereign*, which he reached around noon, it being some ten miles from his own ship. When he arrived, the *Sovereign's* fore topsail was loose, indicating that the enemy were approaching. Rupert had little to say but asked Spragge to get aboard his own ship and make sail ahead.

It was 2.0 p.m. before Spragge had covered the ten miles return trip. All being clear, he made sail. By this time Prince Rupert, with the Red Squadron, had pressed through the French, or White, Squadron which lay anchored 'in the body of the line'. As the Blue Squadron had been ordered to precede it, Spragge had to 'press on more sail'. As a result of all this mismanagement, he was delayed for an hour in engaging; his ships astern were in great disorder, but he continued sailing, hoping to bring them into a good line. He soon saw that there was no chance of achieving this, so he shortened sail to allow Tromp, who had fired a challenging gun, to come up to him. D'Estrées, who was now supposed to follow the Blue Squadron, had not been informed that the Red Squadron was taking the lead. Owing to Rupert's failure to inform the other two squadrons of his intention, the fleet was now in complete disarray.

Meanwhile Tromp, who had the best ships in the Dutch fleet, seemed disinclined, says Spragge, to come to close action with the Blue Squadron. At 4.45 p.m. the main topsail of his flagship, the *Royal Prince*, was shot in pieces from the yard, and he set his mainsail to keep the ship to. At 6.0 p.m. the carpenter told him that there was five feet of water in the hold. At 7.0 p.m. he sent a message to the Vice- and Rear-Admirals of the Blue Squadron letting them know the condition of his ship in case he had to bear away to stop the leaks. But his competent carpenters were able to stop sufficient of the leaks to enable the pumps to prevent the water level from rising. He was thus able to keep in line until 10.0 p.m., when the battle died down. Between 11.0 p.m. and midnight de Ruyter stood away towards his own coasts. Tromp remained until 3 o'clock the next morning, when, noticing that de Ruyter had left, he 'stood away very quietly'. And so ended the Second Battle of Schooneveld.

Spragge commented that there was 'a great want of order in the battle', and that if the main body of the fleet had tacked towards de Ruyter, who was 'very weak in that part' of his line, they would probably have gained a decisive victory. It was probably a justified comment. Rupert had displayed the same impetuosity and lack of control as in his cavalry charge at Naseby which had robbed King Charles I of victory and cost him his throne.

On the following day, 5 June, Prince Rupert called a Council of War, as a result of which the fleet returned to Sole Bay.

21

The Second Battle of the Texel[1]

On 6 July 1673 the King arrived on board the fleet flagship and held a council to decide how to draw the Dutch fleet out of the Schooneveld, for they had too great an advantage in fighting amongst their own sand banks with their shallower draught ships. Count Schomberg, of Louis XIV's army was present, and it was agreed that an attempt to land troops at the Texel should have the desired effect. On the following day it was confirmed that the Allies would land 4,000 soldiers under Schomberg, and in the meantime the fleet would move into the Thames and await the arrival of the transports with their troops.

John Narbrough had rejoined the fleet, taking command, as 'eldest' captain of the *St. Michael*, flagship of the Earl of Ossory, Rear-Admiral of the Blue Squadron (all flagships now had two captains), with a blue flag flying at the mizzen topmast head. He noted that the ship was badly manned with 520 seamen, soldiers, and 'trouncers' (i.e., untrained, and hence troublesome men) out of her complement of 700. By 6 July he had been made up to his complement, having 701 men, of whom 134 were soldiers and 120 trouncers and tradesmen 'which were never at sea and unfit for service'.

On 10 July, according to Spragge, information was received that the Dutch fleet had left the Schooneveld for an unknown destination. The King returned to the fleet on 16 July and called a council. The sailing of the Dutch fleet had altered the situation, and it was agreed that the troops should be embarked but that they should be sent to Yarmouth and remain pending the outcome of the action at sea. It was also agreed that on no account should the Dutch be attacked in the Schooneveld till further orders from the King, under any pretext. (That the King should have taken strategic control of the fleet suggests a lack of confidence in Prince Rupert's ability. It seems unlikely that he would have done so if the Duke of York had still been in command.)

On 17 July, most of the land forces having arrived, the fleet sailed. According to Spragge it consisted of 88 men-of-war, (that is, ships able to

---

[1] 'Journals and Narratives of the Third Dutch War', op. cit.

fight in the line), besides a number of 5th Rates, small frigates (probably 6th Rates), sloops and others. Narbrough gives the strength as 105 English and French men-of-war, of which the smallest had over 40 guns, 38 fireships, and 60 ketches, hoys and tenders. Altogether there were nearly 200 sail and 28,000 men. (The difference between the estimates of Spragge and Narbrough may be that the latter's figure for men-of-war included the 5th and 6th Rates.)

The following day Narbrough recounts what he describes as an extraordinary incident. 'This afternoon the *Greyhound* frigate came into the fleet with a St. George flying at the main-topmast head, Monsieur Schomberg being aboard of her, General of the land forces which are raised against the United Provinces. When the *Greyhound* came near the Admiral, Prince Rupert fired at her and caused her to strike her flag, and put the Captain of her in irons for wearing a flag'. The incident can hardly have endeared Rupert to Schomberg!

On 19 July, writes Spragge, the fleet weighed and steered NE to the northward of the Gabbard, whilst the troop transports with Schomberg steered to Yarmouth. When clear of the Gabbard the fleet steered ESE. Scouts brought information that the enemy fleet of some 100 ships was about eight leagues away to the SE. On 21 July it was sighted at anchor near the Schooneveld. Narbrough's ship, the *St. Michael,* anchored at about 4.0 p.m.; the centre of the Dutch fleet being SE by S about four leagues distant, riding, apparently, about the North point of the sand called the Steenbank, their hulls just appearing above the horizon. A Council of War of Flag Officers was summoned at 3.0 a.m. on 22 July. It was just 8.0 a.m. when Spragge was able to reach the *Sovereign;* Rupert having just fired a gun to weigh anchor. An indignant Spragge wrote: 'We were not consulted about anything, only told we would stand off towards the coast of Holland, in case the enemy did not come to us.' At 10.0 a.m., when Spragge was on his way back to his flagship in his yacht, the wind came 'with a great gust and rain'. It was 12 noon before he was back on board.

Rupert placed the Red Squadron in the van, the White, or French Squadron in the middle, and the Blue Squadron in the rear. The line of battle (with its 89 men-of-war, accompanied by small frigates, fireships, and tenders) was so long that Spragge was unable to see any signal the 'General Admiral' would make, and he considered this 'quite contrary to any custom used at sea before, and may prove of ill consequence to us'. He was quite right, for it was the normal practice for the Red Squadron, under the immediate command of the General-at-Sea, to be in the centre, with his own division of that squadron in its centre — a normal practice that continued up to and including the battle of Jutland (though the squadron was no longer the 'Red').

When the whole fleet had got under way, the order was reversed, with the Blue Squadron in the van, the French in the middle, and the Red bringing up the rear. At 1.0 p.m. Rupert sent his Lieutenant to Spragge with instructions to tack and use his own discretion. After some complicated manoeuvring the Red Squadron was again in the van. Spragge thought that if they had engaged the enemy then, they would have won a decisive victory, because the Dutch had at most only 70 men-of-war. He was obviously furious because he wrote: 'That which was done by us I never saw done before, nor I hope, never will again.' At midnight they anchored, with the French in the middle. Spragge commented, 'Many inconveniences may and do daily happen by putting the French in the middle'.

On 23 July the Blue Squadron was apparently again in the van. Captain George Legge, in the *Royal Katherine*, says that they set sail at 8.0 a.m. with the wind WNW. The course till noon was N by E, and then Spragge tacked. The leading French division, which should have followed him, did not tack as soon as they should, so that a distance of two or three leagues opened between the Blue and French Squadrons. The Prince, with the Red Squadron, manoeuvred to try and rectify this. At noon the Texel bore NE and about 16 leagues off. They anchored for the night with 'Gravesend spire steeple' ESE about four leagues away.

On 24 July it was resolved at a council to send scouts to the Vlie and the Texel. At another council on 28 July it was announced that the primary object was now to surprise the Dutch East Indies fleet. The previous day Rupert had written to the King, asking firstly, if he should send for the land forces at Yarmouth; secondly, if he should go after the Dutch East India fleet if he had news of it; and thirdly, if he had authority to attack de Ruyter in Schooneveld if he though it necessary. It was 9 August before he got the reply to these questions. He was not to send for Schomberg's force until he had beaten the Dutch fleet, and in any case a landing was now considered 'less advisable' than previously thought. As regards the East Indiamen, he was not to go further than between the Dogger Bank and the Texel in search of them, because it would leave the English coast and the Thames exposed to attack, but he could follow them as far as the Elbe. He was on no account to attack the Dutch fleet in the Schooneveld. It is surprising that the day after he had written with his questions Rupert had given his flag officers his own decision on a change of objective.

On 29 July scouts reported the enemy fleet, of about 80 sail, five leagues from the Schooneveld and its course NNE. On 1 August they reported it to be between Goeree and the Maas, and the next day it was decided at a council to get if possible to southward of the enemy and prevent them returning into the Schooneveld.

From 4 to 8 August the weather was too bad to contemplate action. Narbrough says that on 8 August at noon information arrived that the Dutch fleet was in sight SSE from the General. The *St. Michael* was cleared to fight, but the next day the fleet was unable to weigh owing to the high sea. On 10 August at about 8.0 a.m. the fleet, says Narbrough, got under sail and stood SE. Between 10.0 and 11.0 a.m. the Dutch fleet could be seen from the main top, bearing S by W and about six leagues off, standing northwards on the starboard tack. The wind was light and NE. The Allied fleet bore 'lasking down' (that is neither by the wind nor before the wind) towards the Dutch fleet; the French Squadron in the van, the General in the middle with the Red

Squadron, and the Blue Squadron in the rear. The whole fleet was in line ahead, with the Union flag on the mizzen peak of all flagships. Between 3.0 and 4.0 p.m. the wind came E by N 'a fine gale'. 'Our General', Narbrough records, 'bore lasking towards the Dutch fleet' and neared them at a great pace. About 4.0 p.m. the Dutch fleet tacked and stood South on the larboard (i.e., port) tack, as did the Allied fleet — the Dutch bearing to leeward and about three leagues off. At 6.0 p.m. Texel Island bore E?N three to four leagues off.

The fleet sailed all night, but with a short sail and not keeping as near the wind as they could lie, which surprised Narbrough; for the enemy were on the lee bow sailing as near the wind as they could lie which he saw would give them the weather gauge by the morning.

Between midnight and 1.0 a.m. the wind switched to ESE. At 1.0 a.m. the Allied fleet tacked and stood ENE as near the wind as they could lie, it now being SE. At daylight the General hoisted the Union flag at the mizzen peak as a signal to the fleet to fall into line of battle, every flagship repeating this signal. The Blue Squadron was now in the van. The Dutch fleet was SE and to windward on the same course, close by the shore and three leagues distant. The south end of the Texel Island was three leagues away ENE. At full daylight the Dutch fleet formed line and approached the Allied fleet. Narbrough reckoned them not than 88 ships of war as compared with 90 English and French ships. At about 7.0 a.m. the General put a Union flag at the fore-topmast head and at the mizzen-topmast head as a signal for the rear of the fleet to tack and the van of the fleet also to tack. Then the General tacked and the whole fleet stood close by the wind SW by S, the wind being SE by E and SSE. The French were now in the van, the Red Squadron in the middle, and the Blue Squadron in the rear. The Dutch fleet, to windward, had Tromp's Squadron in the line against the Blue Squadron, and de Ruyter, with most of the rest of his fleet, was ranged against the Red Squadron. One division of Bankert's Squadron was sent against Martel's division, which was leading the French Squadron. The other two French divisions were virtually unopposed.

The Dutch being to windward, de Ruyter was making so much smoke with his firing that Narbrough could not see the Red Squadron. At about 8.0 a.m. Tromp's Squadron was 'within fair gun-shot' of the Blue Squadron, which saluted the Dutch with trumpets and three cheers, and then opened fire. Narbrough says that his topsails were very much shot, the fore topsail shot down twice. The shrouds and rigging were cut by the enemy's shot much faster than he could get seamen to make them fast again. He says that the Dutch guns fired more shot than the English, for they plied their guns faster. They fired much 'pound shot' which flew thick and cut much rigging. When the enemy came close Narbrough could see his ship's shot well placed in them, but when they were at any distance the shot fell short.

Between 12.0 noon and 1.0 p.m. the wind came to the SW and the water was so smooth that he could carry out the lower tier of guns without shipping one drop of water. This shift of the wind had put the Dutch to leeward and they fell astern nearly out of range. Narbrough could not see the

Red or White Squadrons, nor hear their guns and wondered what had become of them. Before 1.0 p.m. Narbrough saw 'a great Dutch ship without her masts', and then, at about 1.0 p.m., when his own ship, the St. Michael, had the wind on the beam, her own 'mainmast fell by the board at once', breaking a little above the deck and carrying the mizzen mast overboard with it. However, his headsails were complete, and when the main and mizzen masts were cut away the ship was brought astern on the quarter of Spragge's flagship, the Royal Prince, which was disabled, and, keeping between her and the enemy, the St. Michael continued firing. Spragge transferred to the St. George. Lord Ossory sent Narbrough to the St. George to propose boarding Tromp's flagship. Narbrough delivered the message to Sir Edward Spragge on the quarter deck. Spragge replied that if Ossory boarded Tromp's ship he would second him. The St. Michael then prepared to make the attempt, and at the same time Ossory sent one of his fireships to lie by the disabled Royal Prince with the task of burning any enemy ship that should try and attack her. But Tromp bore away and Spragge could not move in support because the St. George's fore topmast had been shot away, disabling her. Presently the blue flag of the squadron commander was taken down from her main topmast head, and sometime after this Narbrough saw a boat astern of the St. George sunk, and men swimming in the water. He kept looking for the blue flag being hoisted on another ship, unaware that the sunken boat had been carrying the Admiral on the way to transfer his flag and that the gallant Sir Edward Spragge had been drowned.

The St. Michael remained in support of the Prince, receiving much more damage and many casualties. About 3.0 p.m. Tromp's flagship was disabled, forcing him to transfer his flag.

While the Blue Squadron had been engaged in what was almost a private battle between Spragge and Tromp, the Red Squadron had been assailed by de Ruyter's Squadron and all but ten ships of Bankert's. These ten ships comprised Evertsen's division, which had the task of ensuring that the French Squadron did not interfere with the main battle, and so ensure that de Ruyter engaged the Red Squadron with superior numbers. This was a fiercely contested action, during which de Ruyter, in spite of his superior numbers, was unable to gain any advantage.

D'Estrées, with his squadron, only had to contend with the ten ships of one division of Bankert's Squadron under Evertsen. Rupert signalled de Martel to stretch ahead, go about, and get to windward of the Dutch van, so as to place it between two fires. This he did; but as soon as Evertsen saw the danger he charged through the 20 other ships of d'Estrées's Squadron with his own 10 ships and then stood to rejoin de Ruyter. D'Estrées did not follow him and this was the end of French engagement in the battle.

At about 4.0 p.m. Narbrough saw 'a great fleet of ships approaching to windward and SW'. He thought that these were the Red and White Squadrons, but as they got closer he saw that the line of the nearer ships wore Dutch colours whilst those further off wore English. It surprised Narbrough and other observers that the English and Dutch fleets should be sailing together for so long without firing at each other. It transpired, however, that both commanders were sailing to support the commanders of their rear squadrons, about whose fortunes they were worried.

Two Dutch fireships endeavoured to attack the *Prince*, but, as they approached, both the *St. Michael* and the *Prince* opened such a heavy fire on them that they could not grapple the latter and were themselves set prematurely on fire astern of the *Prince*.

Most of the ships of the Blue Squadron were now together and Ossory prepared to pursue Tromp. The majority of his ships were in good enough condition; he had more ships than remained to Tromp and he also had the weather gauge. But he did not know if Spragge had been killed so that the Blue Squadron was without an effective commander.

De Ruyter, in the meantime, was trying to prevent a junction of the Red and Blue Squadrons. Two of the General's fireships (i.e., those attached to the fleet flagship), having the weather gauge, were at about 6.0 p.m., despatched against de Ruyter's Squadron, throwing it into disorder. Unfortunately there was no English follow-up to take advantage of this confusion.

As the French Squadron at last made its appearance, Rupert signalled it to close in on the Dutch rear; d'Estrées disobeyed the signal, bringing his squadron into line where he faced no opposition.

The performance of the French in the battle led to an international row which was probably a major factor in England disassociating itself from its French allies in the war against Holland and bringing Anglo-Dutch hostilities to a close. The single fighting French Admiral, de Martel, wrote a pamphlet charging d'Estrées with having dishonoured France by failing to fight. For this he was sentenced to some months imprisonment in the Bastille. Louis XIV, angry at these accusations, ordered an enquiry, but, questioned by the court, d'Estrées admitted that the King had wished him to 'husband his ships' as he no longer trusted the English.[2]

Narbrough was disgusted at what he saw as the failure of the Allied fleet to destroy the Dutch. He wrote: 'I had rather fall in battle than ever to see the like more, that so mighty a fleet of ships as ours to stand away as now we do'. He added that the Allied fleet had lost no ships and that the Dutch had had the more ships disabled.

That the Dutch were able to stave off defeat was due to three factors — the ability of de Ruyter, the incompetence of Prince Rupert, and the treachery of Louis XIV and d'Estrées.

On 19 February peace was signed between England and Holland. The latter recognised the absolute supremacy of the flag of England from Cape Finisterre in Spain to Norway, and paid a war indemnity.

It was the end of an extraordinary conflict; a conflict which had its roots in the English Civil War and a rivalry in trade which followed England's emergence as a maritime power; a conflict in which neither opponent really disliked each other and in which diplomatic relations were never severed

---

[2] Troude, *Batailles Navales de la France, année 1673*.

(the English and Dutch Ambassadors remained in the respective capitals); and a struggle in which men who had fought respectively for King and Parliament served side by side, or as commander and subordinate, against a foreign foe.

These were wars on which both sides could look back with pride and with some satisfaction, for even in the fiercest encounters chivalry and courtesy were seldom absent for long, and in every battle courage and glory were evenly distributed between victor and vanquished.

For England, during these thirty odd years there was laid the foundation of a Navy which was as said earlier, to be supreme at sea for nearly three hundred years — a Navy of which the principal architect was that extraordinary little man Samuel Pepys.

Index

Notes

1. Some of the Dutch names of persons, ships, and geographical features have been variously rendered by the respective translators of the contemporary documents on which this book is largely based; consequently the spelling in this index is that most frequently used.

2. Names which were successively used for the same ship are shown separated by an oblique stroke.

3. An oblique stroke separating page numbers after the name of a ship, indicates that after the stroke the numbers refer to a new ship of the same name.

4. The word 'Royal' was sometimes omitted in contemporary mentions of a ship's name, e.g. the *Royal Charles* was often referred to as the *Charles*.

A

Admiralty Committee (AC) 6, 32, 43, 54, 60, 63, 65, 74, 76-9, 81, 83-5, 90-2, 95, 98, 99, 100.

Albemarle, Duke of (see Monck).

Allin, Sir Thomas, 107-112, 115, 121-5, 127-9, 131-2.

Ammunition, 47, 68-9, 82, 84-5, 87, 90, 95, 99, 114, 121, 141.

Arlington, Lord, 117, 125.

August 16th, Battle of, 42-3.

Ayscue, Sir George, 3, 38-9, 42-4, 115, 120.

B

Batten, Sir William, 4, 15-7, 20, 22-3, 25-9, 104-5.

Bankert, 128, 136, 143, 152.

Berkeley, Lord, 104-5.

Berkeley, Sir William, 115.

Blackborne, Robert, 65, 77, 81, 83, 91, 94.

Blake, Robert, 2-4, 22, 29, 32, Dover Action 36; 37-8, with Dutch fisherman 40; 41-2, 44, Kentish Knock 45-7; 50-1, Dungeness 52-3; 58, 64, Portland 66-72; 74, temporary retirement 78-9; 84-6, 90, sick 91; 99, 100.
Boatswain, duties of, 11.
Bourne, Nehemiah, 4, 5, 35-6, 45, 74, 76.
Breda, Treaty of, 131, 134.
'Broom', Trump's, 70.

C

Cadiz Bay action, 108-9.
Carpenter, duties of, 11.
Cartaret, Sir George, 8, 13, 104-5, 116, 118, 120, 130.
Charles I, King, 3-5, 8, 12-16, 18, 23-7, 29, 32, 43, 102.
Charles II, King, 1, 4, 5, 8, 15, 26, 28-30, 44, 101-3, 106, 108, 116-9, 124, 127, 131, 133-6, 146, 149, 151.
Clarke, Robert, 83, 108.
Clearing ship to fight, 137.
Council of State (COS), 32, 37-9, 42, 44, 45, 50, 53, 58, 60, 62, 68, 73, 76-7, 86, 96, 99, 100.
Coventry, Sir William, 105-6, 107, 109, 112, 114, 116, 118, 119, 122, 129, 131.
Cromwell, Oliver, 1-3, 5, 27-30, 44, 54, Protector 79; 85, 93, 100-1.

D

Deane, Richard, 2, 3, 29, 32, 54, 64, 66-7, 69-71, 74, 76, 79, 80, 84, killed at the Gabbard 85.
Dover, action off, 36.
Downing, Sir George, 110, 134.
Dungeness, Battle of, 52-6, 95.
Durnford, Robert, 56, 61.

E

Essex, Earl of, 14-15, 18, 22, 24.
d'Estrées, Count, 135-6, 142, 146, 148, 153, 154.
Evertsen, Cornelis, 40, 45.
Evertsen, Jan, 49, 50, 55, 60, 68-9, 83, 92, 96, 125, 153.

F

Fairfax, Sir Thomas, 2, 19, 26, 27-9, 71.
Fighting, instructions for, 123.
Fireships, 10, 38, 43, 58-9, 81, 111, 118, 121-3, 131.
Flag Officers, proposals concerning, 62.
Flags, Dutch naval, 34, 92.
Flags, English naval, 32-3.
Flags, when King on board, 135-6.
Fleet, French, 137.
Fleet organisation, Dutch, 34.
Fleet organisation, English, 33, 122.
Florissen, Peter, 40, 49, 60, 68, 85.
Four Days battle, 116-124.
Frigates, description of, 8, 9.

G

Gabbard, Battle of the, 84-9.
Gerard, Sir Charles, 23-6.
Ghent, van, 134-7, 142.
Goring, Lord, 14, 15, 26.
Grancey, de, 147.
'Great Ships', 8.
Gunner, duties of, 11, 99.
Guns, 7, 8, 100.

H

Harman, Sir John, 112, 115, and the parson 118; 141, 143.
Hatsell, Henry, 63, 65, sends 'Fallstaffian' soldiers 95.
Henrietta Maria, Queen, 4, 13-17, 23.
Holmes, Sir Robert, 3, 112, 125-9, action against Smyrna fleet 134-5; 136, 140.
Hopton, Sir Ralph, 15, 26.
Hotham, Sir John, 13.

J

Jordan, Sir Joseph, 80, 115, 125, 141, 143.

K

Kelsey, Thomas, 57, 84.
Kempthorne, Sir John, 125, 143.
Kendall, William, 65, 95.
Kentish Knock, Battle of the, 45-7.
Ketches, use of, 114.

L

Lambert, John, 3, 28, 101.
Langdale, Sir Marmaduke, 24, 26.
Laws of War and Ordinances of the Sea, 60.
Lawson, Sir John, 4, 69-70, 73, 74, 76-7, 80, 86, 96-7, 99, 101, 107, 112.
Legge, George, 147-8, 151.
Leslie, Sir David, 24, 30.
Line, fighting in, 65, 75, 87.
Loswithiel, Battle of, 24.
Louis XIV, King, 133, 154.
Lowestoft, Battle of, 110-111.
Lyme Regis, 2, 21-2.

M

Maes, van, 131.
Manning of ships, 37, 50, 57, 74, 78, 123, 130.
Martel, de, 152-4.
Martin, Roger, 61, 71.
Master, responsibility of, 10, 11.
Maurice, Prince, 21-2.
Medical stores, 76.
Medway Raid, 105, 130-1, 133.
Merchant ships, 11, 14, 20, 37, 50, 74.

Mildmay, John, 45-6.

Monck, George, 2-4, 20, 54, 64, 68, 69, 71, 74, 76, 79, 80, the Gabbard 84-9; 90, becomes C-in-C 91; 92, 1st Texel 93-5; 96-7, 99, 101-3, 110, 112-6, on breach of security 117; 118, Four Days Battle 120-2; 123, 125, St. James's Day 125-9.

Mothan, P., 76-8.

Mountagu, Edward, 101-2, 112-3, 135, 141.

Myngs, Christopher, 110, 115, 122.

N

Narbrough, John, 135, 137-140, 143-4, 149-152, 154.

Nas, Aert van, 136.

Naval awards, Dutch, 92.

Navigation Acts, 132.

Navy Board, 104, 106.

Navy Commissioners (NC), 20, 32, 43, 53, 57, 74, 76-7, 81, 90-1, 97, 120.

Newcastle, Marquess of, 16, 21, 23.

Northumberland, Earl of, 12, 13, 18, 19.

O

Opdam, Earl of, 110, 111.

Ormonde, Earl of, 19-21.

Ossory, Earl of, 149, 153-4.

P

Paulus, Don, 109.

Pay, arrears of, 58.

Peacock, James, 71, 80.

Penn, Sir William, 4, 25, 35, 37, 45-6, instructions to 64-5; 69, 71, 73, 76-80, 85, 99, 100, 104-6, 111-3, 129, 130.

Pepys, Samuel, 4, 5, 8, 102-110, 112, 118-9, 130-1, 155.

Pennington, Sir John, 13, 14, 17, 18, 23.

Peters, Hugh, 43-4.

Pett, Peter, 9, 63, 104-5.

Pett, Sir Phineas, 9, 43, 135.

Pilots, 57, 68, 70, 123, 124.

Poortmans, John, 81, 83.

Popham, Edward, 2, 29, 32.

Portland, Battle of, 2, 66-72, 73-5, 78.

Pressing for service, 37, 57-8.

Q

Queen, the (see Henrietta Maria).

Quesne, du, 142.

R

Rasbenières, 142.

Rates, explanation of, 6-8.

Ré, Isle of (or St. Martin), 48, 49, 59, 60, 64-5.

Rupert, Prince, 2, 3, 14, 15, 17, 23, 26, 107, 112-9, 122-4, 126, 128, 146-8, 150-1, 153.

Ruyter, de, Battle of 16th August 42-3; 44, 47, 49, 51, 54, 57, 66, 68, 83, 86, 99, 107, 108, 112, 119, 123, 125-8, 130-4, 136-8, Sole Bay 139-144; 145-7, 151-2, 154.

S

St. James's Day, Battle of, 3, 125-9.
Saluting with guns, 107.
Sansum, Richard, 122.
Sandwich, Earl of (see Mountagu).
Schomberg, Count, 149-151.
Schooneveld, 1st battle of, 146-7.
Schooneveld, 2nd battle of, 148.
'Ships and Frigates', 75-6.
Ships, names of prominent:
    Antelope, 16, 107-8, 137.
    Adventure, 27, 136.
    Advice, 67, 107.
    Ann, 127, 137.
    Assistance, 71, 102-3.
    Bear, 76-7.
    Bonaventure, 14, 53, 55, 107-8, 137.
    Bristol, 73, 107, 136.
    Cambridge, 136, 140-1, 146.
    Constant Warwick, 9, 23, 26, 28.
    Diamond, 61, 71, 136.
    Essex, 73, 84, 107, 120.
    Fairfax, 69, 70, 74, 136, 140.
    Fan Fan, 126.
    Garland, 47, 52, 55, 95.
    Greyhound, 16, 98, 150.
    Hampshire, 73, 119.
    Henry, 118, 128, 137.
    James/Old James, 15, 23, 35-6, 46, 111-2, 127, 137.
    Jersey, 125-6.
    Leopard, 25-6, 107, 109, 137.
    London, 131,/ 136, 140, 143.
    Milford, 107-8.
    Monmouth, 132, 136.
    Naseby/Royal Charles, 102, 111-2, 117, 119-122, 125-8, 131,/ 134, 141, 143, 145.
    Nonsuch, 45-7, 70, 107-9.
    Oak, 94-5, 131.
    Phoenix, 107-9,/ 140.
    Plymouth, 107-112, 137.
    Portsmouth, 56, 61, 107, 109.
    Providence, 13, 15, 16, 24.
    Rainbow, 15, 71, 137.
    Resolution, 56, 81, 86, 93, 97, 126, 128,/ 136.
    Revenge, 113, 124, 137.
    Richard/Royal James, 112, 121-2, 126, 128, 131, 137, 139, 142-3, 144.
    Royal Charles (see *Naseby*).

Royal Katherine, 120-1, 126-7, 140, 147, 151.
Royal Prince, 112, 120-1,/ 135-7, 139, 140, 143-5, 148, 153-4.
Ruby, 46, 54, 56, 61, 97, 137, 141.
Rupert, 126, 128, 137.
St. George, 15, 126-7, 137, 153.
St. Michael, 136, 140, 143, 149, 150-1, 153-4.
Sapphire, 50, 53-4, 113.
Sovereign of the Seas/Sovereign/Royal Sovereign, 43, 45, 46, 56, 99, 126, 128, 137, 141-3, 148.
Swallow, 14, 18, 25.
Swiftsure, 8, 100, 102, 120.
Triumph, 52-3, 63, 66-7, 69, 70, 137.
Vanguard, 52-3, 68, 71, 112.
Victory, 8, 52, 71, 94, 136, 140.
Violet, 63, 77.
Warspite, 128, 137.
Signals to the fleet, Dutch, 77.
Signals to the fleet, English, 65, 75, 137.
Slingsby, Sir Robert, 104-5.
Smith, Sir Jeremy, 3, 115, 125, 127.
Soldiers manning ships, 81, 118.
Sole Bay, Battle of, 139-144.
Spragge, Sir Edward, 116, 122, 125, 140, 141, 145-6, 148-151, 153-4.
States General, Dutch, 15, 16, 34-5, 38-40, 44, 47-8, 49-51, 55, 58, 64, 68, 77-8, 81-5, 89, 90, 92-3, 96-8, 100.
Swanley, 21, 23, 25.
T
Teddiman, Sir Thomas, 112-3, 115, 125, 127, 128.
Texel, 1st battle of, 93-5.
Texel, 2nd battle of, 152-4.
Tromp, Maarten Harpertszoon, 2, 16, 17, 34-5, Dover action 36; 37-9, 42, resignation 44; 47, 48-51, Dungeness 52-6; 57-61, 64, 66, Portland 66-72; 75, 78, 81-3, the Gabbard 84-9; 90, 92-3, killed 1st battle of the Texel 94.
Tromp (junior), 111, 125-7, 146-8, 152-4.
'Trouncers', 149.
W
Warwick, Earl of, 4, 5, 9, 13, 15, 17, 18-20, 22-5, 28-9.
Wilde, de, 45-6, 82.
With, Witte Cornelis de, 39, 40, 44-5, 48-9, 50-1, 76-8, 82-3, 92-3, 'Irish' comment 94; 96-8, 100.
Y
York, Duke of, 2, 5, 103, 105, comment to Dutch Ambassador 107; Lowestoft 111-2; 117-8, 121, 127, 129-131, 135-6, Sole Bay 139-144; 145-6, 149.
Z
Zaen, van de, 132.

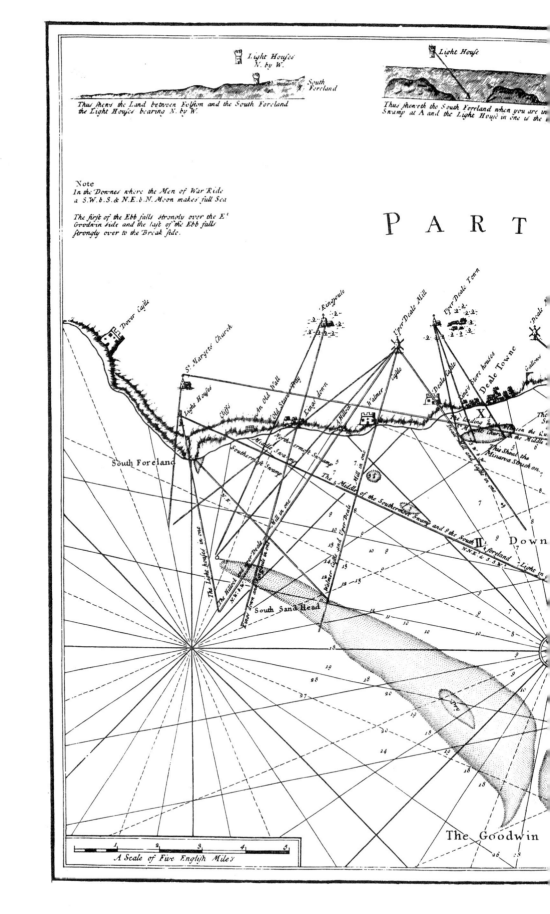

Light Houses
N. by W.

South
Foreland

Thus shews the Land between Folstone and the South Foreland
the Light Houses bearing N. by W.

Light House

Thus sheweth the South Foreland when you are in
Swamp at A and the Light House in one is the

Note
In the Downes where the Men of War Ride
a S.W. b. S. & N.E. b N. Moon makes full Sea

The first of the Ebb falls strongly over the E.
Goodwin side and the last of the Ebb falls
strongly over to the Break side.

PART

Dover Castle

St. Maryces Church

Ringoule

Uper Deale Mill

Uper Deale Town

Deale Towne

Light Houses

Cliffs

An Old Wall

Kings down

Sandhills

Walmer Castle

Deale Castle

Kings Store houses

X

Middle Sea Swamp

Northermost Swamp

Southernmost Swamp

The Middle of the Southermost Swamp and 9 the South

Down

The Light houses in one

The Hilhouse & Uper Deale Mill in one

Walmer Castle and Uper Deale

N.E.

Mill in one

South Sand Head

The Goodwin

A Scale of Five English Miles

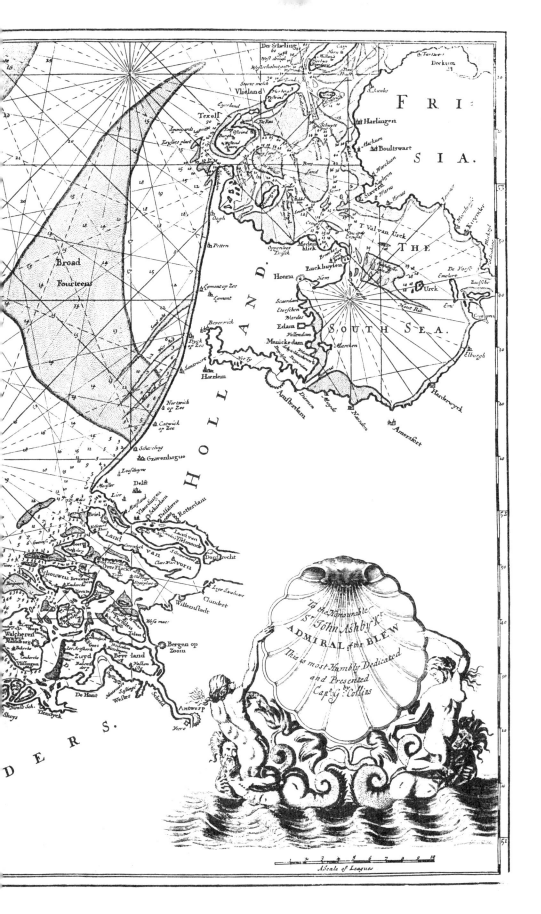

FRI
SIA.

THE

SOUTH SEA.

HOLLAND.

DERS.

Broad
Fourteens

Texell
Vlieland
Des Scheling

Harlingen
Boultswart

T Val van Urck
Urck

Elburgh
Harderwyck

Amersfort

Hoorn
Edam
Monickedam
Amsterdam
Naerden
Weesp

Petten
Egmont op Zee
Egmont
Beverwick
Haerlem
Nortwick op Zee
Catwick op Zee
Scheuling
Gravenhague
Loosduyne
Monster
Delft
Lier
Maesland
Vlaerdingen
Schiedam
Rotterdam
Briel
Land van
Ylelmonde
Dordrecht
Clundert
Willenstadt
Bergen op Zoom
Tolen
Zuyd
Bewland

Walcheren
Middleburg
Vlissingen
De Hont
Welker Schelt
Sluys
Hendyck
Antwerp

To the Honourable
Sr John Ashby Kt
ADMIRAL of the BLEW
This is most Humbly Dedicated
and Presented by
Capt J: Collins

A Scale of Leagues